Envoys of Abolition

British Naval Officers and the Campaign Against
the Slave Trade in West Africa

Mary Wills

Liverpool University Press

First published 2019 by
Liverpool University Press
4 Cambridge Street
Liverpool
L69 7ZU

This paperback edition published 2023

British Library Cataloguing-in-Publication data
A British Library CIP record is available

ISBN 978-1-78962-078-8 cased
ISBN 978-1-80207-771-1 paperback

Typeset by Carnegie Book Production, Lancaster
Printed and bound by CPI Group (UK) Ltd, Croydon CR0 4YY

For Dad

Contents

Illustrations

Acknowledgements

This book would not exist without the rich and diverse archival sources relating to naval officers of the West Africa squadron held by various archives, record offices, museums and private collectors around the UK and abroad. I would like to thank all the institutions and individuals who have granted permission for me to cite from papers in their care, and in particular the private owners of the Blair Adam papers and Henry Rogers's journal. For making this research such an enjoyable experience, I owe thanks to the archivists and librarians at the various institutions I have visited, not least the Caird Library and Archive where I spent many happy hours as a postgraduate student affiliated to the National Maritime Museum. Sarah Walpole, Archivist at the Royal Anthropological Institute, has also been particularly helpful and accommodating. Michael Graham-Stewart has kindly shared his knowledge of the West Africa squadron with me, and his image of the slave ship *Diligenté* is reproduced on the front cover and in Chapter 4 with his permission. The rights to reproduce the other images in this book have been generously granted by the National Maritime Museum, the Royal Anthropological Institute, the Record Office for Leicestershire, Leicester and Rutland and Yale University Press.

This project began with my doctoral research, and I am very grateful to the Arts and Humanities Research Council (AHRC) for their funding of my Collaborative Doctoral Award at the Wilberforce Institute (University of Hull) and the National Maritime Museum, which included financial assistance for research visits around the UK and a fruitful trip to the United States. My position as Postdoctoral Research Fellow on the AHRC-funded Antislavery Usable Past project has since provided me with valuable time for further research and writing. I have also been a grateful recipient of a Caird Short-Term Research Fellowship from the National Maritime Museum.

I am profoundly indebted to four people for their enduring support and guidance in developing the direction of this book. I owe enormous gratitude to Douglas Hamilton, John McAleer and David Richardson, my brilliant PhD supervisors. John Oldfield has been enthusiastic about this research since its beginnings, and for the last five years has been a hugely supportive and understanding boss at the Wilberforce Institute. I would like to thank them all for their invaluable insight, expertise, and unstinting encouragement.

I have profited immensely from the excellent scholarship which feeds into the history of the Royal Navy's campaign against the transatlantic slave trade, and from the various conferences I have attended while presenting this research. For various discussions about the West Africa squadron and advice on the writing of this book, I am grateful to Kevin Bales, Robert Burroughs, Michael Barritt, David Blair, Katie Donington, Nicholas Evans, Bronwen Everill, Richard Huzzey, Andrew Pearson, Nigel Rigby, Suzanne Schwarz, James Walvin and Marcus Wood. Special thanks to Lindsay Doulton for being a great friend and sounding board throughout our respective PhD studies. Thanks too to my friends and colleagues at the Wilberforce Institute and on the Antislavery Usable Past project for all their support. Liverpool University Press has been great to work with. Alison Welsby has been a supportive editor, and I am very grateful to her for taking this project on board.

Finally, thanks to my rock of family and friends, north and south! Special thanks to my mum, Angela, and my sister, Ruby, for always being there. My three children, Kit, Ada and Bobby, have all arrived during the course of this project and have done very little to hasten its completion! They have, however, provided the most important things in abundance, namely love, laughter, and an invaluable sense of perspective. Last but certainly not least, to my husband Dave, thanks for everything.

Seeing this book come to fruition is bittersweet for me in that the person I most want to read it is sadly no longer with us. This book is dedicated to Robert Wills, my wonderful dad and my greatest champion. His passion for literature, language and learning was infectious, and he loved books more than anyone I will ever know. I hope he would have been proud of this one.

Abbreviations

BA	Bedfordshire Archives
BL	British Library
CAC	Churchill Archives Centre, Churchill College, Cambridge University
CRL	Cadbury Research Library, University of Birmingham
CUL	Cambridge University Library
DRO	Derbyshire Record Office
DUL	Durham University Library, Special Collections
GA	Gloucestershire Archives
HUA	Hull University Archives, Hull History Centre
MoD	Ministry of Defence Admiralty Library
NLS	National Library of Scotland
NRS	National Records of Scotland
NMM	Caird Library and Archive, National Maritime Museum
NMRN	National Museum of the Royal Navy
NYPL	New York Public Library
RAI	Royal Anthropological Institute Archive
SHC	Somerset Heritage Centre, South West Heritage Trust
SLNSW	Mitchell Library, State Library of New South Wales
TNA	The National Archives
UIC: SLC	University of Illinois at Chicago Library, Special Collections: Sierra Leone Collection
UKHO	UK Hydrographic Office Archive
USNA	Special Collections and Archives Department, Nimitz Library, US Naval Academy
WC	Wellcome Collection
WSRO	West Sussex Record Office

Introduction

England feels for the woes of Africa, she longs to release her from
those chains of bondage and misery in which she has been bound for
so many years past. She wishes 'Liberty' to be her 'watchword' & all
her children to be happy and free.

> Thy chains are broken, Africa be free!
> Thus saith the Island Empress of the sea
> Thus saith Britannia – oh ye winds & waves!
> Waft the glad tidings to the land of slaves.[1]

This declaration of British paternalism and assistance was written in 1852 by
Royal Navy Commander Arthur Parry Eardley-Wilmot, as part of a long
and passionate letter to the Commander-in-Chief of forces at Abeokuta
(present day south-west Nigeria). Commander Wilmot delivered his message
as a representative of 'HM the Queen' and an officer of the Royal Navy's
West Africa squadron, sent to enforce the terms of the Abolition of the Slave
Trade Act (1807). For six decades, the squadron was active in suppressing
the transatlantic slave trade between West Africa and the plantations of
the Americas, as Britain exerted increasing pressure – diplomatic and
coercive – on other nations continuing the trade. Naval suppression involved
intercepting and detaining slave ships embarked from the West African
coast, and releasing captive Africans found on board.[2] It also encompassed

1 CRL, Church Missionary Society Archive, CA2/08/04, Arthur Eardley-Wilmot
to 'Obba Shoron', 3 April 1852.

2 There are several names in use to describe individuals released from captivity on a
slave ship. Some overlap – for example, 'recaptured slaves', 'recaptives', 'captured slaves'
– but in all the state of recaptivity is regarded as distinct from slave trade captivity. In

an increasingly assertive mission to eradicate the trading in human lives within West African societies. Hence Wilmot offered the people of 'the land of slaves' Britain's protection as a nation 'mighty everywhere'. This proclamation was reinforced by his quotation of the opening couplets of the poem *The West Indies* by the abolitionist poet James Montgomery, first published in 1809.[3] These lines illuminate the new relationship forged between Britain and West Africa in the years following Britain's abolition of the transatlantic slave trade and, later, slavery in the British Caribbean, Mauritius and the Cape (via the Emancipation Act of 1833). Africa is personified as the pleading slave liberated from her slave-trading past; the British have the dominant role in releasing her and dismantling slavery. In his letter Wilmot thus presents concerns and assurances that were at the heart of the British abolitionist campaign in West Africa in the early to mid-nineteenth century. This book is about the unique role played by Wilmot and his naval colleagues in Britain's anti-slavery cause.[4]

Histories of the official operations, tactics and policies of the West Africa squadron and the wider legal and diplomatic framework of the nineteenth-century British campaign against the transatlantic slave trade in which the squadron operated are relatively well known.[5] This book's primary focus is

the British context, the political framework of naval suppression termed them 'liberated Africans', hence the Liberated African Department established in the British colony of Sierra Leone. However, as Chapter 4 of this book examines, terms such as 'liberating' or 'emancipating' are problematic, based on British perspectives of the process of recapturing slave ships and the subsequent fate of those on board. I use these terms in the context of their appearance in original sources.

3 James Montgomery, *The West Indies and Other Poems*, 3rd edn (London: Longman, 1810).

4 Until the Emancipation Act of 1833 many Britons remained slave owners in the Caribbean. Before this date, abolitionist endeavours (including the work of the Royal Navy) focused specifically on anti-slave-trade activity. Naval officers and their contemporaries, however, were not so specific in their terminology. This book will use the term 'anti-slavery' to incorporate the broad spectrum of abolitionist efforts in the early to mid-nineteenth century.

5 Christopher Lloyd, *The Navy and the Slave Trade: The Suppression of the African Slave Trade in the Nineteenth Century* (London: Longman, 1949) and William Ward, *The Royal Navy and the Slavers: The Suppression of the Atlantic Slave Trade* (London: George Allen & Unwin, 1969) continue to be cited as the key general texts for naval suppression. The essays in Keith Hamilton and Patrick Salmon (eds), *Slavery, Diplomacy and Empire: Britain and the Suppression of the Slave Trade, 1807–1975* (Eastbourne: Sussex Academic Press, 2009) analyse British efforts to eradicate slave trading by administrative, diplomatic and naval action. Useful works for the political, diplomatic and strategic background of naval suppression are Leslie Bethell, *The Abolition of the Brazilian Slave Trade: Britain, Brazil and the Slave Trade Question 1807–1869* (Cambridge:

the personal and cultural experiences of the naval officers employed at the operational frontline in implementing British abolitionist policy in West Africa. Rather than regarding their testimonies as peripheral or anecdotal to broader histories of the political or diplomatic context of the work of the West Africa squadron, this study instead places naval officers at the heart of the story by drawing on collections of previously unpublished personal accounts of service in West Africa.[6] These sources are not without their limitations: relatively few serving officers left personal papers, and the narratives that survive are clearly not representative of the experiences of all naval men or of both sides of the varied encounters between naval officers and West African peoples.[7] Nevertheless, these testimonies offer an invaluable insight into the multifaceted nature of naval suppression: a fundamentally different role for officers of the Royal Navy, with extraordinary features of

Cambridge University Press, 1970); David R. Murray, *Odious Commerce: Britain, Spain and the Abolition of the Cuban Slave Trade* (Cambridge: Cambridge University Press, 1980); David Eltis, *Economic Growth and the Ending of the Transatlantic Slave Trade* (Oxford: Oxford University Press, 1987). More recent largely narrative histories of the squadron are Bernard Edwards, *Royal Navy Versus the Slave Traders: Enforcing Abolition at Sea* (Barnsley: Pen and Sword Maritime, 2007); Sian Rees, *Sweet Water and Bitter: The Ships that Stopped the Slave Trade* (London: Chatto & Windus, 2009); Peter Grindal, *Opposing the Slavers: The Royal Navy's Campaign against the Atlantic Slave Trade* (London: I. B. Tauris, 2016). In *Inhuman Traffick: The International Struggle Against the Transatlantic Slave Trade: A Graphic History* (Oxford: Oxford University Press, 2015), historian Rafe Blaubarb and illustrator Liz Clarke have visualized British abolitionist efforts in the style of a graphic novel.

6 These personal testimonies of service in journals, diaries, letters and report books have never been researched as a cohesive group. Outside this collection of personal archives is a vast scope of primary material which is relevant to this research. Complementary papers selected for this book contain personal thoughts and opinions expressed in official records: from each ship (for example, logbooks) or in correspondence with or official reports to government, the Admiralty or other organizations such as the African Institution. Several naval officers published their narratives and memoirs from the West African coast as books or journal pieces. A valuable online source for letters composed by British officials involved in the suppression campaign, including naval officers, is *Visualizing Abolition: A Digital History of the Suppression of the African Slave Trade*, visualizingabolition.org.

7 Where are the other voices in the archive? Regrettably this book contains relatively few African perspectives. While first-person testimonies from recaptives are rare, there is excellent scholarship on the topic which can help build an understanding of what it meant to be a recaptured African in British hands. Similarly, documentation detailing naval officers' encounters with West African peoples on shore remains largely one-sided, and invariably slanted towards British concerns. There is also an absence of surviving archival material from naval ratings (those ranked lower than commissioned officers), although it can be assumed that many experiences were universal throughout HM ships.

service. The glory of battle and victory at Trafalgar was behind them; in its place was employment imbued with notions of humanitarianism and benevolence, which simultaneously exposed men to terrible human suffering. The objectives were impossible to meet at times; officers were tasked with detaining fast and efficient slave ships, captained by those desperate to profit from a still highly lucrative human trade. Climatic extremes and the threat of virulent disease on the West African coast, the so-called 'white man's grave', also affected perceptions of service. Invariably stationed there for two years or more, in the words of one naval officer, many became 'heartily disgusted' with the service.[8]

These narratives dispel the idea that naval officers were no more than the armed presence of the abolitionist movement. Their role was much more nuanced, and a thorough investigation of their attitudes and beliefs provides a valuable vantage point from which to view British abolitionism post-1807 in its varied forms. Presented to the rest of the world as a mission of humanity and enlightened thinking, Britain's international role against the slave trade presented a number of concerns, among which stopping the slave trade at its source in West African societies became paramount. As a result, naval directives to suppress human traffic at sea were bound to an increasingly interventionist approach to advance the anti-slavery message on shore.[9] Britain's humanitarian project to end slave trading in West African societies was tied to the agency of naval officers: these envoys of abolition were Britain's representatives in negotiations with West African rulers, in assisting missionary endeavours and state-sponsored exploration, and in other engagements with West African peoples. Their narratives of these relations are revealing of racial attitudes and Britain's evolving imperial agenda, of the transatlantic exchange of information about the slave trade, slavery and abolition between metropolitan Britain and the rest of the world. This book therefore follows recent trends in maritime history which have sought to include the Royal Navy's role as a social and cultural institution, challenging assumptions that seafarers were insulated from wider themes in British history.

Several scholars have addressed this need to explore cultural connections between navy and empire.[10] This study argues for the representation of naval

---

8 NMRN, 2005.76/2, Binstead diaries, 5 September 1823.

9 Histories of slave-trade suppression are now considered inseparable from the wider imperial context of Britain's anti-slavery campaign. See, for example, Suzanne Miers, *Britain and the Ending of the Slave Trade* (London: Longman, 1975) and the essays in Derek Peterson (ed.), *Abolitionism and Imperialism in Britain, Africa, and the Atlantic* (Athens, OH: Ohio University Press, 2010).

10 Authors such as Marcus Rediker, Isaac Land and Daniel Spence exemplify this

personnel as individuals rather than an anonymous collective. Their personal testimonies, inevitably shaped by their travels, by those they encountered, and by their interpretations of humanitarian discourse, illuminate how naval patriotism, professionalism and notions of duty interacted with anti-slavery rhetoric and imperial impulses.[11] This study therefore personalizes the history of naval suppression to understand what it meant to serve on anti-slave-trade patrols in West Africa, from everyday concerns regarding health, rewards and strategy, to more profound questions concerning national honour, religious belief, cultural encounters, responsibility for the lives of others in the most distressing of circumstances, and the true meaning of 'freedom' for the Africans they 'liberated'. These concerns have not been thoroughly examined in the Atlantic context.[12]

1807: Abolition, empire and identity

The Abolition of the Slave Trade Act marked a turning point in Britain's history as a world power. From its former position as the leading slave-trading nation, after 1807 notions of British identity now stressed abolitionism,

'cultural turn' in the historical scholarship of the Royal Navy, demonstrating how the history of the navy can be used to explore imperial concerns from new perspectives. See, for instance, Marcus Rediker, *Between the Devil and the Deep Blue Sea: Merchant Seamen, Pirates and the Anglo-American Maritime World, 1700–1750* (Cambridge: Cambridge University Press, 1987); Isaac Land, *War, Nationalism and the British Sailor, 1750–1850* (Basingstoke: Palgrave Macmillan, 2009); Daniel Spence, *Colonial Naval Culture and British Imperialism, 1922–67* (Manchester: Manchester University Press, 2015). This strand of historiography has extended to the opinions and motivations of eighteenth-century slave trade seamen and relations to the enslaved on board their vessels – see Emma Christopher, *Slave Ship Sailors and Their Captive Cargoes, 1730–1807* (Cambridge: Cambridge University Press, 2006).

11 These ideas were not specific to the navy in the Atlantic context. For example, Jane Samson, *Imperial Benevolence: Making British Authority in the Pacific Islands* (Honolulu, HI: University of Hawaii Press, 1998), argues that notions of Christian piety and public duty produced an alliance of naval power and humanitarianism in the nineteenth-century maritime Pacific world.

12 Essays which explore some of these ideas can be found in Robert Burroughs and Richard Huzzey (eds), *The Suppression of the Atlantic Slave Trade: British Policies, Practices and Representations of Naval Coercion* (Manchester: Manchester University Press, 2015). On the East African suppression campaign in the later nineteenth century, see Raymond Howell, *The Royal Navy and the Slave Trade* (London: Croom Helm, 1987). Lindsay Doulton, 'The Royal Navy's anti-slavery campaign in the western Indian Ocean, c. 1860–1890: race, empire and identity', unpublished PhD thesis, University of Hull, 2010, assesses the relationship between naval suppression and other imperialist and civilizing discourses on the East African anti-slave-trade patrols.

humanity and philanthropy.[13] Debates about how and why this fundamental transition happened continue to engage historians. In 1808 the abolitionist Thomas Clarkson presented the Abolition Act as Christianity's greatest triumph, regarded as a boost to national self-esteem in the struggles against Napoleon during the French Revolutionary and Napoleonic Wars fought between 1793 and 1815.[14] Historians such as G. M. Trevelyan and Sir Reginald Coupland followed Clarkson's example in representing abolition as a victory of idealism and morality which positioned abolitionists ('the Saints') in direct opposition to depraved plantation owners and slave merchants. Britain's anti-slavery cause was regarded as an indicator of the national character, dedicated to freedom.[15] Naval suppression fitted neatly into this narrative. In 1863 the naval historian C. D. Yonge claimed that suppression efforts 'owed their origin and their persevering resolute continuance to a pure unselfish philanthropy … our motives are as blameless, as honourable, as our exertions have been untiring'.[16] Such self-congratulatory accounts disregarded the darker history of Britain's domination of the slave trade.[17] They also ignored the efforts of other nations to suppress the slave trade, notably the United States and France.[18]

13 Britain dominated the transatlantic slave trade in the decades before 1807, and particularly during the years immediately before the Abolition Act, when it is estimated that Britons traded around 45 per cent of all enslaved Africans embarked from the West African coast. See David Eltis and David Richardson, 'A new assessment of the transatlantic slave trade', in David Eltis and David Richardson (eds), *Extending the Frontiers: Essays on the New Transatlantic Slave Trade Database* (New Haven, CT: Yale University Press, 2008), pp. 1–60.

14 Thomas Clarkson, *The History of the Abolition of the African Slave-Trade*, 2 vols (1808).

15 See, for example, Reginald Coupland, *The British Anti-slavery Movement* (London: T. Butterworth, 1933).

16 C. D. Yonge, *History of the British Navy: from the earliest period to the present time*, 3 vols (London: Richard Bentley, 1863), vol. 2, p. 500.

17 In *Blind Memory: Visual Representations of Slavery in England and America, 1780–1865* (Manchester: Manchester University Press, 2000), Marcus Wood argues that such celebration of the navy's role 'disguised the memory of the two hundred years of British domination of the slave trade' (p. 24).

18 David Eltis and David Richardson, *Atlas of the Transatlantic Slave Trade* (New Haven, CT: Yale University Press, 2010), p. 282, map 185, reveals that the Royal Navy was responsible for four out of five slave vessels captured under bilateral treaties. However, the US Africa squadron (formalized by the Webster–Ashburton Treaty of 1842) was also active in naval suppression. For an overview of US abolition legislation and suppression activities, including first-hand accounts from US naval officers, see Donald Canney, *Africa Squadron: The US Navy and the Slave Trade, 1842–1861* (Washington, DC: Potomac Books, 2002) and Sharla M. Fett, *Recaptured Africans: Surviving Slave Ships, Detention, and Dislocation in the Final Years of the Slave Trade* (Chapel Hill, NC: University of North Carolina Press, 2017), ch. 1. Published narratives from officers of the US Africa squadron

Eric Williams's influential *Capitalism and Slavery* (1944) offered the first challenge to moralistic interpretations of abolitionism, as he identified anti-slavery solely with shifts in Britain's economic interests. While his thesis has since been thoroughly questioned, Williams's conception of the economic as against moral determinants behind abolition has been influential on subsequent studies of anti-slavery which stress the variety of forces at play. Understandings of the origins, dynamics and appeal of the British anti-slavery movement have led to assertions that cultural change on both sides of the Atlantic, rather than economic self-interest, lay at the heart of Britain's abolitionist efforts.[19] The broader social and cultural contexts of the rise of anti-slavery sentiment from the 1780s have been extensively explored, including its relation to popular politics, domestic and imperial reform, urbanization and industrialization, the progress of scientific Enlightenment, and the influence of religious and philanthropic movements, galvanized by the Quakers and other nonconformist groups. Anti-slavery has been regarded as a collective achievement, reflected in mass popular support and resource commitment towards anti-slavery efforts.[20] Histories of Britain's 'age of abolition' in the English-speaking Atlantic world are also interwoven with a tumultuous revolutionary period in former North

include Horatio Bridge, *Journal of an African Cruiser* (London, 1845); Andrew Hull Foote, *Africa and the American Flag* (New York, 1854); Herbert C. Gilliland, *Voyage to a Thousand Cares: Master's Mate Lawrence with the Africa Squadron 1844–1846* (Annapolis, MD: Naval Institute Press, 2003). For the largely unenthusiastic efforts of the French West African squadron (and tensions with British counterparts on the West African coast), see Paul Michael Kielstra, *The Politics of Slave Trade Suppression in Britain and France, 1814–48: Diplomacy, Morality and Economics* (Basingstoke: Macmillan, 2000). A commander of the French forces, Louis Édouard Bouët-Willaumez, published a narrative of his experiences: *Commerce et traite des noirs aux côtes occidentales d'Afrique* (Paris, 1848).

19 See, for example, David Brion Davis, *The Problem of Slavery in Western Culture* (Oxford: Oxford University Press, 1966); David Brion Davis, *The Problem of Slavery in the Age of Revolution* (Oxford: Oxford University Press, 1975); Roger Anstey, *The Atlantic Slave Trade and British Abolition, 1760–1810* (London: Macmillan, 1975); Seymour Drescher, *Capitalism and Antislavery: British Mobilization in Comparative Perspective* (Oxford: Oxford University Press, 1986); Seymour Drescher, *Abolition: A History of Slavery and Antislavery* (Cambridge: Cambridge University Press, 2009).

20 Among others, Howard Temperley, *British Antislavery 1833–1870* (London: Longman, 1972); David Turley, *The Culture of English Antislavery, 1780–1860* (London: Routledge, 1991); Clare Midgley, *Women Against Slavery: The British Campaigns, 1780–1870* (London: Routledge, 1992); J. R. Oldfield, *Popular Politics and British Anti-Slavery: The Mobilisation of Public Opinion against the Slave Trade, 1787–1807* (Manchester: Manchester University Press, 1995); Christopher L. Brown, *Moral Capital: Foundations of British Abolitionism* (Chapel Hill, NC: University of North Carolina Press, 2006).

American colonies, France and Haiti, transforming relationships between nation and empire.[21] The anti-slavery cause became a political tool through which former British involvement in the transatlantic trade was reframed to acclaim the nation's abolitionist achievements, placing the nation, as Joel Quirk and David Richardson have asserted, 'in the vanguard of European civilization and at the forefront of human progress'.[22] The Royal Navy's part in this wider framework of abolition has only recently received the scholarly attention it deserves.[23]

At the beginning of the nineteenth century, the end of the Revolutionary and Napoleonic Wars saw Britain in possession of a vast territorial empire and deploying the dominant naval fleet in Europe, regarded as an integral part of the coercive forces of the state alongside the army and colonial militias.[24] The abolition of the slave trade prompted a multitude of concerns about the appropriate application of this British power and influence. As David Eltis has argued, the 'campaign against the slave trade was fought on two not always compatible levels. There was the physical or naval confrontation and, more important, there was the ideological struggle.' In the years following abolition the goal for abolitionists, alongside the physical suppression of the slave trade, was 'the imposition of a conception of freedom' on others.[25] Britain's elevated moral agenda regarding West Africa and other territories was encapsulated by the three tenets of the 'civilizing' mission: commerce, Christianity and civilization. Abolitionism thus became dependent on the introduction of 'legitimate' commerce (as trade unrelated to transatlantic slavery was termed) and the spread of Christian, 'civilized' values with the assistance of missionaries.[26] The establishment of Sierra Leone as a

21 Linda Colley, *Britons: Forging the Nation, 1707–1837* (New Haven, CT: Yale University Press, 1992). The slave rebellion that broke out in the French colony of St Domingue in 1791 soon became a revolution, leading to the creation of the Republic of Haiti in 1804.

22 Joel Quirk and David Richardson, 'Anti-slavery, European identity and international society: a macro-historical perspective', *The Journal of Modern European History*, 7.1 (2009), pp. 68–92, at pp. 86–87.

23 Richard Huzzey, *Freedom Burning: Anti-Slavery and Empire in Victorian Britain* (Ithaca, NY: Cornell University Press, 2012), positions the Royal Navy's anti-slave-trade patrols in the context of wider British debates about relationships between the state, anti-slavery ideology and imperial interests in the nineteenth century. See also essays in John McAleer and Christer Petley (eds), *The Royal Navy and the British Atlantic World, c. 1750–1820* (Basingstoke: Palgrave Macmillan, 2016).

24 Christopher Bayly, *Imperial Meridian: The British Empire and the World 1780–1830* (London: Longman, 1989), p. 162.

25 Eltis, *Economic Growth*, pp. 102, 104.

26 Robin Law (ed.), *From Slave Trade to 'Legitimate' Commerce: The Commercial Transition in Nineteenth-Century West Africa* (Cambridge: Cambridge University Press,

British Crown colony on the West African coast in 1807 articulated these new priorities. Providing support for the naval attack on slave trading and a settlement for Africans released from slave vessels were major objectives, but so too was a desire to take the message of abolition beyond Sierra Leone's borders. Naval officers worked alongside other colonial officials to promote British conceptions of an improved, civilized society. These beliefs dominated British relations with West Africa throughout the century and invariably served to further British strategic and commercial interests in the region; hence claims by historians such as Robin Law that the push for humanitarian intervention was 'inherently imperialist'.[27]

Historians have also explored how British intentions and objectives changed over time and by the nature of encounters with 'others'. As Christopher Bayly has argued, in the first third of the nineteenth century, the empire was only loosely controlled from the centre: colonial governments, local conditions and metropolitan influences all played a part in formulating imperial policies.[28] Such interpretations of Britain's imperial past have stressed that relationships with empire did not flow in one direction. Identification of the variety of actors – missionaries, explorers, colonial administrators, African rulers – has highlighted how abolitionism and national identity were influenced by the nature of dialogues concerning empire, slavery, religion, race, ethnicity, gender and class.[29] These discourses took place within anti-slavery debates which increasingly took on an international dimension.[30] Discussion of the navy's suppression campaign

1995); Seymour Drescher, *The Mighty Experiment: Free Labor versus Slavery in British Emancipation* (Oxford: Oxford University Press, 2002); Andrew Porter, *Religion versus Empire? British Protestant Missionaries and Overseas Expansion, 1700–1914* (Manchester: Manchester University Press, 2004).

27 Robin Law, 'Abolitionism and imperialism: international law and the British suppression of the Atlantic slave trade', in Peterson (ed.), *Abolitionism and Imperialism*, pp. 150–74, at p. 150. The relationships between abolition, imperialism and humanitarian intervention in Sierra Leone and the US colony of Liberia are examined by Bronwen Everill in *Abolition and Empire in Sierra Leone and Liberia* (Basingstoke: Palgrave Macmillan, 2013).

28 Bayly, *Imperial Meridian*, ch. 7.

29 Catherine Hall, *Civilising Subjects: Metropole and Colony in the English Imagination 1830–1867* (Cambridge: Polity Press, 2002); Catherine Hall and Sonya O. Rose (eds), *At Home with the Empire: Metropolitan Culture and the Imperial World* (Cambridge: Cambridge University Press, 2006); David Lambert and Alan Lester (eds), *Colonial Lives across the British Empire: Imperial Careering in the Long Nineteenth Century* (Cambridge: Cambridge University Press, 2006); Hilary M. Carey (ed.), *Empires of Religion* (Basingstoke: Palgrave Macmillan, 2008).

30 For example, J. R. Oldfield, *Transatlantic Abolitionism in the Age of Revolution: An International History of Anti-Slavery, c. 1787–1820* (Cambridge: Cambridge University

is relatively absent from this historiography, and yet naval officers were in a comparable position to other British representatives on the West African coast to offer insight into Britain's evolving relationship with slavery and empire.[31] As this book explores, naval men were involved in these processes as envoys, information gatherers and negotiators.

The Royal Navy in 1807

The Royal Navy has a long and interrelated history with the institution of slavery in the British Atlantic world. British naval strategy in the eighteenth century was heavily concentrated on the West Indies, to protect the valuable sugar industry that was dependent on slave labour. The ships of the slave trade were also regarded as a 'nursery' for seamen (without the employment of the slave trade, the argument ran, the country would lose the skilled labour which swelled the navy when required for national defence). The Abolition Act overturned this relationship, as the Royal Navy was now tasked with policing and persecuting the transatlantic slave trade, and the main theatre of its interaction with the trade was thus relocated to the West African coast. The officers of the West Africa squadron also belonged to a naval service much changed in nature and purpose. Eighteenth-century naval traditions were associated with prosperity, patriotism and the defence of liberty; as the *Gentleman's Magazine* noted in 1803, 'the anchor of Great Britain' was 'the constitutional courage of her seamen'.[32] However, the post-war years witnessed a shift from public enthusiasm for the navy to despondency, particularly after the failure to win a decisive victory against the United States in the War of 1812. Combined with peacetime reductions after 1815, the mood in naval circles was one of uncertainty and low morale.[33]

Press, 2013); William Mulligan and Maurice Bric (eds), *A Global History of Anti-Slavery Politics in the Nineteenth Century* (London: Palgrave Macmillan, 2013).

31 This study also contributes to a strand of historiography that personalizes the history of Britain's relationship with empire in the use of narratives and individual stories. For example, Linda Colley, *Captives: Britain, Empire and the World 1600–1850* (London: Random House, 2002); Clare Anderson, *Subaltern Lives: Biographies of Colonialism in the Indian Ocean World, 1790–1920* (Cambridge: Cambridge University Press, 2012).

32 Quoted in Gerald Jordan and Nicholas Rogers, 'Admirals as heroes: patriotism and liberty in Hanoverian England', *The Journal of British Studies*, 28.3 (1989), p. 224. See Margarette Lincoln, *Representing the Royal Navy: British Sea Power, 1750–1815* (Aldershot: Ashgate, 2002); Geoff Quilley, *Empire to Nation: Art, History and the Visualization of Maritime Britain 1768–1829* (New Haven, CT: Yale University Press, 2011), ch. 7. For example, monuments erected to honour naval heroes played a pivotal role in influencing British national identity in late eighteenth-century society.

33 Lincoln, *Representing the Royal Navy*, ch. 8. The navy shrank in size from its

Such sentiment reflected the national temper at the beginning of the Regency period: depression, chronic unemployment and social discontent.[34]

The shift in fortune contributed to a different social composition in the commissioned officer class. Officers generally entered the navy directly from school through the 'interest' of family and connections, or via the Royal Naval College, reconstituted in 1806.[35] Fewer vacancies in the post-war years resulted in a decline in the number of lower-class entrants. By mid-century, and reflective of a wider process in British society more generally, a good officer was regarded as both a gentleman and a Christian.[36] In 1840 Midshipman Astley Cooper Key joined the *Pickle* on anti-slave-trade patrols on the West Indies station under the command of Lieutenant Holland, whom he described as 'a perfect gentleman, and has £2000 a year … he is a strictly religious and steady man, and a very good officer and sailor'.[37] Naval hierarchies became more pronounced and stereotypes of ratings as intemperate and uncouth Jack Tars were common in nineteenth-century literary and visual culture.[38] This perceived behaviour from the lower ranks had consequences for a reputation of ill-discipline on the West African coast, and the navy as a whole suffered from poor recruitment and high rates of desertion in this period.[39]

There was also a change in purpose for Royal Navy fleets. The period covered by this book was one of relative peace; it was also a time of

wartime peak of 140,000 to its peacetime norm of about 25,000 men. Many popular publications written after the war offered a negative view of the navy, for example, Admiral Hawkins's pamphlet *Statement of Certain Immoral Practices in HM Ships* (1822).

34 See Eric J. Evans, *The Forging of the Modern State: Early Industrial Britain, 1783–1870*, 3rd edn (Harlow: Longman Pearson, 2001).

35 John Winton, 'Life and education in a technically evolving navy 1815–1925', in J. R. Hill (ed.), *The Oxford Illustrated History of the Royal Navy* (Oxford: Oxford University Press, 1995), pp. 251–52. Commissioned officers held their position by royal commission, usually after passing an examination. They entered the service as midshipmen.

36 C. I. Hamilton, 'Naval hagiography and the Victorian hero', *The Historical Journal*, 23.2 (1980), pp. 386–87; Michael Lewis, *The Navy in Transition 1814–1864: A Social History* (London: Hodder and Stoughton, 1965), p. 22.

37 P. H. Colomb, *Memoirs of the Admiral the Right Honorable Sir Astley Cooper Key* (London: Methuen, 1898), pp. 51–52.

38 Such characterizations were not necessarily legitimate, as argued by Mary Conley in *From Jack Tar to Union Jack: Representing Naval Manhood in the British Empire, 1870–1918* (Manchester: Manchester University Press, 2009). In *War, Nationalism*, Isaac Land stresses the diversity of voices of Jack Tar and argues for the sailor's part in the forging of British national identity.

39 E. L. Rasor, *Reform in the Royal Navy: A Social History of the Lower Deck 1850 to 1880* (Hamden, CT: Archon Books, 1976), pp. 9–10. There were campaigns for the reform of naval recruitment and discipline throughout the century.

increasing British dominance in maritime trade, commerce and shipping.[40] The Royal Navy took a leading role in the suppression of piracy in the eastern Mediterranean, the Aegean, the West Indies, Borneo and in Chinese waters. Officers also served to protect commercial interests in Latin America. In 1848 the West Africa squadron consisted of an equivalent number of warships (27) as the Mediterranean (31) and East Indies and China stations (25 each).[41] The squadron offered paid work at a time when jobs were few, but, as this book explores, many naval officers were sceptical about travelling to the infamous West African coast. The change in purpose contributed to negative comparisons with previous generations who had witnessed the glory of war. An unidentified officer pleaded in 1842, 'Ill-used, time-worn veterans! I cannot share your hardly-earned honours ... Don't *say* that we have degenerated from the gallant tars of old.'[42] However, gallantry and honour in the navy was represented in new forms: Britain's elevated humanitarian agenda contributed to new validations for the navy in its role in policing and protecting the Atlantic empire. As Rear-Admiral Sydney Eardley-Wilmot wrote about the suppression campaign in 1927: 'Great Britain has reason to be proud of what she did in this matter, work, which if less glorious than deeds of war, was of real service to humanity.'[43]

The structure of this book

Envoys of Abolition is a study of the insights and experiences of one key group of individuals tasked with negotiating Britain's nineteenth-century abolitionist campaign in West Africa. As such, the chapters are loosely arranged around the relationships between naval suppression and the themes of anti-slavery, empire and identity. They explore the central roles of naval officers in three arenas: at sea, aboard Royal Navy vessels and captured slave ships; on shore, in West African settlements; and in the metropolitan debates around slavery and abolitionism in Britain. Chapters 1 and 2 introduce the work of the West Africa squadron in detaining slave ships at sea and disseminating the anti-slavery message on shore by examining the individual experiences

40 Paul Kennedy, *The Rise and Fall of British Naval Mastery* (London: Allen Lane, 1976), ch. 6. Between the end of the Napoleonic Wars in 1815 and the Anglo-Russian war of 1854–56 there was peace among the Great Powers; the worst clash was the Opium Wars with China, 1840–60.

41 Kennedy, *Rise and Fall*, pp. 164–71.

42 'The Slaver. From the note-book of an Officer employed against the slave trade', *United Service Magazine*, part I (1842), pp. 375–80, at p. 375. Author's emphasis.

43 *An Admiral's Memories: Sixty-five Years Afloat and Ashore* (London: Sampson Low, Marston and Co., 1927). Sydney Eardley-Wilmot was Commander Arthur Eardley-Wilmot's nephew.

and perceptions of naval officers. Chapter 1 looks at the roles and challenges faced by officers at sea in the pursuit of slave ships, including the difficult conditions of service. Officers' coercive roles at sea became inseparable from their responsibilities to the 'civilizing' mission on shore. Chapter 2 explores their roles in promoting Christianity, legitimate trade and exploration; in the pursuit of anti-slavery treaties with African rulers; and in the increasing use of military force to assert British abolitionist ambitions.

Slavery and the slave trade formed the dominant frame of reference for officers' perceptions of their service in West Africa, and they engaged in constant dialogue with humanitarian ideals and anti-slavery rhetoric. Chapter 3 examines officers' beliefs in relation to the principles of British abolitionism and their commitment to the anti-slavery cause, while Chapter 4 explores their reactions to the human consequences of the slave trade witnessed on slave ships captured as prizes, and their relationships with recaptives. Chapter 6 explores the varied contributions of naval officers to metropolitan discussions about anti-slavery taking place in Britain in the early to mid-nineteenth century, challenging the supposedly isolationist nature of naval service in relation to broader social and cultural movements for change. Key themes throughout these chapters are how officers understood the nature of their role on the anti-slave-trade patrols, their conceptions of duty and professionalism in a humanitarian context, and what was expected of a naval officer in this extraordinary set of circumstances.

Chapter 5 focuses on officers' relationships with West African peoples met on shore, intertwined with ideas of race, gender and class. Officers' narratives of encounters often subscribed to stereotypes about non-Europeans, but also encompass a wide variety of opinions, interactions and connections, and evidence of engagement with different West African cultures reveals how immersed some officers became in their West African mission. Racial identity is key. Chapters 3 and 5 uncover broader shifts in racial attitudes as the century progressed, affecting officers' opinions on slavery, the missionary cause and the necessity of European 'trusteeship' for indigenous peoples.[44] Chapter 4 examines the ambiguities of freedom for Africans 'liberated' by the British. Officers' encounters with slavery and their relationships with African peoples on captured slave vessels and in West African societies may have played out in a military context but were often highly personal and emotional in character and impact. Their experiences illuminate fundamental

---

44 Some of the racial terminology used by naval officers and contemporaries, such as 'savage', 'civilized' or 'heathen', represent cultural and religious chauvinism now recognized as deeply offensive. Such terminology is restricted in this book to quotations or passages in which historical views are summarized.

concerns of the British anti-slavery campaign in West Africa, themes which run throughout the chapters of this book: of national identity, race, humanitarianism, and the true meaning of freedom.

1

Abolition at sea

Broadly speaking, naval officers of the West Africa squadron worked in two distinct but interrelated fields: at sea, detaining slave ships or preventing their embarkation, and on shore, as part of Britain's wider abolitionist mission. This chapter examines the former, through the perspectives of naval officers. As such, it will provide the necessary background for other stories to follow: officers' day-to-day challenges and experiences at sea were hugely influential in how they perceived the wider contexts of their anti-slavery duty.

Background

For six decades, the ships of the West Africa squadron patrolled 2,000 miles of West African coastline lying roughly between the island of Cape Verde in the north and Luanda (or St Paul de Loanda, as it was sometimes known) in the south, in present-day Angola. The British colony of Sierra Leone (and its capital, Freetown) served as headquarters for anti-slave-trade operations, and the squadron was divided geographically into five divisions along the coast (for a period between 1832 and 1840, it was integrated with the Cape of Good Hope station). The number of British ships that patrolled these waters varied. In 1818 Commodore Sir George Ralph Collier had six vessels under his command; the number remained below ten throughout the 1820s before increasing steadily in the 1830s to 27 by 1848. It was invariably the smallest warships that were sent to the West African coast, with crews varying between 60 and 135 men.[1] Steam vessels (in contrast to sail) appeared on the squadron in greater numbers from the 1830s and 1840s. Warrants to search

1 Lloyd, *Navy and the Slave Trade*, Appendix C; www.pdavis.nl/WestAfr.htm [accessed 5 February 2018].

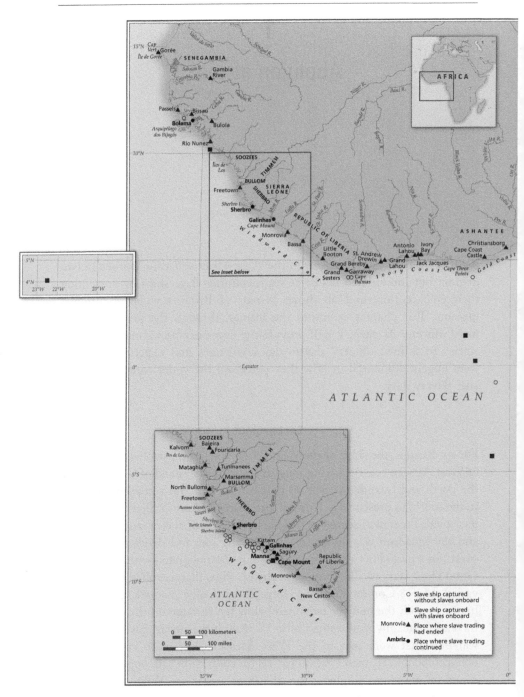

1 'Slave-Ship Captures by the British African Squadron, 1847–1848',
in David Eltis and David Richardson, *Atlas of the Transatlantic Slave Trade*
(New Haven, CT: Yale University Press, 2010), pp. 284–85, map 186

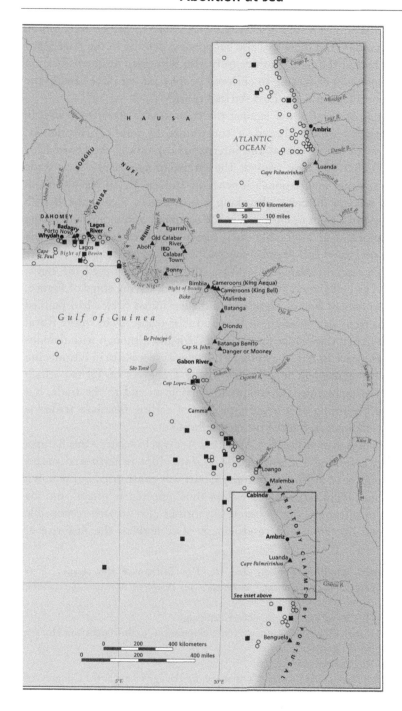

ships suspected of illegal slaving activities were issued to British warships on all foreign stations, and there was also suppression activity in the Americas.[2] The second half of the nineteenth century also witnessed an intensification of naval suppression of trading in enslaved peoples taking place around the Cape of Good Hope and the East African coast.[3]

Britain's use of naval power against the transatlantic slave trade was, in Richard Huzzey's words, 'shaped or constrained by political calculation', in the context of both national and international politics.[4] As David Eltis and David Richardson have argued, 'the campaign against the slave trade always had a strong international dimension', and the Royal Navy's role in suppression was no different.[5] Invoking humanitarian ideals, the British believed they had a right to intervene in the economic and moral endeavours of other nations, and after 1807 they pressured other maritime powers whose citizens were still legally engaged in the slave trade to declare against it. During the Napoleonic Wars, the British exercised the rights they claimed as belligerents to intercept and search enemy ships of France, the Netherlands and Spain. Denmark and the United States had banned their citizens from slave trading, in 1803 and 1808 respectively, so the Royal Navy also searched these ships for enslaved Africans, although with dubious legality. With peace in 1815, the Foreign Office was successful in introducing an anti-slavery agreement in principle at the Congress of Vienna which committed the represented sovereigns to putting an end to the trade, but this was the beginning of a lengthy process of ending the slave trade via international diplomacy, backed by legal reform.[6]

A primary objective of the 1807 Abolition Act was to secure a mechanism for stopping, searching and seizing illegal slave ships in territorial waters and on the high seas. A Vice-Admiralty Court was constituted in Freetown for the trial and adjudication of slave ships thus captured as 'prizes', and the prosecution of offenders. Sierra Leone authorities also became responsible for the formal liberation and resettlement of recaptives; the majority of

2 John Beeler, 'Maritime policing and the Pax Britannica: the Royal Navy's anti-slavery patrol in the Caribbean, 1828–1848', *The Northern Mariner*, 16.1 (2006), pp. 1–20.

3 Doulton, 'The Royal Navy's anti-slavery campaign'.

4 Richard Huzzey, 'The politics of slave-trade suppression', in Burroughs and Huzzey (eds), *Suppression*, pp. 17–52, at p. 17.

5 Eltis and Richardson, *Atlas*, p. 271.

6 It took until 1890, at the Brussels Conference, for the agreement at the Congress of Vienna to become a binding instrument. The League of Nations Convention to Suppress the Slave Trade and Slavery followed in 1926. For a useful overview, see Jean Allain, 'Nineteenth century law of the sea and the British abolition of the slave trade', *British Yearbook of International Law*, 78.1 (2007), pp. 342–88.

those released from British ships remained in Freetown and its hinterland.[7] From 1819 international anti-slave-trade courts, the Courts of Mixed Commission, were constituted there too.[8] The 'right of search' was at the heart of negotiations to create a system of enforcement, and throughout the first decades of the nineteenth century a network of bilateral treaties was signed, the first in 1810, which authorized naval powers to stop and search suspected slave ships of other nations. Treaties signed in 1817 and 1835 between Spain and Britain, and in 1826 between Brazil and Britain made slave trading illegal between Africa, Cuba and Brazil. France began enforcing suppression in its colonies from the 1830s, and in 1836 Portugal was the last nation in the Atlantic world to abolish slave trading (before this date it continued to legally trade 'South of the Line' – the equator). However, excepting the British and Dutch abolitions in 1807 and 1814, a significant delay occurred between the passing of abolitionist legislation and its enforcement on the coast.[9] Part of these treaty negotiations included payments, inducements and bribes as a means by which Britain extracted concessions from other powers. This construction of a diplomatic consensus was administered by a newly created Slave Trade Department which emerged in the 1820s at the Foreign Office – a 'permanent anti-slave-trade bureaucracy', in David Eltis's words.[10]

7 For an overview of the various sites of 'liberation' for formerly enslaved Africans across the Atlantic world in the nineteenth century, see Daniel Domingues da Silva et al., 'The diaspora of Africans liberated from slave ships in the nineteenth century', *The Journal of African History*, 55 (2014), pp. 347–69.

8 From 1817, Courts of Mixed Commission were set up by Britain, the Netherlands, Spain, Portugal, the United States and Brazil to adjudicate cases of suspected slave trading. These courts were empowered to release enslaved Africans and condemn slave vessels and equipment but could not exact penalties against slave ship crews or owners. There were at various times Mixed Commission courts at Sierra Leone, Havana, the Cape of Good Hope, Rio de Janeiro, Surinam and Luanda. See Leslie Bethell, 'The Mixed Commissions for the suppression of the transatlantic slave trade in the nineteenth century', *The Journal of African History*, 7.1 (1966), pp. 79–93. In *The Slave Trade and the Origins of International Human Rights Law* (Oxford: Oxford University Press, 2011), Jenny Martinez ties the work of these international Admiralty courts to the roots of human rights law. See also Tara Helfman, 'The Court of Vice Admiralty at Sierra Leone and the abolition of the West African slave trade', *The Yale Law Journal*, 115 (2006), pp. 1122–56; Farida Shaikh, 'Judicial diplomacy: British officials and the Mixed Commission courts', in Hamilton and Salmon (eds), *Slavery, Diplomacy*, pp. 42–64.

9 Eltis and Richardson, *Atlas*, map 183, pp. 271, 280.

10 Eltis, *Economic Growth*, pp. 96, 111; Huzzey, *Freedom Burning*, pp. 43–45. See also Keith Hamilton, 'Zealots and helots: the slave trade department of the nineteenth-century Foreign Office', in Hamilton and Salmon (eds), *Slavery, Diplomacy*, pp. 20–41.

With responsibility for the military enforcement of these diplomatic commitments, the Royal Navy was thus used as an instrument of state to pursue Britain's international agenda. The navy's role became more prominent as it became clear that the treaty-based system was easy for slave traders to undermine – foreign flags were fraudulently hoisted, the enslaved were disguised as crew members, papers were falsified, faster slave ships were built for purpose, and so on. Agreements in the early decades generally stipulated that ships could be detained and tried only if enslaved Africans were found on board; ships equipped or fitted for the slave trade could not be detained until the introduction of equipment clauses into treaties in the 1830s. Questions over the legal basis of Britain's right to search and detain vessels of other nations created diplomatic tensions and raised issues of intervention by one sovereign state in the affairs of another.[11] As one of the only states with the maritime power to patrol the Atlantic in this way, the British appeared to disregard the rules of state sovereignty and freedom of the seas (which ensured that during peacetime, no state had the right to visit and search the ship of another state without its consent) to serve their purpose.[12] In particular, an agreement with the United States for the mutual right of search of vessels proved elusive and, in Andrew Lambert's words, marked the 'limits of British power'.[13] The American flag was often used as a cover by slave traders, who exploited the diplomatic situation. British efforts were also hindered by accusations of dubious legality by other maritime powers, in the belief that the Royal Navy's authority was being deployed to gain commercial advantage and deny

11 Recent examinations of the Royal Navy as an instrument of foreign intervention in this period include John Bew, '"From an umpire to a competitor": Castlereagh, Canning and the issue of international intervention in the wake of the Napoleonic Wars', in Brendan Simms and D. J. B. Trim (eds), *Humanitarian Intervention: A History* (Cambridge: Cambridge University Press, 2011), pp. 117–38. In the same volume, Maeve Ryan examines the military interventionist aspect of the navy's anti-slavery role in 'The price of legitimacy in humanitarian intervention: Britain, the right of search, and the abolition of the West African slave trade, 1807–1867', pp. 231–56.

12 Andrea Nicholson, 'Transformations in the law concerning slavery: legacies of the nineteenth century anti-slavery movement', in Mulligan and Bric (eds), *Global History*, pp. 214–36; *Slavery in Diplomacy: The Foreign Office and the Suppression of the Transatlantic Slave Trade*, Foreign and Commonwealth Office Historians History Note, 17 (2007), pp. 4–8.

13 Andrew Lambert, 'Slavery, free trade and naval strategy, 1840–1860', in Hamilton and Salmon (eds), *Slavery, Diplomacy*, pp. 65–80, at p. 66. In *Recaptured Africans*, Sharla M. Fett describes how many commentators in the United States charged the federal government with hypocrisy for sanctioning the business of a slaveholding nation and failing to consistently enforce slave trade abolition through granting the mutual right of search (p. 3). Nor was the US Africa squadron particularly effective, with an average of only two slavers per year taken between 1844 and 1861 (Canney, *Africa Squadron*, p. 222).

Britain's international rivals opportunities to profit from slave trading.[14] Such claims were fuelled by Foreign Secretary Lord Palmerston's use of a network of spies and secret-service funds to bribe Brazilian politicians, for example. Many methods of suppression were deemed in breach of international law, the destruction of the property of slave traders in Brazilian waters by the Royal Navy in 1850 being one frequently cited instance.[15]

Changing tactics

The squadron's effectiveness in suppressing slave-trade traffic at sea was severely limited in the first decades of its operations. Captain Edward Henry Columbine was one of the first naval officers charged with fulfilling British abolitionist ambitions on the West African coast; he was also appointed Governor of Sierra Leone in 1810. As Britain was still at war, a permanent anti-slavery squadron did not operate until after 1815, but a small naval force under Columbine's command was employed blockading the coast around the colony, and several slave ships were captured and condemned at the Admiralty courts.[16] In 1809 Columbine appeared confident in the navy's mission, and believed success to be mainly a question of the number of vessels employed to intercept slavers. He wrote in his journal, 'If I had a few tenders, I would very soon put an end to this traffic.'[17] However, the task was made difficult by the equivocal nature of the laws under which crews were operating, and the open defiance of slave traders. Fundamentally, the squadron could not contend with the escalating demand for slaves from the sugar and coffee plantations of Brazil and the Spanish plantation colonies of Cuba and Puerto Rico. As Columbine wrote: 'The temptation is too great for the generality of the mercantile world to withstand. A slave which will not cost above 18 or 20 £ here, is worth 90 £ at the Havannah.'[18] In the decade

---

14 Ryan, 'The price of legitimacy'. Portugal, for example, with an African colonial economy based on the slave trade (and importantly, no real domestic interest in abolition), avoided committing to an agreement to act against the slave trade.

15 Lambert, 'Slavery', pp. 66, 69; Eltis, *Economic Growth*, pp. 115–16. Lord Palmerston was Foreign Secretary three times (1830–34, 1835–41 and 1846–51) and served twice as Prime Minister (1855–58 and 1859–65).

16 Christopher Terrell, 'Columbine, Edward Henry (1763–1811)', *Oxford Dictionary of National Biography*, Oxford University Press, 2004, www.oxforddnb.com/view/article/64853 [accessed 9 March 2017].

17 UIC: SLC, Series III, Folder 10, Columbine journals, 12 March 1810, ff. 62–63.

18 UIC: SLC, Series III, Folder 10, Columbine journals, 23 August 1810, ff. 174–75. For the increase in the numbers and prices of slaves bought in Brazil and Cuba from the transatlantic slave trade, see Eltis, *Economic Growth*, Appendix C, pp. 260–64; Eltis and Richardson, *Atlas*, pp. 200–03.

following Columbine's governorship, several slave ships were captured by the *Amelia* under the command of Captain Frederick Irby between 1811 and 1813, and by Captain Lloyd of the sloop *Kangaroo* in 1812.[19] It was not until 1818, however, that the West Africa station was formally established, with Sir George Ralph Collier of the *Tartar* as its first Commodore. In his reports to the Admiralty, Collier appeared confident in his assertion that the 'detestable traffic is now held in as much abhorrence throughout the British settlements in Africa, as it is by the ... most philanthropic & enlightened person in England'.[20] However, slave trading persisted. Collier wrote that unless naval vessels had 'the full powers of a Belligerent, all prohibitory laws against this trade will become a mockery'.[21] As Samuel Richardson of the *Maidstone* despairingly wrote in a letter home in 1826: 'it is quite ridiculous the attempts we are making against the slave trade. The French we cannot touch at all. The Portuguese are allowed to trade South of the Line; that gives much latitude to false papers that hardly any vessel we find with slaves can be detained.'[22] Despite the best intentions, a fully effectual naval police force would take time and resources.

As the methods pursued by naval vessels at sea appeared ineffective against slave trafficking (which continued at near eighteenth-century levels), Britain's policy towards the suppression of the slave trade began to shift from the late 1820s. In 1830 a Parliamentary Committee had called for a reduction of financial commitments on the West African coast. However, the following decade witnessed popular abolitionism renewed against colonial slavery, and the Reform Act of 1832 shifted parliamentary opinion in response to the new electorate. Reform gave impetus for Britain's policy-makers to involve themselves further in West African affairs, and as a result, the naval suppression campaign became increasingly interventionist. In Andrew Lambert's words, naval policy 'had to deal with supply and demand before the scale of the trade could be reduced to a level where naval force could hope to be effective'.[23] Tactics changed from attempting to capture ships at sea to stopping the embarkation of slave ships in the first place, and expenditure on the West Africa squadron rose by 50 per cent between 1829 and 1841.[24] So-called 'gunboat diplomacy' led to the blockading of points

19 Ward, *The Royal Navy*, pp. 50–58.

20 NMM, WEL/10, George Collier, 'Report of the Forts and Settlements on the Coast of Africa', no folios.

21 MoD, MSS 45, 'Second Annual Report on the coast of Africa by Commodore Sir George Collier, 1820', f. 241.

22 DRO, D8/B/F/66, Samuel Richardson to Jeffery Lockett, 30 June 1826.

23 Lambert, 'Slavery', pp. 77–78.

24 Philip D. Curtin, *The Image of Africa: British Ideas and Action 1780–1850* (Madison, WI: University of Wisconsin Press, 1964), pp. 289–90, 304.

of embarkation; the targeting of barracoons (holding pens for captives) and other inshore slaving establishments; and the destruction of slave-trading vessels, equipment and depots belonging to European traders. Furthermore, as explored in the next chapter, treaties were pursued with African rulers to end the supply of enslaved peoples. The concept of offensive naval action to target the roots of the slave trade was not new. Boat sorties upriver to target slave trading were initiated with the squadron's inception, and the language of combat and war was used frequently. In demanding the release of 50 enslaved people lodged in a house in Accra in 1820, Commander B. Marwood Kelly believed he had 'no chance of reclaiming these poor creatures from slavery without having recourse to prompt measures', and therefore 'cannonaded the town for nearly an hour'.[25] From the 1840s there was an increasing readiness shown by the British to turn to offensive action and the destruction of the settlements of those who refused to accede to a treaty or later broke terms.

Captain Joseph Denman was an experienced officer of the West Africa squadron and a passionate advocate of the anti-slavery cause. He was an influential proponent of the policy of 'preventing the embarkation of slaves', believing that to 'this first great object the capture of vessels should be considered as entirely secondary'.[26] In 1840 ships under Denman's command were engaged in a naval blockade of the River Gallinas (situated near the present-day Sierra Leone/Liberia border) when Denman was instructed to rescue two British subjects detained there by Prince Manna. Denman secured their release and induced the king to sign a treaty whereby the slave trade was abolished throughout his territories. He was also authorized to destroy the slave barracoons, release over 800 enslaved Africans and expel all the (mainly Spanish) slave traders.[27] Denman's 'imposing' policy of blockade was popular with abolitionists. *The Friend of Africa* (the publication of the Society for the Extinction of the Slave Trade and the Civilization of Africa) declared '[t]he effect of this measure on the native and other slave-holders on the coast … entailed on them a multiplied species of distress, to which they had been until then entire strangers'.[28] The action also earned Denman a commendation from Palmerston.

However, a change of government in 1841 led to increasing condemnation of the policy of blockade combined with the destruction of property. The new Foreign Secretary, Lord Aberdeen, was less inclined to assert British power to effect suppression and more concerned with principles of legality. In 1842

---

25 TNA, ADM 1/2027, Commander Kelly to Commodore Collier, 3 September 1820.
26 Quoted in Lloyd, *Navy and the Slave Trade*, pp. 122–23.
27 Lloyd, *Navy and the Slave Trade*, pp. 94–95; Eltis, *Economic Growth*, pp. 120–21.
28 *The Friend of Africa; by the Society for the Extinction of the Slave Trade, and for the Civilization of Africa*, vol. I (London: John W. Parker, 1841), pp. 73–74.

he wrote a letter to the Lords of the Admiralty, which was subsequently published, declaring that 'blockading the rivers, landing and destroying buildings and carrying off persons held in slavery in countries with which Great Britain is not at war cannot be considered as sanctioned by the law of nations'.[29] The news of this change in policy soon reached the African coast. Commander Henry Matson told a Select Committee that 'the slave traders exaggerated this letter to an enormous extent'.[30] The Gallinas slave traders sued Denman personally for damages, compelling him to return to London. Not until 1848 was it laid down that naval officers could not be held personally responsible for action against property.[31]

Denman's stance was vindicated when a government commission to investigate naval suppression concluded in 1844 that tactics of inshore cruising and blockading should be pursued (although with considerations of legality adhered to), and as a result the squadron's ships almost doubled in number.[32] In February 1845 Commodore William Jones was ordered to the Gallinas with a force of '286 men, in 18 boats': a slave barracoon was 'leveled with the ground' and three towns on the river were 'burnt to the ground and utterly destroyed'. The action he described as 'a salutary lesson to those who forget the respect due to our Sovereign'. Jones's description of the action reveals the arrogance associated with Britain's naval strength, and British disregard for international law when dealing with African states on matters concerned with the slave trade. He reported on a subsequent palaver with Gallinas rulers in which he declared: 'England had set her face against the Slave Trade, and was acting against it with a power which would be found invincible, and must prevail at last.'[33] Local rulers were put under severe pressure, forced to sign treaties and accept the imposition of heavy sanctions if they broke agreements. A treaty with the rulers at Bonny in 1844, for example, promised that Britain would carry out 'severe acts of displeasure' if evidence was found of subsequent slave trading.[34]

29 Bethell, *Abolition*, p. 185.

30 Quoted in Joseph Denman, *West India Interests, African Emigration and Slave Trade* (1848), pp. 24–26.

31 Charles Mitchell and Leslie Turano, 'Burón v Denman (1848)', in Charles Mitchell and Paul Mitchell (eds), *Landmark Cases in the Law of Tort* (Oxford: Hart Publishing, 2010), pp. 33–68.

32 Bethell, *Abolition*, p. 199.

33 Commodore Jones to Lieutenant-Governor Fergusson, 7 February 1845 and 18 February 1845, www.pdavis.nl/Jones_3.htm [accessed 21 March 2018]; Huzzey, *Freedom Burning*, p. 142.

34 Quoted in Marcel Van Der Linden (ed.), *Humanitarian Intervention and Changing Labor Relations: The Long-Term Consequences of the Abolition of the Slave Trade* (Leiden: Brill, 2011), pp. 19–20.

Naval personnel were actively engaged in effecting the best means for suppression at sea. Denman lobbied the Admiralty on the benefits of close blockade and became a principal witness to Parliamentary Committees commissioned to examine the slave trade. Although the Foreign and Colonial Secretaries and the Admiralty were fully informed of his intentions, Denman went beyond his official instructions in ordering the destruction of the Gallinas barracoons. Giving evidence before a Select Committee in 1842, he declared that the slave factories 'were not destroyed as a part of the powers with which I was invested'. During the blockade, 'the people upon the shore had been guilty of the most inhuman conduct towards my boats, conduct which a state of war would not justify'. Importantly, then, gunboat diplomacy was a new policy conceived in part by naval officers at the frontline, in response to the apparent failure of diplomatic means. 'Nothing of the sort had been done before, and therefore I did it under very heavy responsibility', Denman argued. 'I could not have struck out a new line without some special grounds to go upon.'[35]

Other officers such as Commodore Charles Hotham championed off-shore cruising, informed by a belief that cruisers sailing close to shore were observed by slave dealers who then moved their captives to another point of embarkation.[36] Denman and Hotham had public disagreements about the best way to enforce suppression; that Denman was willing to defy his Commodore exemplifies his conviction. Denman condemned Hotham's poor management of the squadron, claiming, 'with every thing to learn, he was thus left to grope his way in the dark towards the suppression of the slave trade'.[37] In a private letter, Hotham criticized Denman's 'ignorance' and 'fanciful theories' exhibited before a Parliamentary Committee on anti-slavery measures. He wrote that Denman's recommendations were 'senseless' and 'laugheable [sic]'.[38] However, after the legal judgement of 1848 fell in Denman's favour, blockade became acknowledged as official policy. Naval blockading of major ports of embarkation peaked in 1847 and 1848, when one in nine of the total 1,575 slave vessels captured by the British navy

35 'Minutes of Evidence taken before the Select Committee on West Coast of Africa: Captain the Honourable Joseph Denman, R.N. 22–27 June 1842', in *Trial of Pedro de Zulueta, Jun., on a charge of slave trading. On Friday the 27th, Saturday the 28th, and Monday the 30th of October, 1843 at the Central Criminal Court, Old Bailey, London* (London: C. Wood & Co., 1844), pp. 127, 133.

36 Shirley Roberts, *Charles Hotham: A Biography* (Melbourne: Melbourne University Press, 1985), p. 73.

37 Joseph Denman, *The African Squadron and Mr Hutt's Committee*, 2nd edn (London: John Mortimer, 1850), pp. 41, 44.

38 HUA, U DDHO 10/11, Charles Hotham to Captain Baillie Hamilton, no date [letterbook c. 1847–49].

were taken.[39] The legacy of Denman's action was clear when in 1861 the official objective of the squadron as stated by the Slave Trade Department was 'to prevent the shipment of Slaves at all, not to capture them'.[40]

Conditions of service

The professional roles of naval officers in suppressing the transatlantic slave trade intertwined with their daily experiences of life on 'this abominable coast'.[41] The infamous reputation of West African service led to appointments there being regarded with disdain. Midshipman Augustus Arkwright declared that 'the coast of Africa is the worst station we have'; Lieutenant George Kenyon believed 'without doubt this is the worst station they could send us to, unless it is China'. Lieutenant Francis Meynell declared in letters home: 'I don't care about it. I would rather go to Mexico where there is a bit of a war.'[42] The debilitating tropical climate played its part: violent tropical storms in the wet season were matched by searingly high temperatures at other times of the year, heat that surgeon Alexander Bryson described as provoking a 'wretched state of lassitude'. A further source of environmental hardship was the 'extreme dryness' of the 'Harmattan' wind, which occurred between December and February.[43] These climatic extremes were linked to the prevalence of disease among men of the squadron (and Europeans on the West African coast in general). In his journal Lieutenant George Courtenay quoted this infamous verse to exemplify the 'deleteriousness of the climate':

'To the Bight of Biafra, and Bight of Benin,'
'Few come out, and many go in.'
Which is true enough![44]

Various 'miasma' theories, whereby diseases were believed to be caused by noxious air, dominated discussions as to why ships were stricken by illness. Surgeon Richard Jackson blamed the sickly nature of the 'smokes', described as 'immense fogs exhaled from the marshes', from which 'we imbibe the

39 Eltis and Richardson, *Atlas*, map 186, pp. 284–85.
40 Memorandum by W. H. Wylde, 7 August 1861, in *Slavery in Diplomacy*, pp. 112–15.
41 NLS, MS 12054, phrase used by George Elliot in a letter to Lord Melgund, 6 January 1840, ff. 176–78.
42 DRO, D5991/10/53, Augustus Arkwright to his mother from Portsmouth, [no date] 1841; SHC, DD/X/GRA/1, George Kenyon to his mother from Plymouth, [no date] December 1841; NMM, MEY/5, Meynell letters, 28 January 1844.
43 Alexander Bryson, *Report on the Climate and Principal Diseases of the African Station* (London: William Clowes and Sons, 1847), pp. 2, 197–98.
44 UIC: SLC, Series V, Folder 16, Courtenay journal, no folios.

poisonous vapour'.[45] Disease was in fact spread by insects: Midshipman Cheesman Henry Binstead described how bites from mosquitoes and sand flies caused scratching and swelling, 'until some of the men were perfectly unable to move or see'.[46] Yellow fever (popularly known as Yellow Jack or Black Vomit) and intermittent fever (double tertian or malaria) were responsible for most deaths among Europeans; illness was also caused by dysentery and epidemics of smallpox.[47] As a result, nineteenth-century tropical West Africa was commonly known as the 'white man's grave'. Philip Curtin has argued that this phrase was understood in a literal sense: that Europeans were racially incapable of surviving in the African climate. However, the cause was not climate but the disease environment and a lack of immunity.[48] The greatest danger to sailors' health therefore involved time on shore or on boat service searching rivers (where numerous sites provided cover for slave ships to embark captives). Men experienced poor nutrition, fatigue, and exposure to insect-infested swamps. Commander Hugh Dunlop reported home from the *Alert* in the River Pongas to declare that 'to hunt about in the river with our men would have been certain death to them for the Ponga is the most deadly river on the whole coast of Africa'.[49] Likewise, Sierra Leone was regarded as particularly unhealthy. Among other damning terms, the colony was regarded by officers as 'a most wretched hole', an 'unwholesome hole' and the 'blackguard of all holes'.[50] As a result, Midshipman Augustus Arkwright of the *Pantaloon* declared that 'keeping English sailors at Sierra Leone is next to murder'.[51]

An average of 20 ships were employed on the West Africa squadron between 1830 and 1875, consisting of around 1,600 men, whose sickness, invaliding and mortality rates were significantly higher than those of the Royal Navy as a whole for this period.[52] The Admiralty asked for a report

---

45 R. M. Jackson, *Journal of a Voyage to Bonny River on the West Coast of Africa in the Ship Kingston from Liverpool*, ed. Roland Jackson (Letchworth: Garden City Press, 1934), p. 82.

46 NMRN, 2005.76/1, Binstead diaries, 2 March 1823.

47 Sir James Watt, 'The health of seamen in anti-slavery squadrons', in Andrew Lambert (ed.), *Naval History 1850–Present* (Aldershot: Ashgate, 2007), pp. 69–78, at p. 73.

48 Philip D. Curtin, *Death by Migration: Europe's Encounter with the Tropical World in the Nineteenth Century* (Cambridge: Cambridge University Press, 1989).

49 NMM, MSS/87/002/1, Hugh Dunlop to his sister Fanny, 4 October 1848.

50 NMRN, 2005.76/1, Binstead diaries, 22 March 1823; NRS, GD 219/304/36, Murray letters, 22 September 1847; SHC, DD/X/GRA/1, George Kenyon to his mother, 12 January 1842.

51 DRO, D5991/10/72-73, Augustus Arkwright to his mother, 19 June 1842.

52 Watt, 'Health of seamen', p. 71.

on the matter; the task was passed to Alexander Bryson, who had formerly served as a surgeon on the squadron. Bryson's *Report on the Climate and Principal Diseases of the African Station* (1847) was based on ships' pay books. Due to its restricted circulation, an *Account of the Epidemic Fevers of Sierra Leone* was published for a wider public in 1849.[53] Bryson calculated that the annual ratio of deaths from disease alone between 1825 and 1845 was 54.4 per 1,000 men for the West Africa station, as compared with 18.1 for the West Indies, 9.8 for the home fleet and 7.7 for South America.[54] Fevers spread quickly within the crowded confines of a naval ship. Lieutenant Courtenay wrote of being 'attacked with fever in the most malignant shape' while Commander of HMS *Bann* in 1824. 'My sufferings were very great', he noted, his weight 'reduced so much that my bones had forced themselves though my skin and I anxiously wished for death'. Courtenay survived, but when the *Bann* left the 'pestilential station' in 1825, the vessel had lost '50 by death' in three years, 'in addition to which 51 were invalided for a European climate'.[55] This high proportion of British fatalities was by no means unusual. In his letters home from HMS *Sybille* in 1830, Thomas Butter reported that among the crews of the squadron, 'the Eden lost 200, Sybille 120 lost a great number of men, the Hecla so many as to oblige her to go to England'.[56]

The situation was made worse when recaptives were crowded on to British ships. Diseases associated with enslaved Africans, who might have been held for weeks in terrible conditions in barracoons, were easily transmitted on British cruisers or among prize crews, particularly fever, dysentery, diarrhoea, eye problems and itching diseases caused by worms such as craw-craw.[57] In 1823 Midshipman Cheesman Henry Binstead served on expeditions up the Casamanza, Calabar and Bonny rivers in the boats of the *Owen Glendower* (commanded by Commodore Robert Mends). When Binstead's boat took possession of a Spanish schooner embarking captives in the River Bonny, the 181 Africans were subsequently taken on board the *Owen Glendower* to be conveyed to Sierra Leone. As fever spread Binstead described the ship as 'most beastly and miserable[,] 30 seamen in the Sick List and all very seriously

---

53 Lloyd, *Navy and the Slave Trade*, pp. 131–32.
54 Bryson, *Report*, pp. 177–78. Several scholars have since recalculated and expanded on Bryson's estimates of disease. See Watt, 'Health of seamen', pp. 70, 73; Mark Harrison, 'An "important and truly national subject": the West Africa Service and the health of the Royal Navy in the mid nineteenth century', in David Boyd Haycock and Sally Archer (eds), *Health and Medicine at Sea, 1700–1900* (Woodbridge: Boydell Press, 2009), p. 113; John Rankin, *Healing the African Body: British Medicine in West Africa 1800–1860* (Columbia, MO: University of Missouri Press, 2015), ch. 4.
55 UIC: SLC, Series V, Folder 16, Courtenay journal.
56 NMM, AGC/B/24, Thomas Butter to his father, 1 July 1830.
57 Watt, 'Health of seamen', p. 73. See also Rankin, *Healing the African Body*.

ill with fever also many Mids[hipmen]. Slaves dying from two to three a day what a horrid climate and scene is this.' Within a month, Binstead noted that 'our mess now consists of 6 members having when we left England 27'. He described 'a most melancholy sight ... to see so many poor fellows now laying in their hammocks of fever and little hope of their escaping a watery grave'. Commodore Mends died at sea, while his eldest son, a midshipman, was 'worn down to a mere skeleton' and died later that year. As a result, Binstead, a young and enthusiastic officer, was left 'heartily disgusted with this life and station'.[58]

Some infamous cases of fever on the squadron were publicized in the British press and contributed to a public sense of despondency surrounding suppression efforts. In September 1845 the *Éclair* arrived back in Britain with around two-thirds of the original crew (over 70 officers and men) dead or dying, including its Captain, Walter Estcourt. The ship's boats had been dispatched to the creeks of the Sherbro and Seabar rivers, where the men were exposed to 'malarial exhalations'. After a brief stop at Sierra Leone, the ship was instructed to steam to the Gambia, and then to the Portuguese island of Boa Vista to take on volunteers for its return to England.[59] Commander Estcourt's private journals reveal the extreme physical and emotional distress experienced by many officers. His religious faith appeared to offer some comfort from the sickly conditions on his ship, but as his journal progresses, his analysis becomes more hopeless. His despair was clear: 'My heart has almost sunk within me. Men sick dying dead.'[60] On reaching the English coast, the ship was quarantined at Stangate Creek. Diplomatic complications ensued as the *Éclair* was charged with infecting Boa Vista with a fever epidemic. Naval officers, the press and the public protested the inhumanity of the quarantine, which exposed the crew to further infection. *The Times* called upon the Admiralty 'to relieve us as speedily as possible from the national disgrace we are likely to incur by abandoning a number of our fellow creatures to destruction on board an infected vessel'.[61]

The *Éclair* was one of several high-profile cases indicating that reform of the squadron and its practices was needed for the health of naval personnel; the high rates of fever associated with the unsuccessful Niger Expedition of 1841–42 was another. Most vessels on the squadron were poorly ventilated,

---

58 NMRN, 2005.76/2, Binstead diaries, 4, 7 and 21 July; 30 August; 4, 5 and 28 September 1823.

59 Bryson, *Report*, pp. 181–88.

60 GRO, D1571/F544, Estcourt journals, 27 June, 8 August 1845.

61 *The Times*, 3 October 1845; Harrison, 'Important and truly national subject', pp. 122–24. Publicity was also generated by Walter's father, Thomas Grimston Bucknall Estcourt, MP for Devizes.

proverbially known as 'floating coffins' in the tropical heat. It was also claimed that steam vessels, introduced on the squadron from the 1830s, sustained infection in their engine rooms. Ship commanders were scorned for sending their crews up rivers; the Admiralty was blamed for the poor condition of vessels. Critics claimed it 'most unfair to treat those as dogs, who would willingly risk their lives where the honour or welfare of their country demand them'.[62] Medical reform contributed to new treatments, moving away from the traditional practices of bloodletting and purging, but it was not until the mid-1850s, when naval surgeon William Balfour Baikie proved the use of quinine as a preventative medicine as well as a cure, that the West African coast became a healthier place to live and work.[63]

Threats of violence were another risk to those who served on the squadron. Encounters with slave ship crews angered by naval interference could be perilous, often involving long chases followed by fighting between boarding parties and crews. For example, a midshipman of the *Pheasant* was killed during the transportation of the Portuguese slaver *Vulcano* to Sierra Leone in 1819. Quashie Sam, a 'native sailor' and one of the prize crew, testified that he saw 'the Portuguese Captain in the act of cutting down Mr Castles with a cutlass and saw Mr Castles fall bleeding overboard'.[64] Another infamous case was the murder of Midshipman Thomas Palmer and nine seamen of HMS *Wasp* in 1844 while transporting the slaver *Felicidade* to Sierra Leone. Ten Brazilian and Spanish crew members from the slavers *Felicidade* and *Echo* were tried in Exeter; five were convicted.[65] A local newspaper described the slave ship crews as '[d]esperadoes in character and accustomed to deeds of reckless cruelty, the crew of a slaver presents perhaps a greater amount

62 The medical journal *The Lancet*, quoted in Harrison, 'Important and truly national subject', p. 114. Harrison argues that one consequence of the failure of the Niger Expedition was agreement surrounding the need for naval medical reform between disparate interest groups, including the humanitarian lobby, sailors' welfare campaigners and medical professionals.

63 Watt, 'Health of seamen', pp. 73–77. In *Death by Migration*, pp. 159–60, Philip Curtin argues that the significant drop in mortality among Europeans on the coast was less attributable to quinine, and more to empirical measures such as improving water supplies.

64 TNA, ADM 1/2027, Commander Kelly to J. Wilson Croker, 8 March 1822. The Portuguese crew regained control of the ship, and the captives and the African sailors were later sold into slavery at Bahia, Brazil.

65 *The Times*, 11 July 1845, 14 July 1845; Lloyd, *Navy and the Slave Trade*, p. 86. Two sketches held by the National Maritime Museum depict Janus Majeval, the 'Slaver pirate who ran the knife into Mr Palmer midshipman', and Sobrena (de Costa) from Bahia, a former slave who testified against the slave traders (NMM, ZBA2553 and ZBA2554, unknown artist, c. 1845).

of crime and atrocity than can be met with elsewhere amongst a similar number of men'.[66]

It was not unusual for naval men to engage in combat. A more common experience of life on the anti-slave-trade patrols, with a more significant impact on morale, was boredom. The 2,000 miles of West African coastline patrolled by the Royal Navy were not well charted, nor supplied with many naval bases. Most officers of the squadron spent most of their days at sea: unless they were appointed to expeditions on shore, there were only occasional opportunities for visits to Sierra Leone or the islands of St Helena or Ascension (which served as the infirmary for the sick). Royal Navy vessels often spent months patrolling the West African coast with little prospect of capturing a slave ship. In the earlier years of suppression, empty slave vessels often waited off shore until an opportunity was found to take their cargo on board. British cruisers could, therefore, in Bryson's words, wait 'two, three, or four months in succession, standing "off and on the land" under easy sail'.[67] The situation changed with the introduction of equipment clauses into diplomatic treaties from the 1830s, which made possible the seizure of empty vessels. However, the change in methods in the 1840s, when patrolling the coast was increasingly replaced by blockades of ports and embarkation points, enhanced the squadron's success but led to fewer chases and captures. Midshipman Arthur Onslow wrote about the monotony of his days in his 1852 journal, bemoaning '[m]iserable dull work. There is nothing whatever to do this service is insupportable.'[68]

Normally the period of service for officers between refits was three years, and after 1850 it was reduced to two. In 1842 Captain Broadhead complained that he brought home 11 men who had not been out of the ship for three and a half years.[69] In these circumstances, there were suggestions that continuous months on board vessels led to 'mental disorganisation'.[70] Lieutenant Henry Rogers wrote about his 'monotonous life' in his journal. 'We talk a good deal about our misfortunes and are rather depressed sometimes', he wrote, 'for

66 Quoted in Todd Gray, *Devon and the Slave Trade: Documents on African Enslavement, Abolition and Emancipation from 1562 to 1867* (Exeter: The Mint Press, 2007), p. 81. Violent engagements with armed slave dealers are detailed in Captain Richard Drake's *Revelations of a Slave Smuggler* (New York: Robert de Witt, 1850), pp. 75–76, when the British cruiser *Princess Caroline* took possession of Drake's slaving establishment on the Kambia River, Sierra Leone in 1817.

67 Bryson, *Report*, p. 19.

68 Mitchell Library, SLNSW, MSS 2050, Onslow journal, 5 January 1852; Lloyd, *Navy and the Slave Trade*, pp. 94–96.

69 Lloyd, *Navy and the Slave Trade*, p. 135.

70 Phrase used by Commodore Arthur Eardley-Wilmot in his evidence before a Parliamentary Committee in 1865, quoted in Lloyd, *Navy and the Slave Trade*, p. 183.

my part my feelings have become so blunted by a sea life that I have sunk into a state of care-for-nothingness from which it would require actual or visible danger to rouse me.'[71] In his 1844 journal, Captain Walter Estcourt wrote of his 'melancholy low spirited feeling'. The following year his analysis of service included this fraught and despairing conclusion: 'Hot close damp thundering lightening raining disagreeable nervous leadenly ... enervating debilitating Coast of Africa. Weather either by day or night taking all energy from the men, all interest from our pursuits.'[72] At the Admiralty's request, Captain Claude Buckle wrote a report concerning Estcourt's conduct while in command of the *Éclair*, in particular the decision, against orders, to allow his men on shore at Sierra Leone. Buckle concluded:

> I believe that a depressing effect was produced on the minds of the Éclair's people by an idea which they entertained on leaving England that they were only to remain a short time on the coast of Africa, for a particular service, and were then to be sent to some other Station. The circumstance also of not making a single capture until they had been five months on the station, seemed to cause them to imagine that they were in an 'unlucky ship', and thus added to the feeling of despondency. The uninteresting & monotonous nature of the service they were employed on, no doubt had its effect also.[73]

Such factors, it was alleged, contributed to the squadron's poor disciplinary record. Commodore Charles Hotham believed that in consequence of the service's reputation, 'the worst description of officers find their way to the coast of Africa'.[74] Captain E. J. Bosanquet was similarly concerned. In response to an Admiralty request for the best means to implement abolition, he acknowledged that service on the West African coast was 'unpopular with the best description of officers':

> certainly very many of an indifferent character have always been found serving in it ... should the discipline of the squadron become again as relaxed as it has been at intervals, between 1829 & 1846, it would have a very injurious influence upon the state of the navy, so many young officers receiving their impressions from it, & thus the best nursery for young officers becoming the worst.[75]

71 Private collection, Rogers journal, 22 October 1850.

72 GRO, D1571/F543, Estcourt journals, 2 December 1844; GRO, D1571/F544, Estcourt journals, [no date] March 1845, 15 May 1845.

73 WSRO, BUCKLE/503, Claude Buckle to Captain Baillie Hamilton, 27 April 1846.

74 HUA, U DDHO/10/8, Charles Hotham to Charles Adam, 18 December 1846, f. 43.

75 TNA, ADM 123/173, 'Best means to be adopted for the abolition of the African slave trade, 1850', 11 May 1850.

Public criticism

These circumstances made for a unique set of conditions on the squadron, and despondency increasingly took public form. Morale was undermined by the perceived failures of the labours of the West Africa squadron in the face of relentless supply and demand for slaves; the ambiguities over the Royal Navy's rights of search, capture and condemnation contributed to frustrations. This was particularly the case regarding the perceived continuing intransigence of the United States, the 'rascally Yankees' in Commander Hugh Dunlop's words.[76] The public perception of the anti-slave-trade patrols changed in the 1840s as naval abolitionist policy was increasingly questioned. The growing costs of maintenance, of treaty payments to foreign governments and of running the Admiralty courts compounded misgivings, as did several publications critical of the squadron.[77] Some naval officers published defences of the service in response to such public opinion.[78] Others engaged in a 'spirited and interesting dispute' in the press as to whether to disband the squadron.[79]

Speculation that the squadron was ill-managed added to despondency. In a pamphlet published in 1848, Commander Henry James Matson called the squadron 'a mere paper blockade' and wrote that many ships were 'the very worst description of vessels we have in the service'.[80] The smallest warships,

---

76 NMM, MSS/87/002/1, Hugh Dunlop to his sister Fanny, 4 October 1848. This was particularly the case in the 1850s, when the resurgence of the Cuban trade was mostly carried on by American slavers.

77 Eltis, *Economic Growth*, pp. 7, 27; Huzzey, 'Politics', pp. 25–34. Criticisms of the squadron's methods can be found in Thomas Fowell Buxton, *The African Slave Trade and Its Remedy* (London: John Murray, 1840) and Macgregor Laird and R. A. K. Oldfield, *Narrative of an Expedition into the Interior of Africa by the River Niger*, 2 vols (London: Richard Bentley, 1837).

78 Joseph Denman, *Practical Remarks on the Slave Trade* (London: Ridgway, 1839), *West India Interests* and *The African Squadron*. See also Commander Arthur Eardley-Wilmot, *A Letter to The Right Honorable Viscount Palmerston on the Present State of the African Slave Trade and on the Necessity of Increasing the African Squadron* (London: James Ridgway, 1853). Support also came from outside naval circles, for example from the American missionary the Revd J. Leighton Wilson in *The British Squadron on the Coast of Africa* (London: James Ridgway, 1851), the geographer Sir Henry Yule in *The African Squadron Vindicated* (London: James Ridgway, 1850) and the Revd George Smith, *The case of our West African cruisers and West African settlements fairly considered* (London: J. Hatchard, 1848).

79 For example, Commander Henry James Matson wrote to *The Times* in August 1849 arguing that 'a preventive squadron is absolutely necessary as one of the means to suppress the slave trade', as reported in the *Hampshire Advertiser & Salisbury Guardian*, 18 August 1849.

80 Commander Henry James Matson, *Remarks on the Slave Trade and African Squadron*, 3rd edn (London: James Ridgeway, 1848), p. 64.

mostly sloops and ten-gun brigs, were sent to the West Africa station, and many were considered slow, dangerous and inefficient. The ships that were successful against fast slave vessels were the recommissioned slaver sloops or cutters like the *Black Joke* (formerly the Baltimore clipper *Henriqueta* captured by the *Sybille* in 1827), or small brigs like the *Waterwitch* (an ex-yacht).[81] Rear-Admiral Sir Patrick Campbell was Commander-in-Chief at the Cape of Good Hope during the period when the Cape and West Africa stations combined. In a private letter to First Naval Lord Charles Adam from the *Thalia* in 1836, he wrote that the *Waterwitch* 'sails like a <u>witch</u> ... A few more such as her and we would astonish the Spaniards who laugh at the gun brigs.' In a later letter he requested, 'do not send me any more of these unfortunate gun brigs as you might as well send a cow after a slaver as one of these after the Spanish clippers we have here'.[82]

Disapproval peaked in 1845, when MP William Hutt led an ongoing parliamentary campaign for the squadron's total withdrawal.[83] Hutt and other critics claimed that conditions for the enslaved had been exacerbated by the naval presence as slave traders crowded ships, made longer voyages and kept Africans in barracoons for longer while attempting to evade capture by British patrols. Naval suppression, it was alleged, proved to be 'an enormous fallacy and an aggravation of the evil'.[84] Published letters to the press by naval officers appeared (usually anonymously) in support of these arguments. One from 1845 read:

> We look upon the affair as complete humbug ... The absurdity of blockading a coast 2,000 miles in extent must be obvious to the meanest capacity ... The loss of life and demoralizing effect to our Service are very great ... the naked fact of our exertions in favour of the African slave having increased his miseries to an awful extent, with an immense

81 Andrew Pearson, '*Waterwitch*: a warship, its voyage and its crew in the era of anti-slavery', *Atlantic Studies*, 13.1 (2016), pp. 99–124; Dinizulu Gene Tinnie, 'The slaving brig *Henriqueta* and her evil sisters: a case study in the 19th-century illegal slave trade to Brazil', *The Journal of African American History*, 93.4 (2008), pp. 509–31.
82 Papers of the Adam family of Blair Adam, NRAS1454, Patrick Campbell to Admiral Charles Adam, 12 February and 12 June 1836. Campbell's emphasis.
83 Murray, *Odious Commerce*, pp. 211–12. Hutt's crusade against naval abolitionist policy became tied to several political interests: other so-called 'anti-coercionists' included free traders (who among other causes wished to remove protective duties on non-slave-produced sugar from the West Indies), and members of the British and Foreign Anti-Slavery Society.
84 Captain William Allen and T. R. H. Thomson, *A Narrative of the Expedition to the River Niger in 1841 under the Command of Captain H. D. Trotter, R.N.*, 2 vols (London: Richard Bentley, 1848), vol. 2, p. 411.

sacrifice of life, is uncontradicted by the best-informed advocates of slave measures.[85]

While few challenged the principles of abolitionism in the public arena, the policy of suppression was increasingly regarded as open for condemnation, particularly the loss of British sailors. Cases such as the *Éclair* brought the issue of high mortality before the public, during a period when criticism was beginning to be voiced against philanthropic endeavours more generally. Some officers saw an opportunity to publicize the neglect of sailors' welfare on the West African coast. Writing to *The Times* in 1845, a naval officer wished:

> to direct the public sympathy, which has so long raged in favour of the African blacks, towards their countrymen ... Could their voices reach the ears of those who so inconsiderately urge the employment, or more properly speaking the sacrifice of their countrymen on the pestiferous coast of Africa ... Pity it is that efforts prompted by such holy and noble feelings should be so fatally misdirected.[86]

A Commons Committee under Hutt discussed the squadron in 1848 and 1849, and appeared to favour its withdrawal, but a Lords Committee in 1850 narrowly voted for its continuation. In the meantime, such negativity at home reached officers on the coast. In his private letters, Commander Hugh Dunlop of the *Alert* wrote passionately in support of the squadron, declaring, 'I am in dread of hearing that Government have been driven into withdrawing the Squadron from the Coast, and that the slave trade is to be left to fatten in all its atrocity in future, to the everlasting disgrace of our country.'[87] Dunlop believed it 'quite a mistake' to conclude that the horrors of the Middle Passage (the transatlantic voyage between Africa and the Americas) were increased by the actions of British ships. Indeed, the alternative was that the slave trade would be 'thrown open' to 'people without any capital who would embark in it with every sort of small wretched vessel that could float across from Brazils and Cuba', and thus 'increase rather than diminish the sufferings of the poor negroes'.[88]

In a letter of 1848, Commodore Charles Hotham captured much of the frustration felt by officers. He despaired that:

> this blockade service has been twisted & turned by almost every Politician and naval officer each naturally thinks that if his views were adopted

85 *Hampshire Advertiser & Salisbury Guardian*, 11 October 1845.
86 *The Times*, 'The African Station', 16 October 1845.
87 NMM, MSS/87/002/1, Hugh Dunlop letters, part letter, no date.
88 NMM, MSS/87/002/1, Hugh Dunlop to Alex Monteith, 8 June 1848.

success would be attainable ... You can no more stop the slave trade by y[ou]r present system than you can turn the course of the Danube.[89]

Similarly, while 'devotedly attached' to the service, Commander Matson believed that the squadron's 'efforts have been cramped by proceedings over which they could have no control whatever'.[90] The conditions of this service were unique, and it appeared that efforts to make the squadron a success were floundering, overshadowed by persistent attacks on its existence. In response to this despondency and low morale, many naval officers focused on material rewards as the one positive aspect of anti-slavery service.

Material incentives

Most officers were deployed to the West African coast rather than volunteering to serve there. An incentive structure based around prize money and opportunities for promotion existed to counter some of the hardships they experienced. Since the early eighteenth century, proclamations had been issued at the beginning of each war, allowing the value of captured enemy ships to be divided among the officers and crews of the ships that took part in their capture. Under the Prize Regulations of the Act of 1807, prize money was similarly paid to those engaged in suppression. 'Headmoney' was paid for every recaptured slave and distributed between the crew according to rank. The introduction of equipment clauses into treaties also made possible the seizure of empty vessels as prizes.[91] In the context of redundancies and low rates of basic pay, the opportunity to earn extra money was clearly a motivating factor. The perception of 'good' or 'poor' prizes, referring to the amount of net profit from each capture, frequently features in narratives. Engineer John M'Kie wrote in his memoirs that the 'capture of a full slaver had a very exhilarating effect ... the chief talk being how much prize money it would bring'.[92] For Lieutenant B. King, service on the West Africa squadron had only one objective: 'I can see no other way of freeing myself from debt. My going out is no comfort to me.'[93]

89 HUA, U DDHO/10/11, Charles Hotham to Captain Hamilton, 1 November 1848.

90 Matson, *Remarks*, p. 30.

91 Brian Lavery, *Nelson's Navy: The Ships, Men and Organisation, 1793–1815* (London: Conway Maritime Press, 1989), p. 116; Lloyd, *Navy and the Slave Trade*, pp. 79–84. The situation whereby more prize money was available for taking full slavers was attacked by some officers such as Joseph Denman, because of the possibility that captains might delay making a capture and thus increase the suffering of the enslaved.

92 NLS, MS 24633, M'Kie memoirs, ff. 67–68.

93 Louisiana State University Special Collections, Lieutenant B. King to his creditor, 25 April 1840.

In practice, however, opportunities for accumulating large amounts of prize money were often constrained by the legalities of condemnation and by which section of coast was assigned to each vessel for cruising. Officers wrote about the best parts of the coast to make captures, and therefore add to the prize tally. After taking command of the Southern Division, Commander Alexander Murray was positive about his prospects. 'I may now have better luck in the way of making prizes', he wrote, 'but I don't seem to have any affinity for money or I never should have been involved in a rich man's ruin.'[94] Men only received a share of the proceeds from the sale of a slave ship if it was condemned: as many slave vessels evaded treaty agreements and were released, a capture and conveyance to Sierra Leone could prove fruitless. Furthermore, high costs and long delays in the condemnation of vessels were common.[95] The capturing naval vessel was expected to pay court costs; the recaptives and their associated expenses also remained the responsibility of the vessel and its crew until after adjudication. For example, it cost one ship over £9 to maintain 253 recaptives from the slave ship *Fanny* for one week in 1828.[96] These costs led to frustrations as expressed by Midshipman Edwin Hinde in 1830: 'we have captured a slave vessel but however, it is a very poor prize as the repence [*sic*] of condemning her will be as much as the prize money'.[97] It has been estimated that over £1 million in prize money was paid out between 1807 and 1846, although the sums that reached individuals were relatively small. Michael Lewis has argued that anti-slavery prize money had 'very little inducement value', and for the ordinary rating, the sums of prize money were 'puny' compared 'with the rich prizes of wartime'.[98]

Others welcomed opportunities for promotion and professional satisfaction. An enthusiasm for glory and the thrill of chasing and capturing enemy vessels were common emotions for naval men; suppression took place in peacetime, but the language of war was still prevalent. As Richard Lovell Edgeworth wrote in his *Essays on Professional Education*, first published in 1808, 'no mercenary rewards can supply the place of military enthusiasm,

---

94 NRS, GD 219/304/36-8, Murray letters, 22 September 1847, 5 May 1848.

95 For a study of the bureaucracy of the prize money system in Sierra Leone, see Padraic X. Scanlan, 'The rewards of their exertions: prize money and British abolitionism in Sierra Leone, 1808–1823', *Past and Present*, 225 (2014), pp. 113–42.

96 John Peterson, *Province of Freedom: A History of Sierra Leone 1787–1870* (London: Faber and Faber, 1969), p. 184.

97 NMM, HIN/1, Hinde letters, 26 April 1830.

98 Lewis, *Navy in Transition*, p. 237; Robert J. Blyth, 'Britain, the Royal Navy and the suppression of the slave trades in the nineteenth century', in Douglas Hamilton and Robert J. Blyth (eds), *Representing Slavery: Art, Artefacts and Archives in the Collections of the National Maritime Museum* (Aldershot: Lund Humphries, 2007), pp. 80–81.

and the love of glory'.[99] Such sentiments were expressed by Thomas Eason of the *Black Joke* in a verse from a song he wrote celebrating the bravery and gallantry of his fellow crew members after a violent engagement with the slave ship *El Almirante* in 1829:

> Our men as bold as lions
> Unto their Quarters flew
> With courage bold undaunted
> We hoisted colours blue.[100]

This enthusiasm was particularly common in youthful officers on the squadron who had not experienced war. Alexander Bryson noted that 'young and ardent' officers volunteered for boat service 'in the hope of meeting with a fair opportunity of enhancing their own reputation in the service'.[101] Astley Cooper Key wrote to his family from the West Indies station in 1840. As a teenager soon to pass his lieutenant's exam, his letters are imbued with adventure. He reported on one near-miss:

> what a glorious fight we should have had! ... It would have been a glorious cutting-out expedition – only our ten men against at least thirty or forty on board the slaver ... How glorious! Seeing one's name in the papers for something of that sort! ... I was sharpening my sword in the most butcher-like manner all the chase.[102]

Key's hunting metaphors stress the element of competition, sportsmanship and violence in anti-slavery naval action, narratives linked to demonstrations of masculinity which became more prominent as the century progressed.[103] Letters written home often placed emphasis on confrontation and the author's bravery. In a letter to his brother, Edwin Hinde was keen to stress his 'full determination of shooting one of the Spaniards ... to be able to say that I killed a pirate in action'.[104]

The role of patronage and influence also held sway on the West Africa station as on any other. Francis Meynell was keen to stress his desire for promotion in letters to his father in 1845, asking him to 'exert a little

99 Quoted in Brian Southam, *Jane Austen and the Navy* (London: National Maritime Museum, 2000), p. 131.
100 NMM, LOG/N/41, included in the logbook of HMS *Black Joke* by Lieutenant Henry Downes, 15 March 1829.
101 Bryson, *Report*, p. 200.
102 Colomb, *Memoirs*, p. 52. Key had a distinguished naval career and became First Naval Lord in 1879.
103 Doulton, 'The Royal Navy's anti-slavery campaign', ch. 5.
104 NMM, HIN/1, Hinde letters, 28 May 1831.

influence to get me confirmed to my rank of Lieutenant ... I know you don't like asking favours in that quarter but these things are the custom of the service.'[105] George Augustus Elliot, Commander of HMS *Columbine*, was the son of Rear-Admiral George Elliot and nephew of the 2nd Earl of Minto, First Lord of the Admiralty between 1835 and 1841. In a particularly privileged position to ask for favours, Elliot wrote to his uncle:

> as we are all heartily tired of the Coast of Africa if you could consistently transport us to some more pleasurable and less monotonous part of the world it would be a great relief. The Pacific affords the best prospect both in an enjoyable and lucrative sense unless there is a chance of active service in any other quarter ...

However, Elliot also diplomatically added: 'I can assure you that Columbine can do her duty <u>cheerfully</u> wherever she may be required.'[106]

A position on the West Africa station was still preferable to unemployment; in the post-war 'slump', a lieutenant's prospects for promotion were poor. Discontent was fuelled by the lack of arrangements for the retirement of older officers and continued acceptance of young officer-volunteers. 'Officers complain that they ruin their health in vain', Commodore Hotham noted in private letters, 'that it is a black list station that even vacancies by death are not given.'[107] In his letters of 1842, Midshipman Augustus Arkwright was absorbed with the reshuffling of positions on the station's ships. He wrote from Sierra Leone that he was 'anxious to arrive at the rank of Lieutenant', but despaired of his prospects, particularly when they were so tied to the risks of service:

> It is nonsense going to the coast of Africa for promotion, which is never got now, or very rarely, and when a chance does come up, the party concerned are sure to murder about 50 ignorant Spaniards or Portuguese, or else lose their own heads, arms or legs, which promotion in the navy ... is but a poor substitute.[108]

Later that year, however, Arkwright appeared more optimistic. Now in command of the schooner *Prompt*, he described his time 'cruising for slavers, and boating up rivers' as 'an employment attended with every disadvantage

105 NMM, MEY/5, Meynell letters, 17 August 1845, 27 March 1846. The Meynell family were wealthy landowners in Derbyshire.
106 NLS, MS 12058, George Elliot to Earl Minto, 12 August [1840?], f. 192. Elliot's emphasis.
107 HUA, U DDHO/10/8, Charles Hotham to Captain Hamilton, 24 October 1846, f. 30; Lewis, *Navy in Transition*, p. 134.
108 DRO, D5991/10/72-73, Augustus Arkwright to his mother, 19 June 1842.

except the chance of promotion'. He believed his prospects were directly related to the dangers he encountered. Having 'seen a great deal of life amongst savages', Arkwright perceived such action as equivalent to wartime achievements: 'all little scrapes of this kind, in these days of peace, are thought something of; and as to one's advancement in the service: which must be slow in the Navy just now'.[109] This positive outlook led Arkwright to offer the following broader assessment of his time on the coast:

> Any person who remains a certain time on the Coast of Africa and behaves himself, ought to be rewarded in some manner … the whole manner of living is anything but suitable. Fancy what a life it must be, when, white fellow creatures scarcely ever meet each other. And if they do happen to fall in with each other neither party knows what to say for want of a refined idea. As for society such a word is not known in Africa … Notwithstanding, I can very well manage to put up with every thing that comes across for a time; and I think have a mind sufficiently strong to live amongst these people, without injuring the heart, my feelings, and principles, which are so directly opposite. After a little promotion is gained I hope to look forward to getting a little room on shore; where it will be possible to lead a civilized life, perhaps in Co a wife.[110]

Expressing what he regarded as the alien nature of life in the unrefined colony, far removed from his ideals of British upper middle-class social and cultural norms, Arkwright wished to distance himself from the inhabitants of Sierra Leone and those he met outside naval circles, 'these people' whom he regarded as irreconcilably socially, culturally and ethnically separate from himself.[111] Yet his analysis also revealed an even-tempered and pragmatic attitude towards the service which contrasted with the pessimism of some of his naval colleagues. Others declared that disgust at the nature of life and work on the coast overrode all else, assessments which were based on the extraordinary nature of anti-slave-trade service at sea. As Commander Alexander Murray concluded in 1847, '18 months of the Sierra Leone division ought to count for ten years anywhere else.'[112]

---

109 DRO, D5991/10/74, Augustus Arkwright to his grandfather from Sierra Leone, 7 November 1842.

110 DRO, D5991/10/74, Augustus Arkwright to his grandfather from Sierra Leone, 7 November 1842.

111 Arkwright's family were wealthy Derbyshire cotton-spinning mill owners. He later became MP for North Derbyshire. See www.cromfordvillage.co.uk/arkwrights.html [accessed 2 April 2018]. His condescension was not limited to the people of Sierra Leone. In a letter of 30 April 1841 he declared Portsea (Portsmouth) a 'horrid sea port town … I would much rather be living with the wild Indians in the centre of South America.'

112 NRS, GD 219/304/36, Murray letters, 22 September 1847.

2

Abolition on shore

While the chase and capture of ships at sea represented a natural fit for men of the Royal Navy, officers' concurrent roles on shore in West African territories were more nuanced. Naval officers played a part in a reconfiguration of relations between Britain and West Africa in the early nineteenth century, as British abolitionist ideals and policies were introduced in the colony of Sierra Leone and increasingly rolled out along the coast. These included the pursuit of anti-slavery treaties with African rulers, the encouragement of 'legitimate' trade, a wave of exploration and increased missionary efforts. All were tied to the desire to end the slave trade at source in West African societies via the spread of European ideas of 'civilization'.[1] Officers' narratives are revealing of increasing British intervention in West Africa, and how economic and strategic advantages for Britain became inextricable from humanitarian incentives.

Commerce, civilization and Christianity

As part of Britain's newly assumed humanitarian identity in abolishing the transatlantic slave trade, efforts towards the perceived betterment of West Africa, in a desire to raise the continent from its slave-trading traditions, were based on three guiding principles: commerce, civilization and Christianity. These ideals gathered force as a new phase of the anti-slavery movement gained momentum in the 1820s and 1830s, but they had evolved from ideas put forward in the late eighteenth century. In the 1780s Sierra Leone was first envisaged by British abolitionists as a settlement in which to relocate Britain's

1 Although throughout this book naval officers (and Europeans more generally) discuss 'Africans' as one distinct group, an African identity did not exist in this period. Social organization and customs varied markedly along the coast.

poor blacks, a self-sufficient 'Province of Freedom' in which not only the slave trade but slaveholding would be forbidden. The Clapham Sect, or Saints (the influential group of British philanthropists and social reformers who gathered in south-west London), incorporated the Sierra Leone Company in 1791, attracted to the idea of a free colony as an aid to their cause to advance abolition in West Africa and atone for wrongs committed by Britain in the slave trade.[2] Thomas Clarkson optimistically wrote about the economic potential of the settlement, reflecting his belief that the encouragement of the 'spirited cultivation' of agriculture by Africans on their own land would be the means by which 'the Civilization of this noble continent would be effected in time'.[3] Free labour and competitive trade, it was believed, would generate more profit than slave labour, and hence undermine the institution of slavery.[4] The Company pursued commercial penetration of the interior, formed partnerships with African traders, and increasingly exerted influence over European and Eurafrican trading communities.[5] As Seymour Drescher has argued, the Sierra Leone Company's labour experiment may have turned out to be an economic failure, but it succeeded in laying the groundwork for future British relations with the colony and its borderlands, highlighting the potential for British 'social engineering' overseas.[6]

In response to the settlement's increasing problems, the British government stepped in to declare Sierra Leone a Crown colony in August 1807.[7] In doing so, Britain shifted the rationale of its presence there from commercial to state interests, leading to a new set of priorities and policies driven by abolitionism and idealism, and the desire to make a statement of intent to European

2 Suzanne Schwarz, 'Commerce, civilization and Christianity: the development of the Sierra Leone Company', in David Richardson, Suzanne Schwarz and Anthony Tibbles (eds), *Liverpool and Transatlantic Slavery* (Liverpool: Liverpool University Press, 2007), pp. 252–76. For the history of Sierra Leone in the wider Atlantic context, see Paul E. Lovejoy and Suzanne Schwarz (eds), *Slavery, Abolition and the Transition to Colonialism in Sierra Leone* (Trenton, NJ: Africa World Press, 2015).

3 Quoted in Schwarz, 'Commerce, civilization', pp. 265–66.

4 This argument had its origins in Adam Smith's examination of the structure of wage incentives in *The Wealth of Nations* (1776). See Drescher, *Mighty Experiment*, ch. 2.

5 See Bruce L. Mouser, 'Coasters and conflict in the Rio Pongo from 1790 to 1808', *The Journal of African History*, 14,1 (1973), pp. 45–64, for an example of this interaction.

6 Drescher, *Mighty Experiment*, p. 89.

7 The colony was composed of disparate groups of administrators, officials, traders and settlers, with a mix of vested interests and attitudes towards abolition; the arrival of self-liberated slaves from Nova Scotia and Jamaican Maroons added further tension. Mortality rates of Europeans were high and attempts to establish local agriculture and trade foundered. See Alexander X. Byrd, *Captives and Voyagers: Black Migrants across the Eighteenth-Century British Atlantic World* (Baton Rouge, LA: Louisiana State University Press, 2008), part II.

rivals. The African Institution was founded in 1807 by British abolitionists to support the government in enforcing the new abolition laws, to promote the suppression of the slave trade, and to develop the African economy through legitimate commerce. Furthermore, as the report from its first general meeting in April 1807 noted, members believed a period of social 'development' would spread 'useful knowledge' and encourage Africans to become 'industrious' and hardworking.[8] Britain's maintenance of the colony was therefore supported in humanitarian terms; Sierra Leone, it was believed, exemplified Britain's national honour and was regarded, in Allen M. Howard's words, as 'the beacon of freedom' in Britain's nineteenth-century abolition campaign.[9] As British representatives on the West African coast, naval officers soon became implicated in delivering this abolitionist agenda.

Before his appointment as Governor of Sierra Leone in 1809, Captain Edward Columbine's initial employment was as one of three commissioners charged by the British government with completing a survey of the West African coast from the Gambia to the Gold Coast, to inform an African policy on the future of British forts and settlements, and report on the means of 'carrying into effect the benevolent purpose of the legislature' in the Abolition Act.[10] The other commissioners were Thomas Ludlam and William Dawes, both former governors of Sierra Leone and nominated by William Wilberforce. Reflecting the interaction in purpose of the government and Admiralty at this time, Columbine was selected by the First Lord of the Admiralty, Lord Mulgrave, and his appointment was presumably attributable to his hydrographical experience in the West Indies.[11] As a commissioner, however, Columbine was under government rather than Admiralty instruction. The resulting change in priorities was made clear in a letter from Wilberforce to Lord Liverpool, informing the Secretary of State for War and the Colonies that Columbine and other commissioners had received no instructions for 'the best means of promoting civilization'. Wilberforce added: 'When I said Captain Columbine had <u>no</u> instructions I was substantially but not literally correct', for he had received

8 Wayne Ackerson, *The African Institution (1807–1827) and the Antislavery Movement in Great Britain* (New York: Edwin Mellen, 2005), pp. 17–19, 25.

9 Allen M. Howard, 'Nineteenth-century coastal slave trading and the British abolition campaign in Sierra Leone', *Slavery and Abolition*, 27.1 (2006), p. 23.

10 UIC: SLC, Series III, Folder 9, Columbine journals, 4 February 1809, ff. 1–2; Curtin, *Image of Africa*, pp. 159–60.

11 Columbine completed surveys of St John's and Antigua between 1787 and 1790, and in 1802–04 he undertook hydrographical work off Trinidad. The First Lord was the president of the Board of Admiralty, made up of Lords Commissioners of the Admiralty. From 1806 the First Lord was always a civilian, as opposed to a naval professional, and a member of the Cabinet.

some Admiralty guidance. However, this was for 'a survey of the coast in a nautical way and that it is obvious is a mere nothing'.[12] More importantly, in Wilberforce's words, the commissioners were 'to establish a friendly intercourse' with African rulers and 'turn their minds ... to the new order of things'. They were also instructed to report on the 'Physical and Moral capabilities of Africa and its inhabitants'.[13]

Similarly, Commodore George Collier's introduction to his 1820 report to the Admiralty reveals the multifaceted nature of the work of British naval officers on the coast, a role which went beyond traditional 'nautical' concerns. The report makes clear Collier's initiative and willingness to engage with Britain's wider anti-slavery remit, as he acknowledged that it 'may be thought to embrace many subjects unconnected with the duties of a naval officer'. Nevertheless, he hoped that:

> viewing the increase of our African Colonial prosperity, as the best pledge for the freedom of Africa, their Lordships will receive every communication I make, and information I offer, however trivial, as embracing these combined objects, viz. the general improvement of our western African colonies, and the completion of that desirable result, the abolition of slave trading.[14]

Collier's report exemplifies how naval suppression at sea was tied to information gathering for the purposes of developing the British presence in West Africa. His report included detail on relationships in the settlements between consular officials, merchants, agents and others; and the potential for lawful enterprise and further British territorial expansion.

The opinions of those who had long resided and had commercial interests on the West African coast were not easily altered in this post-abolition environment. 'Quo semel est imbuta recens, servabit odorem, testa diu' [the jar will long retain the odour of that with which it was once filled], Columbine wrote about Governor White of the Gold Coast, affected as he was by 'a remaining tinge of old opinions' regarding the slave trade.[15] In contrast, Sierra Leone was looked to as the model settlement for abolitionist

---

12 TNA, CO 267/25, William Wilberforce to Lord Liverpool, 26 December 1809.

13 TNA, CO 267/25, William Wilberforce to Lord Castlereagh, 19 January 1809.

14 MoD, MSS 45, 'Second Annual Report', ff. 1–2.

15 UIC: SLC, Series III, Folder 9, Columbine journals, 12 January 1810, ff. 51–52. After abolition and the transfer of Sierra Leone to the Crown, the nature of British commercial interests in West Africa changed dramatically. The settlement of the Gold Coast proved particularly problematic, with disagreements over its alleged neutrality and the continued assistance given to slave traders by its British settlers. In 1821 all West African possessions were placed under the rule of the Governor of Sierra Leone.

ideals. The Church Missionary Society (CMS) began work in Sierra Leone in 1804, and the Wesleyan Missionary Society had agents there from 1811. Missionaries encouraged settlers and recaptives in their conversion to the Christian faith.[16] Sir Charles MacCarthy (Governor between 1816 and 1824) was also instrumental in the push to create 'an orderly community of self-respecting Christians', in Christopher Fyfe's words, 'who would pass on to others the religion and European ways they had learnt'.[17] Inseparable from this religious enthusiasm were debates in British society about the obligation to 'civilize' African peoples: Africa's perceived social and cultural deficiencies were inextricably linked to a history of slavery and slave trading. In 1818 Lieutenant Digby Marsh of HMS *Tartar* wrote that Sierra Leone 'is in a most flourishing state'. He believed 'just praise is due' to the 'Governor and Gentlemen of Sierra Leone as well as the missionaries who are appointed to introduce Christianity and civilization amongst the sable savages of Africa, for the progress they have already made'.[18]

In recognition of African agency in the supply of captives for the slave trade, naval officers in the early decades of suppression communicated with African rulers to end slave trading and encourage its replacement with legitimate trade. These first dialogues were a precursor to the official policy of negotiating anti-slavery treaties from the 1840s onwards. Captain Columbine wrote to the Sherbro rulers in Sierra Leone's borderlands to express 'a sincere wish to see Africa in a better condition than it is at present'. He advocated the end of slave trading as 'a noble endeavour to make yourselves, and your children great, and your country happy'.[19] He also reiterated how the slave trade was responsible for many of Africa's ills:

> What has the slave trade produced for any of you? Can any one of you be said to be rich? ... No. Yet all this distress, the depopulation of your country arises merely from the sale of its inhabitants! Instead of keeping the Africans to till their own soil, they are sent to till the Colonies belonging to Europe!

Columbine offered Europe as the great moral example to African society: 'If the inhabitants of Europe had sold each other in a like manner, do you

16 Schwarz, 'Commerce, civilization', pp. 265–66; Andrew Porter, '"Commerce and Christianity": the rise and fall of a nineteenth-century missionary slogan', *The Historical Journal*, 28.3 (1985), pp. 597–621, at p. 599.

17 Christopher Fyfe, 'Four Sierra Leone recaptives', *The Journal of African History*, 2.1 (1961), p. 77.

18 SHC, A/AOV/69, 'Private remarks, occurrences, etc., HM ship *Tartar*, from England to the coast of Africa', c. 1818–19, no folios.

19 UIC: SLC, Series III, Folder 10, Columbine journals, 13 August 1810, f. 167.

suppose that we should have had Ships and Fleets, and Armies and riches as we now have? Certainly not.'[20] Similar language of perceived British superiority framed many officers' narratives throughout the period of naval suppression. Columbine was aided by John Kizell, a former American slave originally from the Sherbro region, who travelled to the region to act as a negotiator and wrote long letters reporting on his mission. Describing the untapped commercial benefits of the area (for trade in coffee, for example), Kizell wrote that the local population needed 'people to bring them into order', a role which naturally fell to Britain. 'God', he wrote, has roused 'the great men of England, and to put it in their hearts to consider the human race. May the Almighty God incline them to persevere; for these men of sin would wish to keep the black people in slavery, and their minds in darkness.'[21] Kizell also reported on entrenched local attitudes and confusion that a slave trade with Europeans was no longer desired or permitted. Similarly, a letter from Commander John Tailour from the *Comus* in the River Calabar in 1815 illustrates the difficulties faced by naval officers as Britain's representatives tasked with meeting African rulers to persuade them to abandon slave trading. 'My language was new to them. I spoke of humanity', he wrote; 'they had never met with any man who thought ill of the slave trade. Their fathers in short their grandfathers – and they knew not how many generations before them they said had been led by King George to consider the trade as then only good.' Tailour recommended that those who may formerly have been sold into slavery 'might become useful to them for life by clearing away & cultivating their country, which will produce almost whatever they will take the trouble to put into the ground'.[22]

Recommendations for non-slave-based trade were imbued with a belief that both African and British manufacturers would prosper from legitimate commerce. Adjustments were made to British trading practices with West Africa after 1807: trade in goods such as ivory, cow hides, gold or beeswax was developed in return for British manufactures, such as cotton cloth, liquor, guns and ammunition.[23] The journals of George Courtenay, Commander of HMS *Bann* in the early 1820s, highlight how the African coast was judged by Britons in terms of mercantile interest, and how naval officers were

20 UIC: SLC, Series III, Folder 11, Columbine papers, [no date] August 1810, ff. 103–05.

21 John Kizell to Governor Columbine, 30 September 1810 and [no date] December 1810, in *West African Sketches: Compiled from the Reports of Sir G.R. Collier, Sir Charles MacCarthy, and Other Official Sources* (London: L. B. Seeley and Son, 1824), pp. 115–26.

22 NLS, MS 9879, copy letter from John Tailour to General Sir Charles Pasley, 3 May 1815, ff. 333–35.

23 Gustav Deveneaux, 'Buxtonianism and Sierra Leone: the 1841 Timbo expedition', *Journal of African Studies*, 5.1 (1978), p. 39.

tasked with collecting information on the economic potential of areas for development. For example, Courtenay reported that the rivers of the Bight of Biafra 'furnish a vast field for commercial speculation'. The inhabitants of Bathurst Town in the Gambia (colonized by the British in 1816) have a 'thriving trade for gold, ivory, bees wax, hides and mahogany'. Courtenay therefore considered the colony as 'advantageous to the mother country, as it not only enriches its own merchants but pays annually some thousand pounds into the public treasury, and likewise takes off British manufacturers to a large amount'.[24] The advocacy of legitimate trade as an end to slave trading, while also providing Britain with a source of commercial potential, had a powerful impact on the direction of Britain's anti-slavery policy in the nineteenth century. It also led to increased exploration in the West African interior.

Exploration

Increasing knowledge about West Africa was aided by an outpouring of geographical accounts between the 1790s and the 1830s. The Association for Promoting the Discovery of the Interior Parts of Africa was founded in 1788 to gather information about the commercial prospects of the African interior. One of its explorers, Mungo Park, journeyed to the River Niger in 1795–97 and published a popular narrative of his expedition. Others followed, such as Thomas Bowdich in his *Mission from Cape Coast Castle to Ashantee* (1819). James MacQueen, a former West Indies overseer, published widely on the geography of Africa in the 1820s, with a particular interest in the River Niger.[25] In their gathering of information about West African societies, some explorers cast themselves as contributors to the anti-slavery cause; in return, the anti-slavery lobby and its allies in government and industry provided financial support for further exploration.[26]

The Royal Navy was also engaged in contributing to increased knowledge of the West African coast. From the end of the eighteenth century, the Admiralty began to recruit scientific expertise to develop the fields of

24 UIC: SLC, Series V, Folder 16, Courtenay journal, no folios.

25 T. C. McCaskie, 'Cultural encounters: Britain and Africa in the nineteenth century', in Andrew Porter (ed.), *The Oxford History of the British Empire: Volume III: The Nineteenth Century* (Oxford: Oxford University Press, 1999), p. 685; David Lambert, '"Taken captive by the mystery of the Great River": towards an historical geography of British geography and Atlantic slavery', *Journal of Historical Geography*, 35 (2009), pp. 44–65. MacQueen was notable in being a self-publicized expert on Africa without having visited the continent.

26 Dane Kennedy, *The Last Blank Spaces: Exploring Africa and Australia* (Cambridge, MA: Harvard University Press, 2013), p. 237.

hydrography and exploration. The Hydrographic Department was created in 1795, and, with peace in 1815, the Admiralty began to commission coastal surveys to chart certain regions of the West African coast – for example, the expedition to explore the rivers around the Bight of Biafra in 1816–17 under the command of Captain James Tuckey.[27] Increasingly, exploration also became a vehicle for suppression of the slave trade and a means to assess the potential of areas to be 'civilized'. Captain Tuckey's instructions from Sir John Barrow at the Admiralty included 'Queries relative to Africa'. Alongside questions about African peoples, their religions, languages and customs, Tuckey was expected to gather information on 18 questions relating to 'Slavery and the Slave Trade', including, for example, 'What are the sentiments of the natives respecting the abolition of the slave trade?'[28]

Many men who led exploratory expeditions had military backgrounds. As Dane Kennedy has remarked, with few other prospects for promotion after the Napoleonic Wars, 'exploration offered a high-risk, high-reward option for those who were especially restive and ambitious', operating in effect as a substitute for war.[29] In 1820 the Scottish naval officer and explorer Hugh Clapperton was recruited by the Colonial Office, together with naval surgeon Walter Oudney and army officer Dixon Denham, to an expedition to discover the course of the Niger, with a view to opening diplomatic and trading relations.[30] Clapperton also acted as the British government's mediator to the Sultans of Sokoto and Borno on the Niger Expedition of 1825–27. In his appointment letter from Colonial

27 Richard Drayton, 'Knowledge and empire', in P. J. Marshall (ed.), *The Oxford History of the British Empire: Volume II: The Eighteenth Century* (Oxford: Oxford University Press, 2001), pp. 231–52, at p. 249; Curtin, *Image of Africa*, pp. 165–66. The African naval survey was carried forward by Captain David Bartholomew in the *Leven* in 1819–21; Captain William Fitzwilliam Owen in the *Leven* and *Barracouta* (1821–26); Commander T. Boteler in the *Hecla* and Lieutenant R. Owen in the *Albatross* in 1827–28; from 1833 by Commander Edward Belcher in the *Aetna*; and between 1835 and 1845 by Captain Vidal in the *Aetna* and the *Styx*. For published accounts of surveying, see, for example, Captain Thomas Boteler, *Narrative of a voyage of discovery to Africa and Arabia performed by HMS Leven and Barracouta from 1821 to 1826 under the command of Capt. W.F.W. Owen* (London: Richard Bentley, 1835); Captain William Fitzwilliam Owen, *Narrative of Voyages to Explore the Shores of Africa, Arabia and Madagascar Performed in HM Ships 'Leven' and 'Barracouta'* (London: Richard Bentley, 1833).

28 NMM, LBK/65/2, letterbook of Sir John Barrow, ff. 122–24. Tuckey's expedition aimed to determine whether the Congo and the Niger were the same river. Most of the crew died of yellow fever.

29 Kennedy, *The Last Blank Spaces*, pp. 66–67.

30 Jamie Bruce Lockhart, *A Sailor in the Sahara: The Life and Travels in Africa of Hugh Clapperton, Commander RN* (London: I. B.Tauris, 2008).

Secretary Lord Bathurst, Clapperton was instructed to stress 'the very great advantages' of abolition, the 'happy results' of which would lead the rulers 'to be ranked among the benefactors of mankind'. He was also to assert the 'mutual benefit' of suppression, including an assurance that British trade in Soudan manufactures would follow.[31] Naval surgeon and naturalist Dr Morrison accompanied Clapperton on the expedition. His incomplete letters of 1825 reveal his optimism about the potential for 'improvement' of African society, and how he was motivated by religious faith and benevolence, stating, 'if I do fail still it is an object worthy the enterprise of the good Christian'. His desire was to 'prove our humble mean by introducing moral & religious improvement to the head of poor Africa & to the hearts of its benighted inhabitants'. Morrison stressed the dual aims of their expedition – to 'civilize' Africa and open trading links to the African interior – which for him were a source of great pride. His language imbued with ideas of heroism and British national honour, he claimed the mission 'is one of those that promises more benefit to the nation than those of Parry or Franklin however new & splendid'.[32]

This drive for knowledge had further consequences. As the Colonial Office, the Foreign Office and the Admiralty all became more directly involved in the broader West African region, an association developed between exploration and imperial policy.[33] Naval officers were involved in debates about new territories and the potential benefits to Britain arising from further colonization.[34] Captain Charles Phillips's letter to retired admiral Sir Richard Keats from HMS *Bann* at Ascension in 1822 uncovers the interlinked nature of naval suppression, commerce and territory in the British anti-slavery enterprise. Phillips suggested British settlement of the island of St Thomas (Sao Tome) in the Gulf of Guinea, then in Portuguese possession. In contrast to Sierra Leone, a 'drain from the mother country', Phillips believed the mountains of St Thomas to have huge economic potential, 'almost equal to the blue mountains of Jamaica'. The benefits would be twofold: the island would 'ensure to England a rich colony', as well as being 'the seat from where Christianity might spring into the

---

31 UKHO, LP 1857/Box M760, Lord Bathurst to Hugh Clapperton, 30 July 1826.

32 UKHO, LP 1857/Box M760, incomplete letter of Dr Morrison, c. 1825. John Franklin and Edward Parry were naval officers and Arctic explorers. Clapperton's journal was later published, as was an account of the expedition by Clapperton's servant, Richard Lander: *Records of Captain Clapperton's Last Expedition to Africa with the Subsequent Adventures of the Author* (London: Richard Bentley, 1830); Hugh Clapperton and Richard Lander, *Journal of a second expedition into the interior of Africa from the Bight of Benin to Soccatoo* (London: John Murray, 1829).

33 Lambert, 'Sierra Leone', p. 108; Kennedy, *The Last Blank Spaces*, p. 112.

34 See also *West African Sketches*, ch. 7.

Western World'. His proposal involved settling formerly enslaved Africans on the island and giving each 'a spot of ground to cultivate, a portion of whose produce might be paid to Government, to repay the ten pounds paid for his emancipation'.[35] What was expected from recaptured Africans in return for Britain's 'gift' of freedom is explored further in Chapter 4. Phillips clearly regarded the process of emancipation as resulting in a debt owed in some form. His proposals for the creation of plantations similar to those in the West Indies also had an uneasy resonance with slavery. British influence was ever-present over the social condition and economic potential of Africans released from the slave trade, but also over physical territory.

Commander B. Marwood Kelly of the surveying vessel *Pheasant* wrote a report for the Admiralty on the potential of colonizing the island of Fernando Po in 1823.[36] Like Phillips, Kelly made comparisons with the prosperous British West Indies, claiming that plantations on Fernando Po 'would be found equally, or more productive than any of the old European Colonial Establishments in the West Indias'. The rivers of the island would facilitate 'the labour of extending the blessings of religion, and civilization, to this long neglected, & much injured quarter of the Globe'. Kelly's vision for Fernando Po was as an anti-slavery utopia of 'social happiness' to effect change across the West African continent, born of British moral instruction and indefatigable Christian faith.[37] Kelly's report reveals how naval officers' experiences informed British policy-makers. He acknowledged that he wrote more than was expected; his remarks were appended to a more traditional survey, and he admitted that he 'embraced matters not immediately commanded by the General Printed Instructions'. The pursuit of promotion or commendation could be at play here; however, Kelly's engagement with the interconnected objectives of both the West Africa squadron and the wider anti-slavery cause are also clear. Kelly wrote that 'as a Public Servant I am bound to render myself as useful to my country as my humble abilities will admit'.[38] He regarded offering his perceptions as to the best ways to further the abolitionist cause as part of this role.

---

35 SHC, DD/CPL/44, Captain Charles Phillips to Sir Richard Keats, 12 August 1822.

36 UKHO, MP 107, Commander B. Marwood Kelly, 'Remarks and observations on the probable value of the island of Fernando Po as a British colony', no folios; Curtin, *Image of Africa*, pp. 162–64. Both Phillips and Kelly contributed to an ongoing debate during the 1820s about the suitability of Sierra Leone as a base for the anti-slavery mission and the need to identify alternative sites.

37 UKHO, MP 107, 'Remarks and observations'.

38 UKHO, MP 107, 'Remarks and observations'.

Increasing intervention

As we have seen, the nature of naval abolitionist policy became increasingly interventionist from the 1830s as new methods were pursued to eradicate the slave trade at its source. At the same time, West Africa was regarded as an area of burgeoning economic interest for Europe, and while reluctant to significantly extend colonial holdings, British agents on the coast were involved in activity to protect these interests.[39] As a result, naval officers were more frequently tasked with missions on shore, working alongside other groups of British representatives in the expansion of the British presence. Wider imperial impulses, the increased drive for civilization and the development of legitimate commerce led to an expanded anti-slavery agenda: through trade expeditions, treaties negotiated with African rulers and increasingly offensive action, naval officers were agents of change in the British grand vision for West Africa in the mid-nineteenth century.

A series of trade expeditions on an increasingly ambitious scale took place in the 1830s and 1840s, several of which focused on the River Niger.[40] Sir Thomas Fowell Buxton's Niger Expedition of 1841 to found an agricultural and philanthropic colony on the confluence of the Niger and Benue rivers was perhaps the most ambitious undertaking in the exploratory and anti-slavery cause. Buxton believed that naval suppression had failed to render the slave trade unprofitable in its policy of targeting slave traders rather than Africans themselves. He called for a more aggressive approach, publishing his views in *The African Slave Trade* (1839) and *The Remedy* (1840), later published as one volume. In 1839 he founded the Society for the Extinction of the Slave Trade and the Civilization of Africa, patronized by the Prince Consort and backed by the influence of Exeter Hall, the meeting place off the Strand in London for missionary and other religious organizations. Buxton's vision for the remedy of the slave trade lay in African societies. 'It is not the partial aid, lent by a distant nation', he wrote, 'but the natural and healthy exercise of her own energies, which will ensure success.'[41] To persuade Africans that

---

39 For African-European economic relations preceding the partition of the continent in the later decades of the nineteenth century, see J. D. Hargreaves, *Prelude to the Partition of West Africa* (London: Macmillan, 1963) and A. G. Hopkins, *An Economic History of West Africa* (London: Longman, 1973).

40 Some were privately financed; others were government-sponsored. For example, Richard Lander and John Lander, *Journal of An Expedition to Explore the Course and Termination of the Niger* (London: John Murray, 1832); Laird and Oldfield, *Narrative of an Expedition*. See Frank McLynn, *Hearts of Darkness: The European Exploration of Africa* (London: Hutchinson, 1992), pp. 27–34.

41 Quoted in Kristin Mann, 'The original sin: British reform and imperial expansion at Lagos', in Robin Law and Silke Strickrodt (eds), *Ports of the Slave Trade: Bights of*

the sale of legitimate produce (for example, cotton, groundnuts or palm oil) would prove more profitable than the sale of people, Buxton looked to the mission stations and schools that proliferated in the African interior from the 1840s onwards.[42] In a familiar theme, 'Buxtonianism' appealed to the high moral virtues of mid-nineteenth-century Britain and also to its economic self-interest: while African regeneration would be aided by British assistance and habits of industry, British manufacturers would at the same time be supplied with raw materials and increasing markets.[43]

The government contributed nearly £80,000 to finance Buxton's expedition, and three specially designed steamers (*Albert*, *Wilberforce* and *Soudan*) carried a total crew of over 300 men. The expedition was led by Captain Henry Dundas Trotter, a senior naval officer who had served with distinction for four years with the West Africa squadron as commander of the *Curlew*. He was advised and assisted in his dealings with local rulers by Commander William Allen and Commander Bird Allen. The accompanying group included missionaries, scientists, doctors and agriculturists recruited and paid for by Buxton and his colleagues. Samuel Ajayi Crowther, a former slave who would become the first Anglican African bishop, was also on board as assistant and interpreter.[44] Buxton's plans to eradicate slave trading involved the establishment of a 'model farm' at Idah, 270 miles inland, to use as a base to make anti-slavery treaties with local rulers, and to offer economic and moral inducements to African people.[45] The mission was a disaster. Trotter later described the 'shattered condition of the expedition, caused by the unusual degree of sickness and mortality'. Of the 145 white men in the

---

Benin and Biafra (Stirling: Centre of Commonwealth Studies, 1999), pp. 171–72; Olwyn Mary Blouet, 'Buxton, Sir Thomas Fowell, first baronet (1786–1845)', *Oxford Dictionary of National Biography*, Oxford University Press, September 2004, www.oxforddnb.com/view/article/4247 [accessed 23 September 2015].

42 Porter, *Religion versus Empire*, p. 150; Susan Thorne, *Congregational Missions and the Making of an Imperial Culture in Nineteenth-Century England* (Stanford, CA: Stanford University Press, 1999), p. 84. The CMS established Fourah Bay College in Freetown in 1827. The college trained missionary teachers such as Samuel Ajayi Crowther, who then travelled to other parts of West Africa. Crowther established the Abeokuta mission in 1843.

43 Deveneaux, 'Buxtonianism', p. 37; Mann, 'The original sin', pp. 171–72.

44 Howard Temperley, *White Dreams, Black Africa: The Antislavery Expedition to the River Niger 1841–1842* (New Haven, CT: Yale University Press, 1991). Eleven of the participants subsequently published journals, including Allen and Thomson, *A Narrative of the Expedition*; John Duncan, 'Some Account of the Last Expedition to the Niger', *Bentley's Miscellany*, 22 (1847); J. F. Schön and Samuel A. Crowther, *Journals of the Rev. James Frederick Schön and Mr Samuel Crowther, Who … Accompanied the Expedition up the Niger in 1841* (London: Hatchard and Son, 1842).

45 Temperley, *White Dreams*, p. 15.

crew, 130 suffered from fever and 40 died.[46] Furthermore, the reality of the model farm was far from its high moral expectations. Lieutenant William Henry Webb of the *Wilberforce* found the settlers 'indolent and lazy, not one ... willing or even disposed to manual labour'. He witnessed two of them armed with whips 'apparently for the purpose of urging the natives to greater exertion'. Hearing of these circumstances, *The Times* declared: 'the Niger ANTI-Slavery Expedition has ... planted a very "model" of the most cruel and iniquitous SLAVERY'.[47]

The expedition's failure added to growing criticism of anti-slavery operations, with disappointment felt by those on the squadron. Midshipman Augustus Arkwright wrote about the 'absurd' expedition in a letter home from the schooner *Prompt*, claiming 'all the people out here knew how little use it was to attempt, and throw away such a sum of money, from the Senior Officer in the Expe. to the lowest boy: all were the worst sort for an employment of the kind'.[48] As a result, some officers remained unconvinced about the efficacy of expeditions into the African interior, with much of the criticism surrounding dangers to health. Commodore Charles Hotham wrote to the First Lord of the Admiralty in 1847 expressing doubts regarding an expedition to the Lagos lagoons. 'I am satisfied we shall obtain some geographical information at an enormous cost of life', he wrote. Hotham did not believe that any expeditionary enterprise could end the slave trade due to its pervasive character, which he regarded as 'Hydra headed, with fascinating qualities which dazzle and eclipse legitimate dealings'.[49]

There was, however, no real slackening of British interest in West Africa, and anti-slavery continued to be regarded in tandem with the spread of Christianity and civilization as inspiration for further explorations of the 'dark continent'.[50] The principle that the slave trade should be superseded by alternative forms of legitimate trade also strengthened and became

46 NMM, BGY/W/2, Henry Dundas Trotter to Captain Baillie Hamilton, 30 June 1847; J. Gallagher, 'Fowell Buxton and the New African Policy, 1838–1842', *The Cambridge Historical Journal*, 10.1 (1950), pp. 55–56.

47 Quoted in Temperley, *White Dreams*, pp. 156–57, 161–62.

48 DRO, D5991/10/74, Augustus Arkwright to his grandfather, 7 November 1842.

49 HUA, U DDHO 10/8, Charles Hotham to the Earl of Auckland, 5 November 1847, ff. 157–58.

50 McCaskie, 'Cultural encounters', p. 673. See Curtin, *Image of Africa*, pp. 308–12 for details of further exploration. There were several more expeditions to the Niger, for example in 1854 undertaken again by the Liverpool businessman Macgregor Laird and led by William Balfour Baikie with assistance from the Revd Samuel Crowther; and in 1857 under Baikie and Lieutenant John Glover. See, for example, Revd Samuel Crowther, *Journal of An Expedition Up the Niger and Tshadda Rivers* (London: Church Missionary House, 1855).

commonplace by mid-century.[51] In his journal of 1845, Commander Walter Estcourt of the *Éclair* put forward British missionary activity and industrial example as the remedies to the slave trade:

> the core [of] our effort should be to prevent the slave trade and above all to encourage the legal trade and raise the moral character of the people, and this is to be done by making settlements where ever there is an opening and making it better worth the native's while to trade in the produce of his land than in his fellow man ... the inhabitants earnestly desire to have Europeans among them and are chiefly desirous of having the English from a belief that we are the most powerful nation and the best traders.[52]

Permeating Estcourt's analysis for the future of the continent was his belief that Africa's revival was impossible without British intervention. Thus legitimate commerce would 'extend morals', embed 'habits of industry' and ensure there was 'a way opened for the introduction of Christianity'.[53]

Similarly, Captain Joseph Denman wrote to Sir John Jeremie, Governor of Sierra Leone, in 1841 to express his desire to see the people of the River Gallinas trade in 'natural resources' of cotton, indigo, pepper, coffee etc., in exchange for 'the luxuries of civilized life' such as flour, wine, tea, butter, clothes, shoes, knives, forks and pans. Denman considered this 'imperatively necessary' as 'the only sure foundation of improvement and civilization'.[54] The trade in palm oil, for example, had for some time existed alongside the slave trade. Introduced by Liverpool merchants before 1807 and expanded after, palm oil became an important trade staple from the 1820s. Due to Britain's industrialization and demand for tropical products (and soap in particular), palm oil imports increased from around 5,000 tons in 1827 to over 30,000 tons by 1853. The trade was at the heart of the British vision for the transformation of the West African economy, and contributed to an increase in British traders, officials and consular officials on the coast.[55] Naval engineer John M'Kie of the *Rattler* reported on the

---

51 Roger Anstey, 'Capitalism and slavery: a critique', *The Economic History Review*, 21.2 (1968), pp. 307–20, at p. 320. It has been argued that this commercial transition posed a 'crisis of adaptation' for African rulers by undermining their control over their income. See, for example, essays in Robin Law (ed.), *From Slave Trade to 'Legitimate' Commerce: The Commercial Transition in Nineteenth-Century West Africa* (Cambridge: Cambridge University Press, 1995).

52 GA, D1571/F543, Estcourt journals, 5 January 1845.

53 GA, D1571/F543, Estcourt journals, 5 January and 26 January 1845.

54 Letter from Denman to Sir John Jeremie, 12 December 1840, in *The Friend of Africa* (1841), p. 105.

55 Martin Lynn, *Commerce and Economic Change in West Africa: The Palm Oil Trade*

palm oil trade from the River Bonny in 1850 which was 'wholly in the hands of Liverpool merchants'. The influence of these traders on local peoples was clear. The 'royal residence' of the King of Duke Town, 'a neat corrugated iron structure', had been presented by the merchants, and 'contained a mixed assortment of presents he had received[:] several large mirrors, lithographs of the Queen and Royal Family'.[56]

One consequence of the encouragement of legitimate trade was the concurrent growth in the use of domestic slaves during the nineteenth century, by Europeans and Africans, in part to service the increasing demand for agricultural exports.[57] Slaves were also employed in coastal areas to produce food for the commercial and urban centres involved in overseas trade. Robin Law and others have argued that the recovery of slave prices after the initial impact of abolition might reflect the expansion in local demand for slaves, whereby it was more profitable for African slaveholders to sell their slaves on the domestic market than for export.[58] An unnamed officer who published an account of his time on the West African coast in 1858 suggested the same in his report of a local ruler who ceased his trade in slaves because 'the demand for ground nuts and other produce having increased, the labour of slaves was more valuable than formerly, in their own country'.[59] The irony of one form of slave trade being encouraged by the suppression of another was not lost on one naval officer, who wrote anonymously to criticize the effect of the trade in gunpowder between Liverpool ships and rulers of the Calabar and Bonny rivers. 'The use thus made of English manufacture is afflicting to humanity', he wrote. 'By us the native kings spread desolation through the country, and extend and perpetuate the very thing we are so anxious to suppress.'[60]

---

in the Nineteenth Century (Cambridge: Cambridge University Press, 1997), p. 3; Martin Lynn, 'The "imperialism of free trade" and the case of West Africa, c.1830–c.1870', *Journal of Imperial and Commonwealth History*, 15 (1986), pp. 22–40, at p. 24.

56 NLS, MS 24634, M'Kie memoirs, ff. 8–11, 17–19.

57 Paul E. Lovejoy, *Transformations in Slavery: A History of Slavery in Africa* (Cambridge: Cambridge University Press, 1983), ch. 8; Paul E. Lovejoy and David Richardson, 'The initial "crisis of adaptation": the impact of British abolition on the Atlantic slave trade in West Africa, 1808–1820', in Law (ed.), *From Slave Trade*, pp. 32–56, at p. 51.

58 Robin Law, 'Introduction', in Law (ed.), *From Slave Trade*, pp. 7, 9, 17.

59 'Journal of a Naval Officer on the West Coast of Africa', *The Colonial Church Chronicle and Missionary Journal* (July 1858), p. 255.

60 Account from the journal of 'a gallant and distinguished naval officer who passed three years on the African coast', in *The Amulet. A Christian and Literary Remembrancer*, ed. S. C. Hall (London: Frederick Westley and A. H. Davis, 1832), pp. 238–39.

Anti-slavery treaties

At the heart of increasing British intervention in the affairs of West African states was the pursuit of anti-slavery treaties with African rulers. Such treaties were intended to end slave trading in their territories and to guarantee the broader goals of a privileged status for British commerce, including freedom to trade and protection of British property. In the relative absence of consular officials on the coast before 1850, naval officers were tasked with such negotiations, known as 'palaver'. By the 1860s, 107 treaties were in existence, often accompanied by subsidies.[61] Naval officers were regarded as Britain's agents, tasked with information gathering and spreading messages of goodwill, abolition, commerce and civilization. However, negotiations invariably required cooperation, compromise and adjustments in policy. As Alan Lester has argued, colonial discourses in this period 'were made and remade, rather than simply transferred or imposed'.[62] African rulers were offered, and demanded, compensation for abandoning the slave trade. Commander Hugh Dunlop of the *Alert* reported on the demands of the rulers of the Sherbro rivers in 1848:

> No sooner was the treaty signed than they requested to know what they were to receive as recompense for having done so!! When it was explained to them that if they strictly adhered to the terms of the treaty ... the sum of three hundred dollars would be distributed amongst them, they at once declared it to be much too small a sum to be divided amongst three kings!!! They were <u>tolerably satisfied</u> however when they were told that their opinion of the smallness of the sum would be made known to Queen Victoria.[63]

Officers' dealings with African rulers were often played out within British hierarchical society models, whereby naval men played the roles of envoys and messengers in the pattern of communication between monarchs. In recognition of African diplomatic conventions, an elaborate exchange of presents was also commonplace, a tradition from earlier European–African slave trade negotiations.[64] For example, the King of Dahomey provided Commodore Arthur Eardley-Wilmot with a long list of presents he

61 Lynn, 'Imperialism', pp. 24–25; Eltis, *Economic Growth*, p. 88.

62 Alan Lester, *Imperial Networks: Creating Identities in Nineteenth-century South Africa and Britain* (London: Routledge, 2001), p. 5.

63 USNA, MS 59, Dunlop remark book, 12 February 1848. Dunlop's emphasis.

64 David Cannadine, *Ornamentalism: How the British Saw Their Empire* (London: Allen Lane, 2001); David Richardson, 'Cultures of exchange: Atlantic Africa in the era of the slave trade', *Transactions of the Royal Historical Society*, 19 (2009), pp. 151–79.

expected in return for a treaty in 1863, which included 'an English carriage and horses'.[65] Naval officers were expected to ensure a treaty by any means possible: in some cases, bribery was also involved.[66]

Commander Dunlop was accountable for several treaties signed between 1847 and 1849, and his intentions for a 'grand palaver' with the Sherbro rulers in 1848 reveal officers' multifaceted roles. Alongside an agreement to ensure suppression, Dunlop sought to 'mediate a peace' between the chiefs to conclude a war that had caused 'great destruction of life & property, as well as to the great detriment of the Sierra Leone trade up the Sherbro river'.[67] A desire to end conflict between African peoples became a key component of the anti-slavery mission, to minimize the practice of rulers selling prisoners of war as slaves; in the case of the Sherbro, such conflict was also disruptive to British trade in the area. Royal Navy vessels blockaded the rivers, but the Governor of Sierra Leone declared himself 'unable to prevent slave dealers receiving what supplies they pleased from the colony'. 'Under these circumstances', Dunlop wrote:

> I resolved to take upon myself the whole responsibility of stopping this infamous trade so disgraceful to a British colony. My great hope of succeeding was by means of the chiefs of these rivers, and to them I now applied to make a Treaty with me for the suppression of the slave trade[68]

According to Dunlop, he single-handedly succeeded in agreeing a treaty of peace and abolition, and as such personified the determination of many of the squadron's officers. Later that year, Dunlop wrote to his sister declaring:

> I have completely put an end to the entire slave trade on my part of the coast from Cape Verd to Cape Palmas ... I have forced the Chiefs to banish the slave dealers, and to deliver up all the slaves to me 1300 in number and 200 prisoners of war.[69]

Naval officers' roles in these negotiations required diplomacy and initiative, and, as Dunlop's rather self-important letters reveal, some appreciation of how various coastal African societies worked. Commander Thomas Forbes was instructed to make 'treaties with all the Chiefs from Grand Popoe to Quitta' in 1852. In a letter to Commodore Henry William Bruce, he reported

---

65 TNA, ADM 123/183, Lord John Russell to Captain Burton, 23 June 1863.
66 Temperley, *White Dreams*, p. 20.
67 USNA, MS 59, Dunlop remark book, 12 February 1848.
68 USNA, MS 59, Dunlop remark book, 5 July 1849. Dunlop's emphasis.
69 NMM, MSS/87/002/1, Hugh Dunlop to his sister Fanny, 17 October 1849. Dunlop's emphasis.

a conversation with a ruler whose income was generated from tax placed on slaves passing through his territory, and who wished 'it would be explained how he was to support himself'. Forbes pointed out to him:

> The benefits of increasing trade ... that he had hundreds of thousands of acres of land, which by a little cultivation would produce a great quantity of palm oil and cotton, and by placing a small duty thereon, he would obtain a larger revenue than the one he at present receives through the slave trade. He appeared to be much pleased with the suggestions, and said he would call upon the English for protection in case of need.[70]

However, not all diplomatic agreements followed this ideal model. Naval officers experienced many fraught attempts at mediation, particularly with the Kingdom of Dahomey, in modern-day Benin. Dahomey was a powerful centre of the transatlantic slave trade; missions to end the embarkation of captives from wealthy port cities such as Ouidah were pursued from the late 1830s to the 1870s, covering the reigns of King Gezo, who died in 1858, and his son and successor Glele. Both rulers were eager to promote legitimate trade in palm oil, and exports from Dahomey rapidly increased in the late 1840s. However, rather than see it as an alternative to the slave trade, the kings wished to pursue both trades simultaneously.[71] As Lieutenant Frederick Forbes acknowledged in 1849:

> The price of a slave ... is very high, being (in goods) from 80 to 100 dollars. Hence with many captures there is great loss; the consequence is, that each slave-merchant counteracts the chances of the losses in some degree, by embarking also in the palm-oil trade, and at this moment not one slave-merchant in Whydah but works both trades.[72]

Although ending slave exports and promoting legitimate trade in Dahomey were the main concerns of naval officers, these objectives became inseparable from the desire to end the practice of human sacrifice, principally of war captives, practised at 'customs' ceremonies. Lieutenant Forbes accompanied British consular officials on visits to Gezo in pursuit of a treaty in 1849 and 1850. He was selected by Commodore Arthur Fanshawe

---

70 TNA, FO 84/893, Thomas G. Forbes to Commodore Bruce, 5 February 1852, ff. 136–37.

71 E. A. Soumanni, 'The compatibility of the slave and palm oil trades in Dahomey, 1818–1858', in Law (ed.), *From Slave Trade*, pp. 78–92. The kings of Dahomey also negotiated with other European powers, for example France in 1851.

72 Frederick Forbes to Commodore Fanshawe, 5 November 1849, in Tim Coates (ed.), *King Guezo of Dahomey, 1850–1852: The Abolition of the Slave Trade on the West Coast of Africa* (London: The Stationery Office, 2001), p. 37.

as 'an officer who has now considerable experience on the African station, and acquired some knowledge of the native languages and habits'.[73] Forbes had by this time already published one account of his service on the West Africa squadron, *Six Months' Service in the African Blockade, from April to October, 1848, in command of H.M.S. Bonetta* (1849).[74] Alongside the message of abolition, he was tasked with relaying Britain's broader vision, which would 'see Christianity introduced into every part of Africa, and thereby to increase the civilisation, welfare and happiness of her people'. King Gezo, however, stressed the intrinsic nature of the slave trade in his society, declaring to his visitors: 'My people cannot in a short space of time become an agricultural people ... All my nation – all are soldiers, and the Slave Trade feeds them.'[75] Gezo signed a treaty in 1852, but it was judged inadequate by the British. A naval blockade to coerce Dahomey was raised that year, although a definitive agreement on ending the slave trade eluded Anglo-Dahomian diplomacy throughout the 1850s.[76]

These relations reveal the diplomatic difficulties and frustrations faced by naval officers. Very often African rulers did not consent to requests for treaties, or else the broader British goals of protection of trade or an end to human sacrifice were rejected. Rulers invariably had their own objectives to pursue and could manipulate British involvement for their own benefit or economic opportunity.[77] The limitations of naval abolitionist strategy were recognized by naval officers and conveyed to policy-makers. At a parliamentary Select Committee in 1842, Captain Joseph Denman stated:

> I believe that all over Africa the natives prefer the slave trade to any other trade ... wherever the slave trade exists people never turn to legitimate traffic at all, unless the slave trade is insufficient to supply their wants ... When the slave trade no longer supplies what they want they are compelled

---

73 Commodore Fanshawe to Lieutenant Forbes, 9 September 1849, in Coates (ed.), *King Guezo*, pp. 15–16.

74 Forbes later published *Dahomey and the Dahomans, being the journals of two missions to the King of Dahomey and residence at his capital in the years 1849 and 1850* (Paris: A. and W. Galignani and Co., 1854), first published 1851.

75 Commodore Fanshawe to Lieutenant Forbes, 9 September 1849; journal of Lieutenant Forbes, 4 July 1850, both in Coates (ed.), *King Guezo*, pp. 15–16, 78–80.

76 Robin Law, 'An African response to abolition: Anglo-Dahomian negotiations on ending the slave trade, 1838–77', *Slavery and Abolition*, 16.3 (1995), pp. 281–310.

77 It has been argued that the eventual demise of the slave trade and shift to commercial agriculture owed more to economic self-interest than to treaties, as it was forced on African powers by the closure of the Brazilian slave market in 1850 and its subsequent impact on demand for slaves. See Lynn, 'Imperialism'; Law, 'An African response'.

to labour and raise produce, and they are then ready enough to engage in lawful trade.[78]

Commander George F. Burgess of the *Hecate* reported on similar limitations of agreements reached in the Bight of Benin in 1857. He believed legitimate commerce to be 'unsecure' because of the intrinsic role of slave trading in African society:

> The older chiefs who value money are attracted to a measure to the more certain mode of making it by employing their slaves in Palm Oil making and trading, but the younger ones are disgusted with so womanish a following as the one named, and sigh for a return of the exciting pursuit of man hunting; and when that becomes worth their while, and when they can succeed in getting a market, no Treaty obligation will be at all binding on them.[79]

It was not only the defiance of African rulers that caused frustrations and tensions. Treaties often included clauses guaranteeing freedom of movement or particular trade policies for European traders; as a result, British merchants made demands on naval officers for protection or assistance in trade disputes. However, the British merchants defended by the navy were not necessarily tied to the anti-slavery cause. In 1863 Commodore Arthur Eardley-Wilmot informed Commander-in-Chief Rear-Admiral Walker about 'the extraordinary opinion' of British merchant vessels concerning the information about slave-trading activity they were bound to provide naval officers, claiming 'they had rather not say a word'. Wilmot declared this truculence 'a reproach to the British Government, and to our squadron out here, as well as a scandal to the British name, that Englishmen go against Englishmen in their efforts to suppress the slave trade'.[80] For very different reasons, naval officers also encountered tensions with missionary groups; their protection was also included in treaty obligations and the navy received frequent requests for assistance from British subjects.[81] By mid-century, naval officers faced a wide array of demands for action, information or protection from

---

78 'Minutes of Evidence', in *Trial of Pedro de Zulueta*, pp. 108, 123–24.

79 CAC, BEAM 1/8, Burgess journal, 1857, no folios.

80 TNA, ADM 123/181, Arthur Eardley-Wilmot to Rear-Admiral Walker, 9 December 1863.

81 Porter, *Religion versus Empire*, pp. 238–39. Examples of these relationships are found in correspondence between naval officers and missionaries of the Yoruba mission of the CMS, with its headquarters in Abeokuta. The settlement of Abeokuta was established in the 1820s as a place of refuge from slave raids initiated by the Kingdom of Dahomey. See CRL, Church Missionary Society Archive, CA2/05 and CA2/08.

differing interests, and the navy's anti-slavery role developed into something much more wide-ranging than that first envisaged post-1807.

Other nations became suspicious that Britain's 'humanitarian' operations were aimed less at the suppression of slave traffic and more at the commercial advantage of the British in the obstruction of other nations' merchant fleets. Both Brazil and Portugal, for example, feared that Britain wished to seize Portugal's African settlements under the cover of abolition, and establish alternative sources for trade in sugar, coffee, cotton and other produce.[82] George Elliot, Commander of HMS *Columbine*, in a letter to his uncle, the Earl of Minto (and First Lord of the Admiralty), declared that abolitionist policy on the coast around Luanda was equally important in deriving commercial advantage against the Portuguese as for its humanitarian motives:

> If we succeed in suppressing the Portuguese slave trade on this coast, I think they will necessarily abandon their colonies ... The native blacks would however soon supply their places as members of the civilised world, and the trade in beeswax and ivory would be opened to the competition of English manufacturers.[83]

That such sentiments were expressed in private correspondence at such high levels of the Admiralty suggests that they drove naval abolitionist policy to some extent. Similarly, Commodore Charles Hotham stressed the interlinked nature of treaties and British trading advantage in a letter to George Eden, First Lord of the Admiralty, in 1847. 'Much time is required to gain an insight and general knowledge of African affairs', he wrote, 'besides the suppression of the slave trade, we have treaties to conclude and mercantile interests ... the trade of Africa is becoming too important to be neglected.'[84] Hotham was appointed as Commodore in large part due to his diplomatic abilities, in a desire from the Admiralty to foster good relations with the French. Hotham acknowledged that he was 'called upon to perform diplomatic duties foreign to my profession, independent of the simple slave question'.[85] He stressed the 'commercial advantages' of anti-slavery treaties in his instructions to Commander Murray in 1846, as Anglo-French relations reached a delicate phase:

82 Lambert, 'Slavery', p. 66.

83 NLS, MS 12054, George Elliot to Earl Minto, 5 January 1840, ff. 170–74.

84 HUA, U DDHO 10/8, Charles Hotham to the Earl of Auckland, 13 February 1847, ff. 62–64.

85 HUA, U DDHO 10/8, Charles Hotham to the Earl of Auckland, 31 August 1847, ff. 136–37; Roberts, *Charles Hotham*, pp. 62, 69. See Kielstra, *Politics*, for Anglo-French diplomacy in the first half of the nineteenth century.

the French have concluded treaties with nine Chiefs on different parts of the Coast thus sowing the seeds for future commercial advantages ... we can neutralize their schemes by a similar course of action ... should you fail in persuading the chiefs to relinquish the slave trade; then you will endeavour to see the treaty entered into with the French and demand the fulfillment of a similar one.[86]

British objectives in naval suppression were constantly evolving, creating scepticism about motives from African rulers and foreign powers. When the pursuit of treaties and negotiations appeared to have limited influence, the navy was called upon for a more aggressive approach to the anti-slavery cause. Nowhere was this more pronounced than in reaction to events in Lagos.

Coercing Africa

The British action against Lagos represents an example of the interaction between abolitionist ideals, commercial expansion and an increased readiness for intervention. All were involved in the attempt to impose social and economic change on African societies, and in the case of Lagos this interference developed into diplomatic and military pressure. This policy of coercion developed from naval strategies of blockade and threats of destruction. During the 1840s Lagos was a centre for slave trading, particularly from the Kingdom of Dahomey. British policy-makers identified the towns of the lagoon as ports from which an alternative trade in palm oil could be developed, and as a gateway for a potentially profitable trade in agricultural products with the Yoruba hinterland.[87] However, Lagos politics were complicated by a long dynastic dispute which culminated in 1845 in the usurpation of Akitoye by his nephew, and a leading slave trader, Kosoko. While in exile Akitoye obtained British support and promised to stop the slave trade at Lagos if reinstated. In 1851 plans were formulated for British intervention with the cooperation of palm oil traders, settlers from Sierra Leone, missionaries, and the chiefs of Abeokuta, who were sheltering Akitoye.[88] Palmerston sanctioned the navy's bombardment of the town and Kosoko was driven into exile.

86 HUA, U DDHO 10/8, Charles Hotham to Commander Murray, 25 November 1846, ff. 36–37.

87 Law, 'Introduction', in Law (ed.), *From Slave Trade*, pp. 23–24; Mann, 'The original sin', p. 176.

88 Mark R. Lipschutz and R. Kent Rasmussen (eds), *Dictionary of African Historical Biography* (Berkeley, CA: University of California Press, 1992), pp. 11–12, 114.

Midshipman Arthur Onslow of the *Samson* was involved in the attack, alongside crews of the *Penelope*, *Bloodhound* and *Teazer*. In his journal he wrote of the 'hard tussle', the shelling 'which blew up about 30 of the niggers', and how 'the town burnt beautifully during the night'. Onslow noted that the town was plundered: 'there was nothing but canoes passing us laden with plunder ... All I got was a piece of county cloth, a grass handkerchief and a bag of coffee which I gave them a bottle of gin for.' This was despite Captain Jones's assertion to Commodore Henry Bruce that it was 'desirable to show that we did not come for pillage, but that our sole object was to stop Slave Trade'.[89] Akitoye was installed as ruler in 1852, signing a treaty of abolition and guaranteeing free trade for British subjects. An authoritative British presence was established with the backing of naval officers. Commander Arthur Eardley-Wilmot reported to Commodore Bruce: 'I made him [Akitoye] put on his kingly robes, mount his horse, assemble all his Warriors, and ride completely round the Town; I went with him and made the people stop every ten minutes, and call out, "Hurrah for Akitoye."'[90] In the following decade, Lagos residents established a new set of allegiances to British representatives, including naval officers, alongside consular officials, merchants and missionaries. The navy's presence was important for security. In 1857, for example, Commodore John Adams informed the Admiralty Secretary that he had specifically stationed a vessel off Lagos to 'warn the chiefs of the risk they will incur by an infraction of their treaties with us'.[91]

Some naval officers involved in the action at Lagos expressed great pride in having expelled slave traders from the area. In 1852 the missionary the Revd Charles Gollmer wrote to Commodore Henry Bruce that the British intervention represented 'an effectual door opened by a gracious God not only for Lagos but central Africa also, you being the honored instrument to effect it'. Bruce expressed satisfaction with the navy's righteous status, declaring, 'I look upon "Lagos" as the child of my old age; and I will not desert it. It will – please God! – yet be established – free and flourishing.' Bruce also made clear his sense of responsibility to the area, adding 'I will make it a point to be here again about the 5 jaws, and "strike a blow" should it be necessary.'[92] However, the Commodore also regarded Lagos as

89 SLNSW, MSS 2050, Onslow journal, 31 December 1851; Captain Jones to Commodore Bruce, 29 December 1851, in Coates (ed.), *King Guezo*, p. 209.

90 Quoted in A. G. Hopkins, 'Property rights and empire building: Britain's annexation of Lagos, 1861', *The Journal of Economic History*, 40.4 (1980), p. 780.

91 TNA, FO 84/1040, Commodore Adams to the Admiralty Secretary, 17 February 1857; Robert Smith, 'The Lagos consulate, 1851–1861: an outline', *The Journal of African History*, 15.3 (1974), pp. 393–416.

92 CRL, Church Missionary Society Archive, CA2/05/12-19, correspondence

an exceptional case requiring British intervention. Informed of a meeting between Captain Heseltine and the Egba rulers in 1853, to discuss 'the very laudable object of making peace with the various native tribes at war', Bruce expressed his disapproval, stating his understanding of British policy 'based upon the principle of non-interference in the disputes of the natives'. The navy's 'moral influence', Bruce believed, 'may well be used to put a stop to wars detrimental to commerce, and calculated to retard the diffusion of Christianity and civilisation', but naval officers must not go 'beyond what his instructions authorized him to do'.[93] Bruce's commentary reflects the constraints on naval officers charged with anti-slavery diplomacy, whose freedom to effect change, should they wish to, was limited by their professional status and obligation to follow orders.

In 1861, following a deterioration of the political situation in the interior, Britain annexed Lagos and appointed a Governor to protect its interests, a policy designed to initiate a complete suppression of the slave trade from the region.[94] Historians have urged that British interference in West Africa must be regarded within the wider context of European imperialism and commercial change in the mid-nineteenth century. Kristin Mann and others have argued that in the bombardment of Lagos, as in the anti-slavery movement more generally, activists and policy-makers understood morality and commercial self-interest as interconnected elements of one broader process of imperial reform, reinforcing Britain's sense of superiority in its relations with West African peoples.[95] Some African rulers certainly viewed British actions as driven by arrogance rather than philanthropic concern, often encouraged in this opinion by other foreign powers. Glele, King of Dahomey, for example, wished Captain John Proctor Luce and his naval colleagues to know:

> that the white men at Wydah & also here – Brazilians, Portuguese, Spanish & French, had always been endeavouring to poison his mind against the English who they represented as being a powerful & rapacious

between Commodore Bruce and Revd C. A. Gollmer, 6 January 1852, 10 November 1853. Bruce's emphasis.

93 CRL, Church Missionary Society Archive, CA2/05/12-19, correspondence between Commodore Bruce and Revd H. Townsend, 11 January 1853, 16 February 1853.

94 Hopkins, 'Property rights', p. 795.

95 Law, 'Abolition', pp. 150–74; Mann, 'The original sin', p. 169; Hopkins, 'Property rights', p. 781. Imperial expansion in West Africa was not solely a British enterprise, as Europeans and Americans established settlements and trading posts, and displayed a new curiosity about the African interior. See J. F. Ade Ajayi and B. O. Olorunt-imehin, 'West Africa in the anti-slave trade era', in John E. Flint (ed.), *The Cambridge History of Africa*, vol. 5 (Cambridge: Cambridge University Press, 1976), pp. 200–21.

nation, who no sooner obtained a footing in any country than they dethroned its lawful King & took possession of it – for instance at Lagos.[96]

Further intervention was always under consideration in the 1850s and 1860s, and naval officers were looked to as sources of information in the planning of coercive measures. For example, in 1860, the Foreign Secretary Lord John Russell requested 'careful inquiry' from officers on the coast regarding 'rooting out the nest of slave dealers' established in the River Pongas. Reporting from the river, Commodore William Edmonstone proposed that 'the severe displeasure of the Govt. should be conveyed' to rulers who broke treaty agreements, and 'in the event of any recurrence of such conduct … his town will be destroyed'. Edmonstone's recommendations were adopted as policy and Stephen Hill, the Governor of Sierra Leone, wrote to the Commodore to commend his strategy: 'our mild rule is misunderstood & nothing but using force or the demonstration of force can be effectual in such cases'.[97]

Due to time spent travelling in the interior, communicating with local peoples and implementing the squadron's objectives, tactics and strategies, naval officers were regarded as experts in their fields, able to inform the policy-making process. The Admiralty sent circulars and questionnaires to senior officers to obtain 'information or suggestions which may contribute, and render more effectual' efforts towards naval suppression.[98] In a Foreign Office memorandum of 1861, the head of the Slave Trade Department, William Henry Wylde, suggested that a 'conference' of naval officers who had 'recently returned from Africa' would assist the government to 'take more efficient steps' towards suppression, proposing that 'some practical measures might be suggested for rendering our efforts for the suppression of the Slave Trade considerably more effective than they now are'.[99] Commodore Arthur Eardley-Wilmot certainly put forward his views on future relations with Dahomey, arguing in 1861 in a letter to the Foreign Secretary in favour of a close blockade and a mission to persuade Glele to give up the slave trade.[100] Wilmot first served on the West African coast

96 RAI, MS 280, Luce journals, vol. 4, ff. 52–54.

97 TNA, ADM 123/181, Under Secretary of State for Foreign Affairs to the Secretary of the Admiralty, 26 November 1860; William Edmonstone to the Lords of the Admiralty, 7 May 1861; Stephen Hill to William Edmonstone, 25 October 1861.

98 See TNA, ADM 7/606, 'Observations as to the most effectual mode of checking the Slave Trade', c. 1850, and replies from officers to the circular 'Best means to be adopted for the abolition of the African slave trade' in TNA, ADM 123/173.

99 Memorandum by W. H. Wylde, 7 August 1861, in *Slavery in Diplomacy*, pp. 112–15.

100 Murray, *Odious Commerce*, pp. 302–03.

from 1850 to 1853 in the *Harlequin*, and pursued treaties with Gezo in 1852. He returned to the West African coast as Commodore between 1862 and 1866. He prided himself on his knowledge of African affairs. In a published letter to Palmerston to tell him the 'truth' about the slave trade in 1853 he wrote:

> Without presumption, I may here state that few officers that have served upon this coast are so well acquainted with the slave dealers personally as myself. I have landed upon *every part* of the western coast, when it was considered dangerous and impracticable ... I have made it my business to know these people *personally*.[101]

Wilmot's recommendations for blockade were to become the basis for future policy, although objections were raised at first. Wylde instead favoured a policy of 'active measures on shore', and neither he nor Palmerston supported Wilmot's suggestion for a mission to negotiate with the king, Palmerston declaring Glele 'a brutal savage'.[102] A year later, however, Wilmot travelled to Dahomey on his own initiative to deliver messages of abolition, legitimate trade, the end to human sacrifices and peace with Abeokuta. At the end of January 1863, he wrote to Rear-Admiral Walker that since his last communication in November the previous year, 'much has transpired that will naturally cause the liveliest interest in all quarters'. The tone of Wilmot's report regarding the mission suggests that his decision to visit the king was taken without seeking approval from higher authorities. He prepared for an absence of fourteen days but was away for over fifty, which may explain why on his return the Commodore was instructed 'to abstain from undertaking any mission into the interior which might interfere with the execution of his more immediate duties'.[103]

While a treaty with Glele for the abolition of the slave trade was not forthcoming, the mission was successful in other ways. Wilmot reported on the 'friendly disposition' of the king:

> 'From henceforth', he said, 'the King of Dahomey and the Queen of England are one; you shall hold the tail of the kingdom, and I will take

---

101 Arthur Parry Eardley-Wilmot, *A Letter to The Right Honorable Viscount Palmerston on the Present State of the African Slave Trade and on the Necessity of Increasing the African Squadron* (London: James Ridgway, 1853), p. 8. Wilmot's emphasis.

102 Memorandum by W. H. Wylde, 7 August 1861 and memorandum by Lord Palmerston, 9 August 1861, in *Slavery in Diplomacy*, pp. 112–16.

103 TNA, ADM 123/183, Commodore Wilmot to Rear-Admiral Walker, 29 January 1863; Secretary of the Admiralty to Rear-Admiral Walker, 23 March 1863.

the head:' meaning that we should have possession of Whydah for trading purposes, and supply him with everything.[104]

The economic potential for Britain of these relations clearly entered the minds of policy-makers. Wilmot's decision to visit the king was later vindicated when in 1863 the explorer Richard Burton was instructed to continue 'to cultivate the friendly relations which have been established' on a return mission to Dahomey.[105] Burton was similarly unable to reach terms with Glele, but Wilmot was placed in charge of implementing the subsequent blockade, which lasted for the remainder of the decade and played a large part in bringing an end to the vestiges of the Atlantic slave trade in the region.[106]

Officers of the Royal Navy played key roles in delivering policies and promoting ideals on shore which were perceived as fundamental to Britain's anti-slavery cause: supporting exploration and information gathering; encouraging the development of legitimate commerce; pursuing anti-slavery treaties; and urging 'civilization' via religious conversion and adoption of Western standards.[107] Anti-slavery framed British policy towards Africa in the mid-nineteenth century, but other factors were at play. A hesitancy to intervene in the internal affairs of African states was increasingly set against a desire to protect and develop economic interests.[108] However, Britain's burgeoning imperial presence in West Africa faced numerous limitations, including finance, communications, disease and limited knowledge of the interior.[109] Fundamentally, many African states, Dahomey being a good example, proved reluctant or unwilling to conform to the British dictate.

104 Commodore Wilmot to Rear-Admiral Walker, 10 February 1863, in 'Despatches from Commodore Wilmot respecting his visit to the King of Dahomey in December 1862 and January 1863', *UK Parliamentary Papers*, 1863 (3179).

105 TNA, ADM 123/183, Lord Russell to Captain Burton, 23 June 1863. See Richard Burton, *A Mission to Glele, King of Dahome* (London: Tinsley Brothers, 1864).

106 Murray, *Odious Commerce*, p. 304.

107 As Bronwen Everill has argued, the ideas of commerce, Christianity and civilization were constantly shifting in the nineteenth century, and over time were interpreted as a loose coalition of ideas, connected to colonization, humanitarianism and anti-slavery rather than dictated by them. Everill, *Abolition and Empire*, pp. 12–13.

108 Huzzey, *Freedom Burning*, ch. 6; A. G. Hopkins, 'The "new international economic order" in the nineteenth century: Britain's first development plan for Africa', in Law (ed.), *From Slave Trade*, pp. 240–64.

109 Lynn, 'Imperialism', pp. 27–29, 35. In 'Emperors of the world: British abolitionism and imperialism', in Peterson (ed.), *Abolitionism and Imperialism*, pp. 129–49, Seymour Drescher has argued that while the suppression campaign entailed 'imperialist' methods of coercion, imperialism was the 'last thing on the minds of British policy makers' during this period.

As Andrew Porter has argued, the study of British imperial activities in this period must be regarded as 'alive to varied processes of interaction, adaptation, and exchange'.[110]

As the abolitionist mission on shore diversified and intensified, naval officers were responsible for communicating the British anti-slavery vision. At times their role was anything but diplomatic and peaceful, as they were tasked to punish perceived belligerence 'with a very wholesome terror' in the destruction of African settlements.[111] Officers fed back their experiences to the government and the Admiralty, and as Commodore Wilmot's experiences in Dahomey testify, officers also served as envoys in the development of relationships between African rulers and the British establishment. Their narratives highlight the reality checks and adjustments required in the operation of the British anti-slavery agenda. As we shall see, the task of implementing this agenda was also highly subject to personal experiences and beliefs.

---

110 Andrew Porter, 'Introduction: Britain and empire in the nineteenth century', in Porter (ed.), *Oxford History*, p. 4.

111 Commodore William Jones, quoted in Huzzey, *Freedom Burning*, p. 4. Jones was referring to his action against Prince Manna in the River Gallinas in 1845, in which the towns of Tindes, Tainah and Minnah were destroyed by fire.

3

Officers' commitment
to the anti-slavery cause

The *Instructions for the Guidance of Her Majesty's Naval Officers Employed in the Suppression of the Slave Trade* (1844), issued to all serving officers on anti-slave-trade patrols, began with the assertion: 'The Slave Trade has been denounced by all the civilized world as repugnant to every principle of justice and humanity.'[1] This chapter examines how far naval officers agreed with and were inspired by this sentiment. The navy's campaign against the transatlantic slave trade was one part of a complex history of British abolitionism, a multi-dimensional blend of religion, morality, philanthropy, politics, economics, national identity and public opinion. Furthermore, in the aftermath of the upheavals of the Revolutionary and Napoleonic Wars, the mood of despondency in Britain – born of economic decline, unemployment and social unrest – was given focus by an enthusiasm for naval suppression, as a distraction from domestic affairs.[2] But how far did individuals serving in the navy subscribe to abolitionist ideals? As the majority of nineteenth-century naval officers came from the middle or upper-middle classes, most would be exposed to a culture of anti-slavery sentiment in popular politics, literature and the press, as part of the wider middle-class evangelical reform movement during this period, which included free trade, temperance and the reform of manners.[3] This is not to say that the lower ranks of the naval hierarchy were unresponsive to abolitionism.[4] Anti-slavery was at various

---

1 *Instructions for the Guidance of Her Majesty's Naval Officers Employed in the Suppression of the Slave Trade* (London: T. R. Harrison, 1844), p. 1.

2 Colley, *Britons*, pp. 321–22, 359–60.

3 David Turley, *The Culture of English Antislavery, 1780–1860* (London: Routledge, 1991).

4 Nor political radicalism, as the naval mutinies of 1797 at Spithead and Nore against poor living and working conditions in the navy demonstrated.

times a popular movement, with the involvement of all classes and both men and women in generating pressure for the abolition of the slave trade and, later, slavery in British colonies. Many testimonies of naval suppression offer emotion, insight and conviction regarding the anti-slavery cause, often driven by religious belief. However, others held more ambiguous views, particularly as attitudes regarding anti-slavery and race evolved and hardened as the century progressed.

Religiosity and the navy

The historical links between anti-slavery and religious dissent are well established. The eighteenth-century evangelical revival initiated by the writings of John Wesley, George Whitefield and others laid the foundation for a wide variety of nonconformist reform movements in Britain, including those led by Quakers, Baptists, Unitarians and Methodists.[5] The new spirit of evangelical religion became active in political protest, finding expression in the anti-slavery cause. This interpretation of the Bible condemned slavery as contrary to the will of God; such condemnation also had a moral dimension, as the evangelical sense of providential judgement focused on the slave trade as a national sin. Abolition was therefore regarded as the only way to pay the nation's moral debt to those who had been enslaved.[6] As a religious and moral movement, evangelicalism infiltrated the institutions of Great Britain and dominated the political agenda at the highest levels. As Richard Blake has argued, there was a concurrent surge in evangelical sentiment in the Royal Navy by the beginning of the nineteenth century, a movement which promoted religious observance, morality and humanitarianism for the reformation of maritime society.[7] The influence of evangelical naval officers was significant enough to earn them the pejorative title 'Blue Lights', named after night-time flares. Lower-deck seamen with Methodist convictions, so-called 'psalm-singers', also established prayer and Bible-study gatherings.[8]

Prominent evangelicals in the navy included Sir Charles Middleton, appointed First Lord of the Admiralty in 1805. While serving in the West

---

5 Elie Halévy, *The Birth of Methodism in England*, trans. and ed. Bernard Semmel (Chicago: University of Chicago Press, 1971).

6 Roger Anstey, *The Atlantic Slave Trade and British Abolition, 1760–1810* (London: Macmillan, 1975), ch. 8.

7 Richard Blake, *Evangelicals in the Royal Navy 1775–1815: Blue Lights & Psalm-Singers* (Woodbridge: Boydell Press, 2008) and Richard Blake, *Religion in the British Navy 1815–1879: Piety and Professionalism* (Woodbridge: Boydell Press, 2014).

8 Blake, *Evangelicals*, p. 112.

Indies in 1759, Middleton was in command of the *Arundel* when the British slave ship *Swift* joined his fleet for protection. James Ramsay served as naval surgeon under Middleton and witnessed the horrific conditions on the slave ship. Both men had a 'conversion' experience and were increasingly involved in the abolitionist movement.[9] Ramsay left the Royal Navy in 1761 and sought ordination in the Church to enable him to work among slaves in the West Indies. Later installed as vicar on Middleton's estate in Kent, Ramsay wrote the first statement of the abolitionist cause to be argued on first-hand evidence, *An Essay on the Treatment and Conversion of African Slaves in the British Sugar Colonies* (1784).[10] Ramsay and Middleton, later created Lord Barham, were key members of the influential evangelicals who met at Barham Court: their social circle included William Wilberforce, Granville Sharp, Thomas Clarkson and other leading abolitionists.[11]

Lord Barham's evangelical principles found expression in his *Regulations and Instructions Relating to His Majesty's Service at Sea* (1806), in which for the first time a naval chaplain's duties were outlined.[12] His nephew, Admiral James Gambier, was also associated with this intersecting world of naval politics and religion. Gambier gave support to the distribution of Bibles and to the establishment of dedicated missions and floating chapels. In retirement, he became the first president of the CMS in 1812 and the British and Foreign Seaman's Friend Society and Bethel Union in 1820.[13] The Commissioner of Portsmouth Dockyard, Sir George Grey, and his wife Mary were enthusiastic supporters of the Seamen's Missions, after witnessing 'the grievous neglect of religion and morality which prevailed in the navy'. In 1817 Grey became the president of the Portsmouth Dockyard Bible Association.[14] The spiritual mission at sea was also given impetus by 'Bo'sun Smith' – the Baptist minister Revd George Charles Smith – and encouraged by junior officers such as Lieutenant the Revd Richard Marks, who wrote his spiritual reminiscences, *The Retrospect* (1816), to convey the

9 Simon Schama, *Rough Crossings: Britain, the Slaves and the American Revolution* (London: BBC Books, 2005), pp. 168–69; John E. Talbott, *The Pen and Ink Sailor: Charles Middleton and the King's Navy, 1778–1813* (London: Frank Cass, 1998), pp. 129–30.

10 J. Watt, 'Ramsay, James (1733–1789)', *Oxford Dictionary of National Biography*, Oxford University Press, 2004, www.oxforddnb.com/view/article/23086 [accessed 4 October 2016].

11 Brown, *Moral Capital*, pp. 341–44.

12 Southam, *Jane Austen*, p. 193.

13 Richard Blake, 'Gambier, James, Baron Gambier (1756–1833)', *Oxford Dictionary of National Biography*, Oxford University Press, 2004, www.oxforddnb.com/view/article/10321 [accessed 4 October 2016].

14 Mandell Creighton, *Memoir of Sir George Grey, G.C.B.* (privately printed, 1884), p. 12.

Christian message. By mid-century, scripture reading, study groups and prayer meetings had become a key part of maritime religious observance. Sunday service was compulsory throughout the navy and ships introduced voluntary daily prayers.[15] However, reconciling religious observance with the living and working conditions on an active naval ship was difficult, as the recruitment and freedom to preach of naval chaplains was in the hands of ships' captains. Officers with deep religious convictions were often dismissed as dour by the ship's company; Gambier was known as 'Dismal Jimmie' to his men. Edward Mangin was chaplain of the *Gloucester* in 1812. He perceived that 'nothing can possibly be more unsuitably or more awkwardly situated than a clergyman in a ship of war; every object around him is at variance with the sensibilities of a rational and enlightened mind'.[16]

Nevertheless, young evangelical officers began to gain recognition in mid-ranking appointments, demonstrating, in Richard Blake's words, 'the feasibility of combining piety with high professionalism'.[17] Commander Walter Estcourt and Captain Claude Henry Mason Buckle, contemporaries serving on the West Africa squadron, were considered men of 'deeply earthed Christian principle'.[18] Estcourt was Commander of the fever-ridden *Éclair* from August 1844 until his death in 1845. His journal entries for his time on the squadron reveal how he relied on his faith for comfort. His daily commentaries frequently included 'read prayers' or 'read the liturgy and a sermon', but it was in times of distress that his religious belief was most openly revealed. Following the deaths of several of his crew he wrote that he urged survivors 'to place all their hope & all their confidence in the Almighty'. Two months later, with disease rife on board, Estcourt's personal interpretation of his situation was relayed through profound religious expression:

> we are however in the hands of our Almighty Being who ... will in His own good time stay the plague of body but it is very very trying now ... very trying of our faith GOD however knows what is best for us and can bring that to pass; our present affliction may be waking in us a sincere repentance & a finer faith ... all therefore should unite in prayer to GOD, that he may be pleased to withhold the hand of the destroying angel.[19]

15 Blake, *Evangelicals*, pp. 245–47, 275, 286–91.
16 Quoted in Lavery, *Nelson's Navy*, pp. 116, 209; Blake, *Evangelicals*, p. 3.
17 Blake, *Religion*, p. 11.
18 Quotation from Estcourt's obituary in *The Nautical Magazine* (1845), GRO, D1571/F530.
19 GRO, D1571/F544, Estcourt journals, 25–26 April and 4 June 1845.

Estcourt's faith remained undiminished. In the final journal entry before his death, he wrote, 'I always trust in the Lord that he will in His own good time and in His own way save us out of trouble.'[20]

Captain Buckle served on anti-slave-trade patrols between 1841 and 1845 in command of HMS *Growler*, and again in 1849–50 as captain of the *Centaur*. An experienced officer, he had previously served in Burma and on the South American and West Indies stations.[21] Buckle and Estcourt were good friends; Estcourt wrote that he admired Buckle 'as a zealous officer and an intelligent man and felt a sincere friendship for him as a gentleman'.[22] Buckle's journals also reveal a deeply religious man. His private reading was invariably composed of evangelical texts, including 'Scott's Bible and Commentary' and 'Cooper's heart stirring sermons' (likely Edward Cooper's *Practical and Familiar Sermons*, first published in 1809). Writers such as Thomas Scott, a founder of the CMS, condemned virtually all forms of slavery. In his *Commentary* on Exodus 21:2–11, perhaps a passage that Buckle read aboard the *Growler*, Scott wrote that slavery was 'inconsistent with the law of love'. Buckle was a great admirer: 'How truly scriptural, spiritual and practical is Scott, how opposed to the mere nominal Christian.'[23] Among Buckle's personal papers is an engraving of the abolitionist Granville Sharp and a handwritten copy of the inscription found on Sharp's memorial tablet in Westminster Abbey, erected by the African Institution in 1816, in which Sharp is described as 'among the foremost of the honorable band associated to deliver Africa from the rapacity of Europe'. There is also a handwritten copy of the epitaph on Sharp's tomb in Fulham churchyard.[24] An admiration of Granville Sharp suggests an appreciation of his anti-slavery ideals, and in a rare reflection on his employment, Buckle linked the nature of his 'duty' to an idealized perspective of the service: 'I must keep in the path of duty, and free the wretched African!'[25]

However, Buckle scorned the lack of religiosity of the *Growler*'s crew. One Sunday he noted that he 'performed divine service on deck & read one of

20 GRO, D1571/F544, Estcourt journals, 6 September 1845.

21 Biographical information provided by West Sussex Record Office.

22 GRO, D1571/F544, Estcourt journals, 18 January 1845. The first volume in the series of John Marshall's *Royal Naval Biography* (1823) held by the Caird Library and Archive at the National Maritime Museum is inscribed: 'CHM Buckle, March 1846 ... Presented to me by Bucknall Estcourt Esq. as a memento of his son, my late lamented friend.'

23 WSRO, BUCKLE/470, 7 October, 14 October 1844; Anstey, *Atlantic Slave Trade*, pp. 188–89.

24 WSRO, BUCKLE/524. It is not clear who transcribed the memorials, although the handwriting does not resemble Buckle's as seen in his journals.

25 WSRO, BUCKLE/476, 3 February 1850.

Cooper's sermons to ship's co.' However, 'I fear to very little purpose, they are very practical and scriptural and truly evangelist, not what our ignorant and polluted & thoughtless men like to hear, nor I believe the officers either.'[26] While Buckle was clearly influenced by evangelical ideology, his journals offer few insights into his personal views about the slave trade. His accounts of captured slavers contain little emotion and are somewhat detached in reporting. Typical journal entries include: 'at 8PM we captured the Sherbro Schooner now called the *Erquador* with between 3 and 400 slaves on board – and have her now in tow'.[27] In contrast to other accounts of suppression, there is little commentary on interaction with enslaved Africans. Furthermore, Buckle does not relate any of the emotional miseries that frequently appear in other officers' narratives. His reasoned and prudent journal entry for one New Year's Eve on the squadron is a good example: 'Thus closes the year 1844 in which I have had many occasions of feeling grateful for undeserved mercies and benefits conferred and for much personal prosperity[;] would that I could duly consider these things, and so profit by them.'[28] The lack of sentiment in Buckle's journals offers an example of the inherent difficulties in attempting to gauge attitudes and beliefs from personal narratives. This is not to assume that evangelical religious belief automatically equated to anti-slavery sentiment, as shall be explored later. There were, however, many naval officers who publicly expressed a commitment to abolitionism with benevolent and Christian purpose.

Abolitionist beliefs on the West Africa squadron

Within a generation, naval personnel witnessed a shift from a national economy flourishing on the profits of slavery, and a political structure in large part supportive of it, to abolition and moral condemnation of the trade the navy was once instructed to protect. The career of Captain Edward Columbine exemplifies this change. In the decades before 1807, Columbine's service in the West Indies brought him into close contact with slavery. In one letter he described the rescue of slaves from a ship wrecked off the coast of Trinidad. He wrote, 'it is impossible to dismiss this narrative without reflecting on the interposition of Providence by which we were thus inabled [*sic*] to contribute to the deliverance of so large a number of our fellow creatures'.[29] However, as expected of British naval personnel in the

26 WSRO, BUCKLE/470, 6 October 1844.

27 WSRO, BUCKLE/476, 21 October 1844.

28 WSRO, BUCKLE/476, 31 December 1844.

29 UKHO, MP 46/Ac 8, pp. 376–78. I am grateful to Captain Michael Barritt for information on Columbine's service in the West Indies.

years before abolition, Columbine also served to protect the slaveholding interests of the islanders. An engraved sword was presented to him by the merchants and inhabitants of Trinidad, 'as a mark of the high sense they entertain of his services in protecting and defending the island in the years 1803 & 1804'.[30] Reflecting the shift in British society more generally, by 1810 (and now integrated into abolitionist circles via his role as Governor of Sierra Leone), Columbine believed that complicity in the 'atrocious traffic' represented 'an indelible stain' on Britain's moral integrity. 'No man who is alive to the honour of his country', he wrote, 'but must feel the Disgrace, not the <u>Dignity</u>, of permitting its flag to wave for so many years over a line of Slave-holes.' Columbine also referred to the shame brought upon the navy by its former protectionist role. He exclaimed, 'Oh! That the same flag should fly triumphant over the head of our immortal Nelson; and be prostituted to protect the Slave-dealer in his den.'[31] That Nelson himself had little time for abolitionist arguments is illustrative of the ideological conflicts surrounding naval suppression during this early period.[32]

Sir George Ralph Collier had a distinguished naval career prior to his employment as the first Commodore of the West Africa squadron, serving in the Revolutionary and Napoleonic Wars and the American War of 1812. He had earned the patronage of the Admiralty and high-profile members of society, notably Prince William of Gloucester.[33] Collier was a passionate abolitionist and deeply committed to the work of the squadron, as evidenced by his various reports and official correspondence. Declaring that British naval officers under his command worked with 'commendable zeal in the cause of humanity', Collier wrote ardently that the slave trade 'is more horrible than those who have not had the misfortune to witness it can believe, indeed no description I could give would convey a true picture of its baseness & atrocity'. For example, he reported, 'the sickening and desponding appearance of most of the wretched victims' of the Spanish slaver *Anna Maria*, taken by the *Tartar* in the River Bonny in 1821. He described how the males were shackled and bound and 'several had their

30 Presentation sword held by the National Maritime Museum (Object WPN1254).

31 UIC: SLC, Series III, Folder 9, Columbine journals, 12 January 1810, ff. 50–52. Columbine's emphasis.

32 In private letters, Nelson asserted that he was 'taught to appreciate the value of our West Indian possessions ... while I have an arm to fight in their defence, or a tongue to launch my voice against the damnable doctrine of Wilberforce and his hypocritical allies'. Quoted in Hugh Thomas, *The Slave Trade: The History of the Atlantic Slave Trade 1440–1870* (London: Picador, 1997), pp. 545–56.

33 Andrew Lambert, 'Collier, Sir George Ralph, baronet (1774–1824)', *Oxford Dictionary of National Biography*, Oxford University Press, 2004, www.oxforddnb.com/view/article/58443 [accessed 3 March 2018].

2 Sir William Beechey, *Captain Sir George Ralph Collier, 1774–1824*, c. 1814

arms so lacerated by the tightness, or long continuance of this restraint, that the flesh was completely eaten through'. His views on slave traders were clear, denouncing them as 'beyond all question, from the captain to the cabin-boy, the vilest and most depraved class of human beings'.[34]

34 MoD, MSS 45, 'Second Annual Report', f. 13; George Collier to the Lords of the Admiralty, 27 December 1821, George Collier to the Registrar of the Court of Mixed Commission, 26 March 1821, George Collier to J. W. Croker, 31 March 1821, in *British*

Collier was notable in linking humanitarianism to his understanding of the nature of 'publick [sic] duty' on the West African coast. He believed that in the three years of his command he had 'endeavoured to perform with zeal, and to the best of my ability, the very varied, and not unfrequently, distressing duties arising out of it'. His actions against slavers were performed with 'no view to personal merit, for I did what humanity, and therefore my duty, only required and I am satisfied that every British Officer on the Coast of Africa would have done as much'.[35] Collier's understanding of his professional duty was imbued with humanitarian imperative and a moral responsibility to release the enslaved, and he highlighted similar motivations in the crew of the *Tartar*. He wrote that a fast sailing vessel was purchased, 'at the joint expense of myself and some of the officers', to search the rivers of the Windward Coast for slave ships. Collier attributed this willingness to share in the expenditure to:

desire springing from the best feelings of the heart, and which had been roused in this instance into active benevolence by the dreadful scenes occasionally witnessed in the suffering misery of the unfortunate captives from the African shores. I have felt it due to the character of my officers to shew [sic] that the same philanthropic feelings, which actuate the conduct of so large a proportion of our country men are not confined to those resident on shore.[36]

Collier further reported that 'the whole crew of the Tartar have come forward ... in the most decorous but urgent manner' to offer their pay 'as a security for their proportion of the expense in case of the non-condemnation of the [slave] vessel'. He concluded:

It therefore strongly proves what the misery and sufferings of the slave must be, until he may reach his point of destination, when they could produce such strong effect upon so many unlettered and uneducated minds, as the crew of a man of war may be supposed to be composed of.[37]

Rejecting the popular stereotypes of British seamen as uncouth and unfeeling, Collier portrayed an entire crew affected by witnessing conditions 'so appalling and distressing to our feelings'.[38]

and Foreign State Papers, 1821–1822, compiled by the Foreign Office (London: J. Harrison and Son, 1829), pp. 178–80, 191, 272–73.

35 George Collier to the Lords of the Admiralty, 27 December 1821, in *British and Foreign State Papers, 1821–1822*, pp. 215–16.

36 MoD, MSS 45, 'Second Annual Report', ff. 108–11.

37 MoD, MSS 45, 'Second Annual Report', ff. 111–12.

38 Collier's perceptions of his crew are in stark contrast to those of naval surgeon

While he believed that it was benevolence and humanitarian zeal that motivated the men under his command, Collier himself undoubtedly inspired abolitionist sentiments among those he led. In 1824, three years after his time on the coast, Collier committed suicide by cutting his own throat. At the inquest into his death he was described as a 'zealous and gallant officer' but also 'a man of very sensitive feeling and mind'. The jury was unanimous in their verdict that Collier had suffered 'a state of temporary derangement'. This was unofficially attributed to aspersions cast against his professional conduct in the recently published *James's Naval History* (Collier, it was alleged, had allowed the escape of an American frigate in Porto Praya in 1815). An unidentified naval officer quoted in the *Royal Cornwall Gazette* implied that his anti-slavery service may also have contributed to his unstable mental condition. The officer remarked that the 'many and severe wounds he [Collier] received had long afflicted his bodily health, and his subsequent services on the coast of Guinea could not but prove injurious to a mind more than commonly sensitive, and to a constitution thus debilitated and weakened'.[39]

As explored further in Chapter 6, Collier's narratives provide evidence of how individual officers' experiences on the West African coast contributed to metropolitan debates about anti-slavery in Britain. That his heartfelt and unfettered views were publicly expressed in official reportage (and therefore directed at the Admiralty and government) rather than in private narratives is important. Extracts from his reports were subsequently published in British newspapers. Similarly, the emotional anguish in Commodore John Hayes's flag-officer reports from HMS *Dryad* in 1830–31 is striking. By then in his late fifties and a naval officer with much experience, Hayes had previously served on the Jamaica station.[40] He described conditions for enslaved Africans on two French slave vessels detained by the *Black Joke* in a letter to Captain George Elliot, Secretary of the Admiralty:

> the <u>scalding perspiration</u> was running from one to the other, covered also with their own filth, and where it is no uncommon occurrence for women

Peter Leonard in his *Records of a Voyage to the Western Coast of Africa, in His Majesty's Ship Dryad* (Edinburgh: William Tait, 1833). Leonard believed 'Jack' a thoughtless 'animal' whose only notion of 'duty' is conflict: 'it is not to be supposed that any notions concerning the inhumanity of slave-dealing, or the boon of emancipation which he is about to confer on so many hundreds of his fellow-creatures, enter his thoughtless head … He is ordered – it is his duty' (pp. 131–32).

39 'Melancholy Suicide', *Royal Cornwall Gazette, Falmouth Packet & Plymouth Journal*, 3 April 1824; *The Morning Post*, 26 March 1824.

40 J. K. Laughton, 'Hayes, John (1775–1838)', rev. Roger Morriss, *Oxford Dictionary of National Biography*, Oxford University Press, 2004, www.oxforddnb.com/view/article/12758 [accessed 3 March 2016].

to be bringing forth children, and men dying by their side, with full in their view, living and dead bodies chained together, and the living, in addition to all their other torments, labouring under the most famishing thirst.[41]

Hayes denounced the 'nefarious traffic' and the 'horrible crimes, worse than murder, perpetrated on those wretched creatures'. One officer, Hayes claimed, 'found not only living men chained to dead bodies', but other cases, 'too horrible & disgusting to be described'. His compassion for the enslaved led him to plead with the Admiralty to 'reflect on what must be the sufferings of upwards of five hundred of these miserable people chained together, and crammed in between the decks of a vessel only half the tonnage of a Ten Gun Brig. Gracious God! Is this unparalleled cruelty to last for ever?'[42]

Hayes, like Collier, wrote with emotive and rhetorical language in his correspondence with the Admiralty, echoing the emotional Romantic sensibility characteristic of abolitionist writing in the late eighteenth and early nineteenth centuries. Their subjective language fits within a wider narrative of abolitionist beliefs sparking personal transformations, following the experiences of Thomas Clarkson, for example.[43] In adding details of their distress, there is a sense that both Collier and Hayes wrote with emotion beyond what was expected for official reportage in order to persuade their superiors how vital and worthy they believed the work of the squadron to be. Collier claimed that he reported on the terrible conditions, 'to show how frightful the situation of the Slaves is, when in charge of the Spanish and Portuguese Slave-masters and their Crews'.[44] Hayes was keen to stress that men under his command were seeing things unimaginable to people in Britain. He wrote,

these notions, where blood is spilt, I am aware are viewed in England by many (who reflect not on, or take into their consideration, the sufferings,

---

41 TNA, ADM 1/1, John Hayes to George Elliot, 20 January 1831, ff. 259–61. Hayes's emphasis.

42 TNA, ADM 1/1, John Hayes to George Elliot, 20 January 1831, ff. 259–61.

43 Brycchan Carey, *British Abolitionism and the Rhetoric of Sensibility: Writing, Sentiment, and Slavery 1760–1807* (Basingstoke: Palgrave Macmillan, 2005). Clarkson's preoccupation with the slave trade began with his prize-winning essay published in 1786. He subsequently mobilized public opinion by reporting on his visits to slave ships in the major British ports associated with the slave trade, and by collecting evidence about the trade and Africa. See Oldfield, *Popular Politics*, ch. 3.

44 George Collier to the Lords of the Admiralty, 27 December 1821, in *British and Foreign State Papers, 1821–1822*, pp. 215–16.

the unspeakable sufferings, of the poor unhappy Africans,) as most horrid affairs, but when their sufferings be considered, I think it will appear in another light.[45]

Joseph Denman was one of the most publicly committed abolitionists to serve on the West Africa squadron. He was Lieutenant of HMS *Curlew* off the coast of South America when in 1833 it captured the Portuguese slaver *Maria de Gloria*, with 423 enslaved Africans on board. As there was no court in Brazil with jurisdiction over Portuguese ships, Denman conveyed the ship to Sierra Leone, a voyage of 46 days. The Anglo-Portuguese court there took several months to conclude that the ship was seized south of the equator and was therefore permitted to trade under Portuguese law, and so the vessel was returned to Rio and its owner. By this time, 104 recaptives were dead, while a further 169 died on their third Atlantic crossing. 'I was 46 days on that voyage', Denman wrote, 'and altogether 4 months on board of her, where I witnessed the most dreadful sufferings that human beings could endure.'[46] Subsequently, Denman dedicated himself to improving the efficacy of the squadron. As we have seen, Denman's destruction of slave barracoons at Gallinas (and the example his actions presented to other officers) became a contentious issue in the 1840s, and he was criticized for his 'somewhat mistaken zeal in the cause of suppression ... arising doubtlessly from the most philanthropic motives'.[47]

Denman's publications in support of naval abolitionist policy were driven by a belief that the slave trade 'was a custom manifestly unjust, unlawful, and in violation of the law of nature'.[48] His notion of abolitionism was intimately tied to ideas of liberty and individual freedom, as he condemned the continuance of slavery in 'a Cuba plantation or in a Brazilian mine' as 'a blow aimed at the very foundation of human society; for what title to any mere external possession can hold good if the natural right to freedom is denied?' Denman also believed in Britain's spiritual duty to end slavery, based on considerations of religious morality and humanity, demanding that European rulers 'prove by their acts ... that they are worthy to lead mankind in the paths of religion, justice, and humanity'. Like many of his contemporaries, Denman believed that Britain alone could bring about the change needed on the continent. If Britain was to withdraw anti-slavery

45 TNA, ADM 1/1, John Hayes to George Elliot, 6 May 1831, ff. 418–30.

46 Quoted in Lloyd, *The Navy and the Slave Trade*, pp. 92–93; Robert Burroughs, 'Eyes on the prize: journeys in slave ships taken as prizes by the Royal Navy', *Slavery and Abolition*, 31.1 (2010), pp. 99–115, at p. 110.

47 Bryson, *Report*, p. 255.

48 Denman, *The African Squadron*, p. 64.

efforts, he asserted, 'she leaves Africa to her fate, and that fate is the "EXCESS OF THE EVIL," the Slave Trade recognized, unlimited, and perpetual'.[49] Several naval officers who published accounts or remarks about the suppression of the slave trade focused on British moral superiority and high spiritual purpose in the abolitionist mission on the West African coast, whereby morality was regarded as inseparable from national honour. For example, Commander John Foote asserted the un-Christian behaviour of the Brazilians, who, 'disregarding alike the principles of religion and morality, the faith of treaties, and the execration of the whole civilised world', continued to practice 'the nefarious traffic in human flesh; and in pursuit of their guilty speculations practise greater cruelties ... than the minds of Christian men can conceive'.[50]

The notion of the slave trade as a direct challenge to Christian principles was also propounded by Captain William Fitzwilliam Owen, who first encountered the trade while serving in Java as senior officer of the Batavia squadron in 1811–12. In deploying his ships to intercept slave-carrying vessels, he claimed to have liberated 1,500 slaves.[51] Later engaged in surveying the West African coast, Owen believed that abolition was God's will. In 1825, on witnessing the arrival of chained captives in Benguela, Angola, Owen was outraged by the 'scene of human suffering produced by human agency ... mankind should know what manner of people they are, who call themselves men and Christians'.[52] Owen's understanding of professional duty was inseparable from his sense of spiritual obligation to act in defence of the enslaved. As superintendent for the proposed new naval base on Fernando Po in the late 1820s, Owen captured more than 20 slave ships, albeit with a reputation for unorthodox methods, including ignoring treaty agreements and torturing captured ships' officers. Owen's abolitionist zeal caused further controversy when he released captured Africans on the island without first sending them before the Mixed Commissions, and then set them to work manning his ships and administering the island. He also pressed into service

---

49 Denman, *The African Squadron*, pp. 49, 68, 70. Denman's emphasis.

50 'A Few Remarks on the Slave-Trade in the Brazils by Commander Foote R.N.', *United Service Magazine*, part II (1845), pp. 378–87, at p. 378. For a wider discussion of ideas of 'cultural imperialism', see Howard Temperley, 'Anti-slavery as a form of cultural imperialism', in Christine Bolt and Seymour Drescher (eds), *Anti-Slavery, Religion and Reform* (Folkestone: Wm Dawson & Sons, 1980), pp. 335–50.

51 E. H. Burrows, *Captain Owen of the African Survey, 1774–1857* (Rotterdam: A. A. Balkema, 1979), p. 44.

52 Quoted in Burrows, *Captain Owen*, p. 161; Robert T. Brown, 'Fernando Po and the anti-Sierra Leonean campaign: 1826–1834', *The International Journal of African Historical Studies*, 6.2 (1973), pp. 253–54.

the crews of captured slavers.[53] Considering the role of naval suppression in framing Britain's abolitionist position on the international stage, it is perhaps unsurprising that senior officers subscribed to Lord Palmerston's belief that 'Great Britain is the main instrument in the hands of providence' for putting an end to the slave trade.[54] However, the emotion and moral worth of the words and actions of these officers suggests more than just following the party line.

These officers personified the close connection between military virtue and moral stature present in concepts of the nineteenth-century naval 'Christian hero'.[55] In 1813 Commodore Charles Penrose published a letter in *The Naval Chronicle* noting how the 'most able and zealous … Christian heroes' were to be found in the navy. He believed they could become 'powerful engines for the dissemination of knowledge and truth' in carrying the Christian evangelical message around the world.[56] As we have seen, many naval officers supported the Christian philanthropic mission to eradicate the slave trade from African society and 'civilize' the continent. The abolitionist cause, imbued with the idea of 'trusteeship' for the betterment of non-European peoples, was part of a wider force of religious enthusiasm that extended to indigenous peoples across the globe, a missionary impulse that directed attention to the moral and spiritual condition of 'the heathen'. Emphasis was placed on how Christian Europe might save non-Europeans from themselves, hence the influence of 'imperial stewardship'.[57] These perceptions took British superiority for granted, and clearly had a racial subtext. When in 1835 MP Thomas Babington Macaulay called for an educational system in India whereby the English language would take precedence over 'poor and rude' Indian tongues, he was proposing that

53 Brown, 'Fernando Po', pp. 258–60.

54 Quoted in Colley, *Britons*, p. 360. However, as J. R. Oldfield notes in 'Palmerston and anti-slavery', in David Brown and Miles Taylor (eds), *Palmerston Studies II* (Southampton: Hartley Institute, University of Southampton, 2007), Palmerston's stance against the slave trade was more pragmatic (and in Britain's national interests) than passionate.

55 Hamilton, 'Naval hagiography', pp. 381–98. See also Jane Samson, 'Hero, fool or martyr? The many deaths of Commodore Goodenough', *Journal for Maritime Research*, 10.1 (2008), pp. 1–22.

56 Quoted in Blake, *Religion*, pp. 154–56.

57 Andrew Porter, 'Trusteeship, anti-slavery, and humanitarianism', in Porter (ed.), *Oxford History*, pp. 198–221; Christopher Bayly, 'The British and indigenous peoples, 1760–1860: power, perception and identity', in Martin Daunton and Rick Halpern (eds), *Empire and Others: British Encounters with Indigenous Peoples, 1600–1850* (London: UCL Press, 1999), pp. 19–41. For example, from the early nineteenth century, missionary activity in India focused on the perceived degradation of Indian society and religion, condemning 'heathen' practices such as sati, the rite of widow-burning.

Indians be educated into civilization. He looked forward to future relations (and opportunities for trade) with this new generation of cultural intermediaries, 'a class of persons, Indian in blood and colour, but English in taste, in opinions, in morals, and in intellect'.[58]

Naval officers praised expanding missionary activity in West Africa. *West African Sketches* (1824) was a series of essays compiled from the reports of Commodore George Ralph Collier and Sierra Leone Governor Charles MacCarthy, among others. The volume was intended to inform the reader about 'the many amusing and interesting details of Western Africa', and was part of the copious literature produced about the continent during this period. It is unclear which author penned which 'sketch', but the tone of the publication regarding the British role in Africa is unequivocal. The destructive effects of the slave trade had caused 'habits of violence and insecurity' and a 'dismembered' society; these conditions were tied to the 'moral turpitude' of heathenism and a lack of Christianity. According to the authors, this dire situation would only be alleviated by British example, by 'our genuine philanthropy' and 'our humanity and pity':

> The chain which bound Africa to the dust ... has been broken by British energy and perseverance; be it then our heaven-directed employ to teach her the exalted use of her liberated faculties, and to impart the boon by which she may continue to raise herself from the ruin and degradation, the misery and the crime, we have alas! so greatly contributed to bring upon her.[59]

As part of Britain's obligation to introduce Christianity to the continent, European standards of education were considered as key to dispersing the influence of indigenous beliefs. As Collier wrote, education of the children of 'these gross idolaters' was 'the best way of arriving at that important desideratum, the quiet and silent introduction of Christianity into that part of Africa'.[60] Admiral Robert Wauchope declared he had shed 'tears of gratitude and thankfulness' while contemplating the impact of Sunday School teaching in Sierra Leone: 'I felt what a blessing our West Coast cruisers had been in bringing the parents of these children into such blessed

---

58 Thomas Babington Macaulay, 'Minute of 2 February 1835 on Indian Education', in *Prose and Poetry*, ed. G. M. Young (Cambridge, MA: Harvard University Press, 1957), pp. 721–24, 729; Catherine Hall, 'Troubling memories: nineteenth-century histories of the slave trade and slavery', *Transactions of the Royal Historical Society*, 21 (2011), pp. 147–69. Thomas was the eldest son of Zachary Macaulay, but did not share his father's evangelical beliefs, instead endorsing secular notions of civilization.

59 *West African Sketches*, pp. 3–5, 24.

60 MoD, MSS 45, 'Second Annual Report', ff. 113–15, 215–16.

circumstances.'[61] In 1842 Midshipman Augustus Arkwright wrote from Sierra Leone of his support for the 'moral education' and 'correct information about religion' provided by the missionaries in the colony, declaring them 'more deserving and by far the most useful portion of our country-men out here'.[62] Lieutenant Frederick Forbes was also deeply committed to the anti-slavery cause as a humanitarian Christian mission; in his account of his expedition to Dahomey in 1849 he declared that the 'crusade against the slave trade is a holy one'. He tied suppression of the slave trade at sea to the spread of the anti-slavery message on shore, as he asserted that slavery was 'the offspring of ignorance', which required 'the light of civilisation' to conquer it. Ideals of 'treaty, trade and the advancement of civilisation' constituted the 'moral course whereby to check this great evil', which 'will in time crown with success the most philanthropic undertaking ever entered into in this world'.[63]

Notions of British identity were key to these beliefs, inseparable from the Christian mission, and from ideas of freedom from slavery for African states. Commander Arthur Eardley-Wilmot's long letter to the Commander-in-Chief of the forces at Abeokuta in 1852 propounded the elevating example of the Christian faith, which promoted 'peace, friendship, kindness, charity'.[64] Wilmot's perception of 'charity' took the form of encouraging the African people to 'do good & endeavour to benefit their fellow creatures', including an end to 'making slaves of others'. Religious faith was integral to his beliefs. 'May the great God above us, in whose eyes the white man and the black man have equal claims, take you into His Holy keeping', Wilmot wrote, '& open your heart to see in his own good time, the wonderful works that he doeth for the children of men.' Wilmot expressed great confidence and pride in the British anti-slavery mission, especially in comparison to other European nations. For example, the Portuguese, he claimed, 'have no interest in the permanent prosperity of your country. If all of you were to die tomorrow, they would laugh & sing as usual.' On the contrary, the English had died in numbers on the coast, he wrote, in order to 'make you & all Africa like England & the rest of the civilised world. To teach you what real happiness is & to shew [sic] you how you can make your country the richest upon earth.'[65] Wilmot clearly articulated Britain's sense of moral

61 Robert Wauchope, *A Short Narrative of God's Merciful Dealings* (privately printed, 1862), pp. 107–09.

62 DRO, D5991/10/72-73, Augustus Arkwright to his mother, 19 June 1842.

63 Forbes, *Dahomey and the Dahomans*, pp. 31, 90.

64 CRL, Church Missionary Society Archive, CA2/o8/o4, Arthur Eardley-Wilmot to 'Obba Shoron', 3 April 1852.

65 CRL, Church Missionary Society Archive, CA2/o8/o4, Arthur Eardley-Wilmot to 'Obba Shoron', 3 April 1852.

responsibility to African society. He also stressed the need for continued paternalism, based on a blinkered vision that only Britain could save African peoples.

Ambiguities surrounding abolitionism

Other officers of the West Africa squadron, however, held different views about the anti-slavery cause. The navy as an institution remained inherently conservative, and many officers regarded suppression of the slave trade as a professional duty they were required to perform without dwelling on any humanitarian purpose. At its most extreme, a lack of commitment is highlighted by examples of British officers' involvement in selling enslaved people on the West African coast. In 1810 Lieutenant Bourne was placed in charge of a detained slave brig and directed to Sierra Leone. Instead, Bourne proceeded to Princes Island where Captain Columbine reported that he 'sold her & the slaves to a Portuguese merchant; taking in payment bills on Rio Janeiro, 1300 dollars & a small schooner'.[66] Naval surgeon Robert Flockhart implied that a fellow naval officer was willing to profit from the slave trade regardless of Britain's abolitionist position. In letters from 1838, Flockhart recounted the discovery of an American captain of a slave ship, who 'turns out to be a man of the name Graham who served for two years on this coast in the Lynx one of our cruisers, and who said he was an Englishman'.[67]

It is impossible to know the number of similar occurrences, but examples of such disregard for abolitionism by some in the navy are significant.[68] Racial beliefs in the innate inferiority of non-European peoples clearly influenced some officers' commitment; a position against the slave trade did not necessarily equate to a belief in racial equality.[69] Paul Cuffe was a free black American, a Quaker sea captain who sailed to Sierra Leone from Massachusetts in 1811 with a plan to transport settlers from America at his own expense.[70] Writing his journal from Freetown, Captain Columbine was unenthused about Cuffe's chances of success, based on his own preconceptions about African peoples:

66 UIC: SLC, Series III, Folder 10, Columbine journals, 10 December 1810.

67 NRS, GD 76/458, Flockhart letters, 12 November 1838.

68 While trading in enslaved people was illegal for Britons, some British individuals and companies continued to profit from the slave trade by other means throughout the nineteenth century – providing credit and insurance for slave vessels, for example. See Marika Sherwood, 'Britain, the slave trade and slavery, 1808–1843', *Race and Class*, 46 (2004), pp. 54–77.

69 As Catherine Hall has argued in *Civilising Subjects*, many evangelicals hated slavery but accepted racial inequality (p. 361).

70 Ackerson, *African Institution*, pp. 72–73.

as to any effect he can produce on the savages beyond the narrow limits of this little town, it seems to me to be quite out of the question ... I will never join in those flattering representations which have been made of this place, in order to delude ignorant people to it, to their ruin.[71]

Columbine's reflections were linked to his understanding of West African societies. There was a developing awareness of Africa in Britain in the early nineteenth century, promoted in books, pamphlets, newspapers and accounts of exploration. Abolitionists sought to weaken the assumption that Africans were innately savage and therefore suited to nothing more than slavery. Columbine was keen to stress that he supported every 'benevolent intention' to rid the continent of the slave trade. However, writing from Bance Island (the former British slave fort), Columbine was sceptical of efforts to civilize the domestic slaves of the settlement, because of what he regarded as deficiencies in the African character. 'They are excessively indolent, insolent & even mutinous', he wrote, 'the produce of their labour amounts to a mere nothing.' Here his language echoed that of the directors of the African Institution, whose discussions on Africa were based around beliefs that idleness and a lack of morality among its people were a result of the slave trade.[72] Columbine, however, did not believe that African people were capable of change. 'People in England may talk as they please about the natural excellence of the African disposition, when unshackled by slavery', he wrote; 'as far as I am able to judge, they have as strong a natural & cultivated bias to craft & rascality as any knaves I ever met with'.[73] His thoughts differed from those he expressed to the Sherbro rulers praising the benefits of agriculture and legitimate trade, illuminating the difference between opinions expressed in public and private papers.[74]

Columbine exemplified some of the racial tensions and moral ambiguities regarding concepts of slavery, servitude and freedom for African people. While he fully supported an end to the slave trade, Columbine held little faith in Africans' ability to repair their own society, and advanced the case for outside (British) rule as the only way to redress the innate problems of the African character. Such attitudes were unsurprising, considering that black people were regarded as objects of ridicule and racial caricature in British print, literature and popular culture throughout the late eighteenth

71 UIC: SLC, Series III, Folder 12, Columbine journals, 2 March 1811.

72 Ackerson, *African Institution*, p. 23; UIC: SLC, Series III, Folder 10, Columbine journals, 27 February 1811.

73 UIC: SLC, Series III, Folder 10, Columbine journals, 27 February 1811.

74 See Chapter 2, pp. 45–46.

and early nineteenth centuries.[75] For example, George Cruickshank's print *The New Union Club, Being a Representation of What Took Place at a Celebrated Dinner, Given by a Celebrated – Society*, published in 1819, purports to show a dinner held at the African Institution. It employs many common nineteenth-century racial stereotypes, including criticism of the idea that black people could aspire to behave like Europeans.[76] As Columbine wrote with cynicism in 1811, he held no regard for the plan to instruct Africans 'to wear breeches? Or part with their wives?' He added: 'Hope is so rapid & sanguine on this head, that she totally loses sight of Experience.'[77]

As the century progressed, racial arguments from a new group of scholars and scientists increasingly asserted the innate inferiority of non-European peoples. One outward expression of these renewed racial prejudices was a retreat from humanitarian ideals, and a rejection of philanthropic hopes for the moral and social improvement of African societies.[78] Enthusiasm for the anti-slavery movement was diminished by the abortive Niger Expedition in 1841, while other events in the colonies challenged established humanitarian ideas. This was particularly the case with regard to attitudes towards former slaves in the British West Indies 'freed' under the Emancipation Act of 1833.[79] In an account published in 1832, Captain Frederick Chamier (who served on anti-slave-trade patrols on HMS *Arethusa* in the 1820s) expressed doubt that 'in the event of a sudden emancipation, men with minds uninformed' would 'go cheerfully and manfully to work for their own support'.[80] By mid-century it had become evident that the sugar colonies had continued to decline economically and that 'freed' slaves – the majority now subject to strict terms of forced labour known as apprenticeship – had failed to live up to missionary expectations of self-improvement and self-discipline. Planters and their allies highlighted humanitarian naivety;

75 Curtin, *Image of Africa*, pp. 363–64; Catherine Hall, 'An empire of God or of man? The Macaulays, father and son', in Hilary M. Carey (ed.), *Empires of Religion* (Basingstoke: Macmillan, 2008), pp. 64–83.

76 For a discussion of *The New Union Club*, see Hamilton and Blyth (eds), *Representing Slavery*, pp. 290–92.

77 UIC: SLC, Series III, Folder 10, Columbine journals, 27 February 1811.

78 Quirk and Richardson, 'Anti-slavery', pp. 87–88; Curtin, *Image of Africa*, ch. 15.

79 See the essays in Catherine Hall, Nicholas Draper and Keith McClelland (eds), *Emancipation and the Remaking of the British Imperial World* (Manchester: Manchester University Press, 2014). Disillusionment with humanitarianism in the colonies has been explored in, among others, Andrew Bank, 'Losing faith in the civilizing mission: the premature decline of humanitarian liberalism at the Cape, 1840-60', in Daunton and Halpern (eds), *Empire and Others*, pp. 364–83.

80 Frederick Chamier, *The Life of a Sailor by a Captain in the Navy*, 2 vols (London: Richard Bentley, 1832), vol. 1, pp. 268–69.

it was claimed that ex-slaves were doomed through innate incapacity, indolence and superstition to always be 'mastered'. Hence Thomas Carlyle, in his vitriolic, and widely distributed, pro-planter pamphlet *Occasional Discourse on the Nigger Question* (1849), argued, in effect, for the reintroduction of slavery in the West Indies.[81] In 1865 the riot over vacant land in Jamaica's Morant Bay resulted in the declaration of martial law by Governor Eyre, under which 469 black people were executed and another 650 flogged. The revolt and the controversy caused by humanitarian attempts to have Eyre prosecuted were widely publicized and held the attention of metropolitan, middle-class Britons.[82] In 1866 Commander Bedford Pim, a retired naval officer, presented a paper in Eyre's defence to the Anthropological Society of London in which he claimed that freedom and equality were the cause of discontent in Jamaica, because in slavery, 'a decidedly inferior race was rescued from a state of barbarism scarcely human, and compelled to take a useful position'.[83]

In popular culture, enthusiasm for humanitarianism gave way to apathy and renewed racial prejudices. Charles Dickens, reviewing Allen and Thomson's *Narrative of the Niger Expedition* (1848) in *The Examiner*, attacked Buxton's aims and declared the civilizing mission as absurd, as his description of the negotiations makes clear:

> Obi, sitting on the quarter-deck of the *Albert*, looking slyly out from under his savage forehead and his conical cap, sees before him her Majesty's white Commissioners from the distant blockade-country gravely propounding, at one sitting, a change in the character of his people ... the entire subversion of his whole barbarous system of trade and revenue – and the uprooting, in a word, of all his, and his nation's, preconceived ideas, methods and customs.

Dickens's critique was against blind philanthropy abroad when he believed more worthy subjects suffered at home. Hence in *Bleak House* (1853), Mrs Jellyby expended all her energies caring for the poor black children of the

---

81 Hall, *Civilising Subjects*, ch. 6. The impact of the principles of apprenticeship in the West Indies also affected perceptions of liberated Africans in West Africa. As Richard Huzzey has argued, expectations of cheap 'free' labour in India, the Caribbean and in Africa in turn shaped racial beliefs, highlighting an uneasy relationship between anti-slavery ideology and racial prejudices. Huzzey, *Freedom Burning*, pp. 200–02.

82 Hall, *Civilising Subjects*, pp. 57–65. This was true of other uprisings in the empire, including the Cape frontier wars, the 1857 Indian Mutiny and the New Zealand wars.

83 Quoted in Douglas A. Lorimer, *Colour, Class and the Victorians: English Attitudes to the Negro in the Mid-nineteenth Century* (Leicester: Leicester University Press, 1978), pp. 150–51.

Niger while her own family lived in squalor.[84] Like most white, Victorian, male, middle-class commentators, Dickens's attitudes towards race and empire were complex, but the racism inherent in his article *The Noble Savage* (1853) and his outspoken responses against the Indian Mutiny of 1857 are revealing about the popular attitudes of British society, which held him in such admiration.[85]

In his published account of slavery in Brazil, naval surgeon Thomas Nelson attacked apologists for slavery, and in particular the 'invidious comparison' of conditions of slavery with the situation of the labouring poor in Britain, which 'can only serve to illustrate to what absurdities men will be driven'.[86] But these popular sentiments against humanitarianism abroad reflected other changes in British society from mid-century, in particular the emergence of new standards of gentility and attitudes towards social status. The significance of masculinity hardened, particularly in the public schools that produced naval officers, and sentiment assumed a less positive sense. Young, middle-class gentlemen increasingly wished to be perceived as virile, unsentimental and racially superior, and were less inclined to tolerate the emotional appeals of an earlier generation. 'Nigger philanthropy', as it was now often called, suffered in consequence.[87] As the narratives of Lieutenant Forbes or Commodore Wilmot make clear, many officers in the mid-century continued to be committed to the missionary cause, and there was a renewed surge of popularity for missionary activity in the 1840s and 1850s.[88] However, these decades also reveal diminished

84 Quoted in Temperley, *White Dreams*, pp. 166–67; Patrick Brantlinger, 'Victorians and Africans: the genealogy of the myth of the Dark Continent', *Critical Inquiry*, 12.1 (1985), p. 175.

85 Grace Moore, *Dickens and Empire: Discourses of Race, Class and Colonialism in the Works of Charles Dickens* (Aldershot: Ashgate, 2004), pp. 4–5, 45, 70. Catherine Hall has written of the 'liberal ambivalence' exemplified by commentators such as Dickens and Thomas Babington Macaulay, whereby slavery was hated as an institution as the antithesis of freedom, yet racial inequality was accepted as a necessary foundation for a stable society (Hall, 'Troubling memories', p. 158).

86 Thomas Nelson, *Remarks on the Slavery and Slave Trade of the Brazils* (London: J. Hatchard and Son, 1846), pp. 57–59. William Cobbett, for example, the period's most widely read popular journalist, wrote with virulent racism about the miseries of Britain's labouring poor in contrast to the perceived comfort of colonial subjects.

87 J. A. Mangan and James Walvin, 'Introduction', in J. A. Mangan and James Walvin (eds), *Manliness and Morality: Middle-class Masculinity in Britain and America 1800–1940* (Manchester: Manchester University Press, 1991), pp. 1–2; Lorimer, *Colour, Class*, pp. 113–18; Alan Lester, 'British settler discourse and the circuits of Empire', *History Workshop Journal*, 54 (2002), pp. 22–48, at p. 44.

88 In *The Civilising Mission and the English Middle Class, 1792–1850: The 'Heathen' at Home and Overseas* (Basingstoke: Palgrave Macmillan, 2009), Alison Twells argues

faith in philanthropic endeavours on the part of some naval officers. This was related to the beginnings of a shift towards duty as exemplified by muscular Christianity and specifically naval forms of masculinity and endurance which characterized naval officers of the later Victorian period.[89]

Captain John Proctor Luce was Senior Officer in the Bights in 1862–63. In his journals, he wrote extensively about the African societies he encountered, and was notable for criticizing missionary projects on the continent as flawed and ill-handled. Of the missionaries at Cameroon River he wrote, 'their self sacrifice & martyrdom to the good cause is generally speaking, Exeter Hall bosh'. The site of many meetings of the anti-slavery lobby, Exeter Hall in London represented, for many, philanthropic hypocrisy. Integral to Luce's criticisms was the increasingly common belief in the indolence of African peoples. He wrote that missionaries 'make but few converts' because 'in the nigger mind there is so much to be eradicated before the simplest truths of our religion can be received, that the case seems almost hopeless'.[90] African missionaries also came under fire. After visiting the settlement in the River Niger led by the Revd Samuel Ajayi Crowther, Luce condemned 'the lazy wretches', who:

> have not cleared away an acre of ground or sown an ounce of seed. Why should they as long as they have a lot of muffs in England who under the fond idea that these Sierra Leone angels are civilising & Christianising Africa, keep them well supplied with necessaries & luxuries.[91]

Beliefs that Britain's philanthropic efforts were misguided became more commonplace with the increasing disillusionment regarding the squadron's perceived inefficacy expressed in the British press and various publications. For example, many condemned abolitionist policies in relation to the death of British sailors. One naval officer wrote to *The Times* in 1844 to make a 'plea for the white victims of philanthropy on the coast of Africa'. He condemned the ships of the squadron as 'the annual hecatombs of our fellow-countrymen, so uselessly, so wantonly, nay so mischievously, sacrificed in that deadly climate'.[92] Such divisive sentiments polarized naval

---

that these decades witnessed conflicting currents of continuing commitment to the missionary cause alongside increasingly popular notions of racial difference.

89 In 'The Royal Navy's anti-slavery campaign', chs 2 and 5, Lindsay Doulton stresses the significance of the public school education system in the promotion of militarism, patriotism and Protestantism in the world view of naval officers in the later nineteenth century.

90 RAI, MS 280, Luce journals, vol. 3, f. 165.

91 RAI, MS 280, Luce lournals, vol. 3, f. 203.

92 *The Times*, 'Attempts to Suppress the Slave Trade', 29 August 1844.

personnel and the abolitionists who directed their work on the coast, a 'them and us' mentality that contrasts to the commonalities in purpose expressed elsewhere. Philanthropy assumed a negative character. A naval officer wrote to *The Times* in 1846 to condemn the 'canting and ranting of the Exeter-hall gentry! Every one of those Mawworms [parasitic worms] should be sent out here to man the squadron. We should then see what would become of their egregious philanthropy.'[93]

Others believed that British charity would be better extended to the West Indian planters affected by the consequences of the Emancipation Act. Lieutenant Gordon Macdonald of HMS *Childers* served on anti-slave-trade patrols in the West Indies in the 1820s and wrote in defence of 'the rights of the colonies' in his memoirs. While Macdonald opposed 'this horrid system of slavery', he held contempt 'for those people in England termed or known as Abolitionists who have no justice or charity on their side towards their fellow creatures and subjects the West Indians'.[94] The phrase 'fellow creatures' was used many times by other officers to describe enslaved Africans; Macdonald instead switched sympathy to the planters, presenting them as the victims of hostile action from abolitionists. Indeed, many in Britain were mindful of planters' property rights and supported gradual rather than immediate emancipation.[95] A West India meeting in 1833 featured the contribution of Admiral Sir Thomas Byam Martin, who condemned 'an act of gross injustice' against the sanctity of property. The admiral had formerly served in the West Indies, which justified him, he believed, in declaring 'that there never were more iniquitous and false statements than those which I have seen put forth by the Anti-Slavery Society'.[96] In other letters, Byam approved of the Abolition Act of 1807 – 'a proposition that no Christian legislature could resist' – but he perceived an end to the trade in enslaved Africans as quite separate to the 'emancipation of 800,000 slaves ... a thing that cannot be contemplated without a dread of its consequences'.[97]

While some naval officers condemned the principle of abolition, others took such attitudes further and believed that slavery was the rightful condition for African peoples. Pro-slavery ideas remained a potent force in Britain

93 *The Times*, 'Service on the Coast of Africa', 22 May 1846.

94 NYPL, Macdonald memoirs, c. 1832, pp. 100–03.

95 Including Lord Palmerston. See Oldfield, 'Palmerston and anti-slavery'.

96 *The Morning Chronicle*, 28 May 1833.

97 *Letters and Papers of Admiral of the Fleet Sir Thomas Byam Martin*, ed. Sir Richard Vesey Hamilton, vol. 1 (Navy Records Society, 1903), pp. 87–88. The West India interest still had a powerful voice in Parliament and the City and in 1833 negotiated a sum of £20 million in compensation for the loss of property (enslaved men, women and children).

throughout the nineteenth century.[98] Several naval officers were plantation and slave owners themselves, as evidenced by the list of claimants and awardees of compensation listed on the Legacies of British Slave-ownership database. This list includes Sir Charles Adam, First Naval Lord three times between 1834 and 1847, awarded compensation for plantation slaves in British Guiana.[99] A naval officer's letter to *The Times* in 1845 declared that African people were 'sunk in the lowest barbarism ... whose condition as human beings is undoubtedly improved by slavery'.[100] On board the *Bristol* off the West African coast in 1866, naval surgeon Fleetwood Buckle recounted in his journal a discussion with a clergyman, the Revd Pemberton, 'about the negro and his position – he quite agrees with me that he was intended for a slave & must be made to work'. Echoing Thomas Carlyle, Buckle too believed that slavery was the natural state for black people. He aggressively asserted the indolent stereotype when he discussed the black crewmen on board with vehement racism: 'I will not have charge of the stinking niggers they won't work – you cannot get them to without a stick at their backs.' Buckle's opinions illustrated the debate in this period about what constituted philanthropy, charity and goodwill towards others when he later wrote that Pemberton was 'really the most liberal minded clergyman I ever met with. The most charitable.'[101]

In letters to his brother from HMS *Favorite* in 1847, Commander Alexander Murray supported the continuance of the transatlantic slave trade in a more measured but similarly offensive way, advocating the benevolence of the system of slavery for the future progress of the African continent. 'The more I see of the whole system the more I am convinced that the attempt to stop the emigration of Africans is an error', he wrote; 'if ever any progress is made in our day in the civilization of Africa it will be by using slavery as

---

98 Paula Dumas, *Proslavery Britain: Fighting for Slavery in an Era of Abolition* (Basingstoke: Palgrave Macmillan, 2016). For example, Sierra Leone was increasingly attacked by pro-slavery writers. See David Lambert, 'Sierra Leone and other sites in the war of representation over slavery', *History Workshop Journal*, 64 (2007), pp. 103–32, for an examination of the 'war of representation' over Sierra Leone as exemplified by the exchanges between Kenneth Macaulay, cousin of Zachary Macaulay, and James MacQueen, a geographer of Africa and spokesman for the anti-Sierra Leoneans, in 1826–27.

99 https://www.ucl.ac.uk/lbs/person/view/8659 [accessed 21 November 2017]. The database lists 55 individuals with an occupation of 'Sailor (Royal Navy)' and 49 individuals with a connection to the term 'naval officer'. Many estates were legacies of plantations that were gifted to naval officers in the eighteenth century.

100 *The Times*, 'The African Station', 16 October 1845.

101 WC, MS 1395-6, Fleetwood Buckle diaries, 8 July, 6 August and 25 October 1866. Buckle's emphasis.

an assistant therein instead blindly shutting the eyes and waging war against the social institutions of a continent which are coeval with the races in which they exist'. In reframing the slave trade as 'emigration', Murray removed the suggestion of enforced movement of Africans and the cruelties associated with it. He continued with an attack on the views of the Exeter Hall lobby, claiming that this 'superb coast wants nothing but human industry to make it the richest tropical region in the world ... Exeter Hall would call this slavery and so it is – but the same sort of slavery existed in England within the memory of history.' He added: 'Were I, Mr Colonial Government, I would become a slave owner myself.'[102] Murray's support for this form of 'human industry' appeared undiminished by any barbarities he may have witnessed on the coast. Writing two years later, after the completion of his service there, he wrote that 'my opinions are for nothing much less than a return to the old slave system as far as Africa is concerned'.[103]

Murray's views are in stark contrast to those of some of his contemporaries on the squadron such as Joseph Denman. Clearly, even considering the impact of abolitionism on British society, there was an endurance of eighteenth-century pro-slavery rhetoric among some naval personnel, suggesting a deeper vein of conservative political views in the navy more broadly.[104] It is notable that Murray made these comments in private correspondence. Many officers who did express pro-slavery views publicly, in letters to newspapers for example, did so anonymously. This distinction between publicly and privately expressed views shows how far anti-slavery was perceived as the dominant ideology by mid-century, entrenched in the public consciousness. It also supports the idea that there were certain opinions concerning slavery and the slave trade that naval officers were not permitted to express in public in order to avoid prejudicing their professional position.

More common was an expression of ambivalence towards abolition. Commander George Augustus Elliot of the *Columbine* was seemingly indifferent to the plight of the enslaved, a state of mind induced by concerns for his own hardships. In a letter to Lord Melgund, the private secretary to the First Lord of the Admiralty (and his uncle) the Earl of Minto, Elliot declined to offer much reflection on his experiences:

102 NRS, GD 219/304/36, Murray letters, 22 September 1847.
103 NRS, GD 219/304/39, Murray letters, 8 May 1849.
104 For example, Captain Robert Fitzroy served in South American waters in the 1820s and 1830s and encountered the slave trade and slavery first-hand, particularly in Brazil, yet continued to believe in the 'benevolence' of the slave system. See Adrian Desmond and James Moore, *Darwin's Sacred Cause: Race, Slavery and the Quest for Human Origins* (London: Allen Lane, 2009), ch. 4, for Fitzroy's disagreements with Charles Darwin over slavery during the *Beagle*'s voyage around South America.

were I to write you a detail ... of the vile state of the Portuguese colonies, the improving condition of the blacks, the arrival of the slavers, with a list of those that escape and those that are captured, it could afford you very little amusement and there is not an object within my reach which you ever have or ever will know or care about. Unless by the by you are contemplating a speech on antislavery and in that case I shall feel great pleasure in forwarding you all kinds of information relative to their state and condition previous to transportation, and the inhuman treatment they are subjected to before they reach their destination.[105]

The tone of the letter suggests that neither he or Melgund were interested in fuelling anti-slavery debates. He continued:

One idea I will give as a sample of the rest which rather amused me at first. The Portuguese keep the slaves as they buy them in barracoons or sheds until they are embarked. They are chained together to prevent escape and therefore cannot work consequently they are twice a day compelled to holla for an hour without stopping by way of exercise, you can fancy the sort of row perhaps a thousand of them together and the Portuguese applying the lash if they leave off or don't holla loud enough. You can hear the poor wretches for miles off.[106]

A sympathetic tone can be traced here, but at the same time Elliot's amusement is revealing. While he accepted that his experiences would strengthen anti-slavery arguments, he also appeared detached from and indifferent to the distress of the captive Africans.

In a later letter, Elliot described his 'strict blockade' off the Guinea coast, and concluded: 'the slave merchants are mostly ruined, the slave crews have perished from fever and the slaves have fared no better for when their owners could no longer feed them they put an end to them – but this is all unavoidable'.[107] Elliot gave the death of enslaved Africans the same emphasis as the ruination of slave merchants, and he appeared to care little about either. He wrote of his disgust at the nature of service on 'this abominable coast' and suggested that it was strong enough to outweigh any commitment to the anti-slavery cause. 'One or two of my chases have been rather interesting and some of the boat work has also afforded excitement', he wrote, 'but all other points connected with this service is disgusting enough, unless one happens to be impressed with an extraordinary degree of philanthropy.'[108] For Elliot, unlike many of his naval colleagues, a

105 NLS, MS 12054, George Elliot to Lord Melgund, 6 January 1840, ff. 176–78.
106 NLS, MS 12054, George Elliot to Lord Melgund, 6 January 1840, ff. 176–78.
107 NLS, MS 12054, George Elliot to Lord Melgund, [no date] March 1840, ff. 180–83.
108 NLS, MS 12054, George Elliot to Lord Melgund, 6 January 1840, ff. 176–78.

personal commitment to suppression required an incomprehensible level of compassion and support for the anti-slavery cause.

George Elliot's letters provide a pertinent conclusion to this chapter. While a successful 'suppressionist' – for example, he successfully enforced blockades at Luanda and Ambriz during his service there between 1838 and 1840 which consequently ruined the trade of slave merchants – Elliot cannot be described as an enthusiastic abolitionist. His case makes it clear that a passion for anti-slavery was not a prerequisite for this service and did not necessarily make an officer any more successful in his role. In this respect, what constituted 'zeal' in the maritime context? While some officers believed fervently in the anti-slavery cause, others expressed an equal level of dedication to their professional duty, demonstrating the same enthusiasm for chasing slavers as they would for work on any other naval station. When Lieutenant Edmund Gabriel wrote of the 'spirited and gallant conduct' of a colleague and the 'hearty spirit' of the crews under his command who 'justly merited ... the proud title of British sailors and marines', it was in the context of their resisting fire and capturing an enemy vessel rather than any sense of celebration in the release of captives.[109] Pride in captures was as likely a result of professional achievement and patriotic honour as commitment to passionate abolitionism.

Margarette Lincoln has argued that from the eighteenth century naval officers 'were becoming the repositories of social virtues', with representations of officers as exemplars of British virtue and manhood.[110] However, it must not be assumed that all naval men were, or aspired to be, humanitarians motivated by the moral imperative to end slavery. The official obligations of the navy must be remembered: protecting and expanding the empire was very much a naval responsibility in the nineteenth century, and in this context humanitarianism and idealism did not always sit well with other professional qualities.[111] Many officers were not self-confirmed abolitionists,

---

109 SA, DD/X/GRA/6, Edmund Gabriel to George Kenyon, 23 July 1842. Gabriel was referring to the capture of the Brazilian barque *Ermelinda Secunda* in the River Congo with 118 Africans on board.

110 Lincoln, *Representing the Royal Navy*, p. 4.

111 See Samson, 'Hero, fool or martyr?', pp. 1–22, for an examination of the conflicts between idealism and professionalism in the career of Commodore Goodenough in the Pacific Islands in the later nineteenth century. In 'Too zealous guardians? The Royal Navy and the South Pacific labour trade', in David Killingray and David Omissi (eds), *Guardians of Empire: The Armed Forces of the Colonial Powers, 1700–1964* (Manchester: Manchester University Press, 1999), pp. 70–90, Samson argues that officers active against the South Pacific labour trade were 'naval humanitarians' who sought to influence public opinion in support of the Pacific islanders. However, as on the West Coast of Africa, preconceptions about naval duty connected with the enforcement of

but simply performed the role for which they had been appointed. Hence, they could express revulsion at what they had witnessed in the slave trade, and yet display racial prejudice.

However, the existence of anti-slavery beliefs among many of these officers is significant. So, too, is the variation in opinions, particularly as the century progressed, reflecting perceptions of middle-class men in British society more widely. To early Victorians, manliness embraced qualities of chivalry and patriotic virtue, demonstrated by earnestness and integrity; terms to describe the written word of George Collier or John Hayes, for example. The concept's transition to virility and 'the cult of manliness' meant that by the 1860s, to be sentimental or philanthropic was no longer considered an ideal.[112] For the Royal Navy, as defenders of British values, the nature of duty can be seen to shift accordingly, from one where professionalism converged with a spiritual responsibility that stressed humanity and the religious imperative to end slavery, to one of stoicism and detachment. For those charged with upholding abolition, the impact ·of this shift was significant on their understanding of their role. Naval officers' sense of duty and perceptions of the anti-slavery mission were also affected by the brutal reality of prize voyages and the ideological challenges they faced regarding conceptions of freedom for African peoples.

'British humanitarian sensibility' were impacted by shifting realities about race and what constituted philanthropy.

112 Norman Vance, *The Sinews of Spirit: The Ideal of Christian Manliness in Victorian Literature and Religious Thought* (Cambridge: Cambridge University Press, 1985); Mangan and Walvin, 'Introduction', pp. 1–2.

4

Prize voyages and ideas of freedom

To witness the brutality and human trauma of the transatlantic slave trade on a detained slave vessel was extraordinary employment for British naval officers. This chapter uncovers their reactions to such service and explores the extent to which officers engaged with the individuals they were 'liberating' – on captured slavers, on Royal Navy ships, or while stationed at the British territories of Sierra Leone or St Helena. The Royal Navy has long associations with concepts of freedom: Britain's maritime supremacy in the eighteenth and nineteenth centuries was regarded as an upholder of Christian freedoms, crucial to national identity. As P. J. Marshall has argued, 'Protestantism, commerce, maritime power and freedom were seen as inextricably linked.'[1] The Royal Navy was now responsible for granting liberty (or British perceptions of liberty) to captive Africans. As we shall see, officers' ideas about freedom, its limits and its applicability to African people were concepts bound to racial attitudes and their understandings of different African societies.

Officers' experiences of prize voyages

Nothing can exceed the horrors of those slave vessels: the poor wretched negroes may be said to be almost stowed in bulk, for they are laid on their backs along the slave-deck in rows, the head of one between the legs of another, all chained together; so you may conceive the horror, the filth, and abomination of those slave-decks after a long passage; and though the slavers we captured had only left the Bonny the day before, yet when our

1 P. J. Marshall, 'Empire and British identity: the maritime dimension', in David Cannadine (ed.), *Empire, the Sea and Global History: Britain's Maritime World, c.1763–c.1840* (Basingstoke: Palgrave Macmillan, 2007), pp. 41–59, at p. 46.

men went down below to get some of the poor creatures on deck, such was the stench and want of pure air that they could not remain below above a few minutes.[2]

In his memoirs of service on the West Africa squadron, Admiral Robert Wauchope gave this distressing account of the capture in 1836 of the Spanish slave schooner *Atylia*, with 119 captives on board. It was the task of only a small number of nominated officers and men to form a prize crew, instructed to transport detained slave vessels to the nearest port at which an international Court of Mixed Commission (or from the 1840s, a Vice-Admiralty Court) would establish the legality of its capture. On the West African coast, this invariably meant Freetown.[3] The inhumane conditions described by Wauchope were not easily alleviated by British naval personnel, either on a slave vessel taken as a prize or if recaptives were taken aboard a Royal Navy ship for transportation to Sierra Leone. Several factors contributed to this. First, Freetown was a considerable distance from the major sources of slave exportation in the Bights of Benin and Biafra. Between 1819 and 1826, for example, it took prize crews an average of 62 days to sail to Sierra Leone from the point of capture.[4] In 1821 Lieutenant Christopher Knight wrote to the Admiralty Secretary from the *Snapper* in the Old Calabar River to stress that the distance to Sierra Leone

cannot fail to produce a great mortality among the Slaves ... and to be a great risk to the lives and healths [*sic*] of our Seamen and officers who have to navigate them up ... Eight weeks is by no means to be considered a long time to perform this difficult Passage.[5]

Indeed, many transatlantic crossings were of equivalent length or shorter (and the Middle Passage actually decreased in duration during the nineteenth century).[6] In the 1820s there were moves to transfer the Mixed Commission courts to Fernando Po, regarded as a healthier and more geographically suitable location. Captain William Owen was sent to the island in 1827

---

2 Wauchope, *A Short Narrative*, pp. 116–17.

3 Bethell, 'The Mixed Commissions', pp. 79–93.

4 Brown, 'Fernando Po', p. 250.

5 Lieutenant Knight to J. W. Croker, 5 August 1821, in *British and Foreign State Papers, 1821–1822*, pp. 185–86.

6 Voyage lengths on the Middle Passage varied from six weeks to three months depending on places of embarkation and disembarkation. The nineteenth-century decrease is associated with improvements in oceangoing technology. See Eltis and Richardson, *Atlas*, maps 123–24, pp. 160, 180–81.

to establish a settlement there, but the scheme was abandoned when the Spanish refused to sell the island to the British.[7] Voyage times for ships taken as prizes south of the equator were reduced when the island of St Helena began to be used by the British as a Liberation Establishment from the 1840s onwards.[8]

Pestilential conditions aboard slave ships invariably continued during a prize voyage. Naval surgeon Alexander Bryson identified the illnesses which commonly afflicted those on board: 'dysentery, fever, small-pox, ophthalmia, and diarrhoea … engendered by filth, insufficient food, and the over-crowding of many people into a small, badly-ventilated space'.[9] Such circumstances are vividly illustrated in this officer's account of conditions on the Portuguese prize brig *Corsico* in 1841:

> I certainly never beheld such a scene of complicated misery as our prize presents this morning; 392 wretched creatures crammed into a small vessel of 80 tons, nearly all children; 12 cases of small-pox, and about 50 cases of itch … Most of them are living skeletons, mere skin and bone … I dread sending away an officer and men in such a floating pest house![10]

Poor provisions contributed to problems. In 1823, 181 recaptives from a Spanish schooner detained in the River Bonny were taken on board the *Owen Glendower* for transportation to Sierra Leone. The crew and passengers subsequently suffered an epidemic of fever. Midshipman Binstead noted that declining health was exacerbated by the poor state of provisions; three weeks into the voyage, naval personnel were surviving on 'only one meal a day being on quarter of allowance', there being 'little or no bread in the ship'.[11] It can be assumed that the recaptives were provided with similar rations or worse.

Furthermore, as seen in Chapter 1, critics of the squadron claimed that shipboard mortality rates increased in response to suppression efforts. Naval blockades of embarkation points caused a delay in captives being loaded on to slave vessels, leading to long periods of confinement in barracoons

---

7 Brown, 'Fernando Po', pp. 249–64. Former naval officer James Holman accompanied Owen and later published his experiences on the island in *A Voyage Round the World: including travels in Africa, Asia, Australasia, America*, 2 vols. (London: Smith, Elder and Co., 1834).

8 Andrew Pearson, *Distant Freedom: St Helena and the Abolition of the Slave Trade, 1840–1872* (Liverpool: Liverpool University Press, 2016), p. 79.

9 Bryson, *Report*, pp. 255–56, 259.

10 'Letter of an officer on board HMB *Water-Witch*, dated off Benguela, 4 August 1841', published in *The Friend of Africa* (1841), p. 207.

11 NMRN, 2005.76/2, Binstead diaries, 24–25 July 1823.

on shore and severe cases of disease and malnourishment. Samuel Ajayi Crowther wrote that he spent four months in chains at Lagos waiting for his Portuguese owners to see an opportunity to begin embarkation and shipment to Brazil.[12] When the opportunity for departure arose, captives were embarked quickly without being checked for diseases; overcrowding of ships was common, as was the precautionary measure of locking captives in the hold for the first few days of a voyage, to avoid detection.[13] As a result, naval officers offered much commentary on the emaciated and exhausted condition of the enslaved, even though most slave vessels were captured near the coast and had therefore not been at sea very long. Lieutenant Digby Marsh of the *Tartar* was involved in the capture of a Portuguese slave schooner off Princes Island in March 1819. In his book of private remarks, he wrote that the enslaved Africans 'were in such a debilitated state as to require being carried to the boats'. He recorded the emaciated weights of two men aged 20 and 26 as 64 lbs and 81 lbs respectively; a 14-year-old boy weighed only 45 lbs. Marsh added that the other captives from the slave schooner were 'so sick and debilitated that they could not undergo the exertion of being weighed'.[14]

In consequence, the death of a significant proportion of recaptives was common. David Northrup has identified 'astonishingly high losses between capture and adjudication' due to mistreatment before embarkation and the length and trauma of prize voyages.[15] For example, in 1826 the slaver *Invincival* arrived in Sierra Leone after being detained in the Cameroon estuary with only 250 survivors from the 440 captives embarked. Commodore Collier reported that 46 of 266 recaptured Africans aboard the *Anna Maria* had died during its two months' passage to Sierra Leone.[16] In 1826 Samuel Richardson of the *Maidstone* arrived in Sierra Leone from the Bight of Benin in charge of a prize with 176 recaptives on board, and declared in a letter home, 'it really is the most distressing sight you can possible imagine ... I was very fortunate in bringing all the slaves in harbour except one who

12 Samuel Ajayi Crowther to the Revd William Jowett, Secretary of the CMS [no date] 1837, in Philip D. Curtin (ed.), *Africa Remembered: Narratives by West Africans from the Era of the Slave Trade* (Madison, WI: University of Wisconsin Press, 1967), pp. 298–316, at p. 310.

13 Sylviane A. Diouf, *Dreams of Africa in Alabama: The Slave Ship Clotilda and the Story of the Last Africans Brought to America* (Oxford: Oxford University Press, 2007), pp. 62–63.

14 SHC, A/AOV/69, 'Private remarks, occurrences, etc., HM ship *Tartar* – from England to the coast of Africa', c. 1818–19, no folios.

15 David Northrup, 'African mortality in the suppression of the slave trade: the case of the Bight of Biafra', *Journal of Interdisciplinary History*, 9.1 (1978), p. 47.

16 Northrup, 'African mortality', p. 57; Peterson, *Province of Freedom*, p. 183.

jumped over board and drowned himself – it is quite a common thing to lose thirty or forty during their passage'.[17]

While a prize voyage ended at Sierra Leone, the emancipation process could not begin until the slave ship had been officially condemned; this usually took a few days, but could take weeks, during which time recaptives remained on board the slaver.[18] In January 1861 naval surgeon Richard Carr McClement visited the *Clara Windsor*, recently arrived at Freetown after being detained by the *Espoir* near Ascension. The vessel, under American colours, was bound for Cuba from Cabenda with 840 enslaved Africans on board, including over 400 children.[19] McClement wrote in his diary:

> It would be utterly impossible to describe the sight which presented itself to us when we first went on board;– and; it would be equally difficult for anyone who had not seen it, to comprehend the amount of misery, the suffering and, the horrors, that were contained within the wooden walls of that little craft.

Reporting that only 616 recaptives had survived the passage to Sierra Leone, McClement portrayed 'men, women, and, children, huddled together; some emaciated to skeletons; some lying sick and heedless of all around; and, some on the point of passing into another world ... All were naked and had their skins besmeared with the filth in which they lay.'[20] The significant number of children on board reflected the increased proportion of those younger than 13 or 14 years of age captured in the slave trade in the nineteenth century.[21]

Naval officer James Edward Bowly wrote to his parents from Sierra Leone in March 1863, describing conditions on an American-built schooner commanded by Spaniards and captured by the *Brisk* off Princes Island. Of the 540 captives on board at embarkation, many had 'died at a dreadful rate', with only around 200 of the 320 released by the *Brisk* then surviving the passage to Sierra Leone:

17 DRO, D8/B/F/66, Samuel Richardson to Jeffery Lockett, 30 June 1826.

18 Northrup, 'African mortality', p. 49.

19 The Trans-Atlantic Slave Trade Voyages Database, www.slavevoyages.org, voyage 4336 [accessed 20 January 2018]; 'Return of Slavers Captured by Her Majesty's Cruizers on the West Coast of Africa', *UK Parliamentary Papers*, 1860 (2598), p. 79.

20 SCA, GB 0240 FA/67/3, McClement diary, 7 January 1861, pp. 118–21, www.scottishcatholicarchives.org.uk/Learning/DiaryofRichardCarrMcClement/DiaryExtracts/Empire/tabid/186/Default.aspx [accessed 20 June 2018].

21 Eltis and Richardson, *Atlas*, map 115, p. 166. The proportion of children from West Central Africa in the slave trade after 1807 – 50 per cent – was almost double the share of the previous century. This was possibly because faster voyages made the transportation of lower-priced slaves economically feasible.

The poor wretches had been on board the slaver 48 days ... they were in the most dreadful condition that human beings could be in. I should never have believed that anything could have been so horrible. The slave decks were not more than 5 feet 6 inches high, and how they managed to cram in 540 I cannot conceive ... we landed the poor things, and now was the worst part to see them come up from below, labouring under every imaginable disease, and some of them mere walking skeletons, with their bones protruding through their skin. A great many were too weak to get up, and we were obliged to send the white men below to pass them up like sacks.[22]

Witnessing the distressing realities of the Middle Passage – extreme disease, emaciation and suffering – was for many a transformative experience. Lieutenant James Stoddart's obvious anguish at discovering an emaciated African – 'a bundle of what I took to be rags ... a living skeleton' – hidden on deck was not unusual; as he later wrote, 'the sight of the poor fellow haunted me for years'.[23] In his published *Remarks on the Slavery and Slave Trade of the Brazils*, naval surgeon Thomas Nelson included long passages describing the horrors he witnessed on the slave ship *Dois de Favereiro*, intercepted by HMS *Fawn* en route to Brazil. He declared himself in disbelief that conditions on slavers – 'disease, want, and misery' beyond 'all powers of description' – could be 'so easily overlooked or so readily forgotten, by the apologists for slavery'.[24] Nelson called the slaver *Vencedora* a 'floating Pandora box'; of the appearance of the recaptives on board, 'no pen can give an adequate idea ... most of them look like animated skeletons'. Nelson described his experience as disturbing in the extreme:

So painful and revolting was every object that met my sight, so much beyond the average amount of human suffering, the mass of loathsome misery and disease which surrounded me, destitute of a single trait upon which the mind could rest for a moment's relief, that now, after the lapse of a few days ... the whole scene floats in my mind more like the phantoms of a frightful but impressive dream than the sober event of every day reality.[25]

Conditions were so severe that naval officers could often do little to relieve them. These narratives support the notion that considering shipboard

22 GA, D4582/6/6, James Edward Bowly to his parents, 16 March 1863. This capture was reported in *The Times*, 13 April 1863, which reported the total number of deaths on the slave ship as 284.

23 James Stoddart, 'A Cruise in a Slaver. From the Journal of Admiral James Stoddart', *Blackwood's Magazine*, 1480 (1939), p. 194.

24 Nelson, *Remarks*, pp. 42–46.

25 Nelson, *Remarks*, pp. 47–50.

mortality rates, passage duration and conditions on board, experiences on prize voyages could constitute an alternative Middle Passage for the enslaved. This comparison must be qualified; as Emma Christopher makes clear, the fundamental difference was that the Middle Passage was intended to prepare people for sale as property, to 'alter human being to thing'.[26] However, while in some cases naval officers were powerless to ease the discomfort of recaptives, in others there is evidence that they contributed to these circumstances.

Treatment of recaptives

Prize voyages were by their nature extremely challenging commissions for naval officers. In some published accounts, relations between officers and recaptives were depicted as harmonious and amicable. For example, an officer of the *Black Joke* described how recaptives from the slaver *Marinerito* 'took every opportunity of … testifying their thankfulness to the English, and by their willingness to obey and assist, rendered the passage to Sierra Leone easy and pleasant to the officers'.[27] Medical officers assigned to a commission to inquire into the state of liberated Africans at Sierra Leone in 1830 described 'the kindness with which these poor wretches have been invariably treated by the naval officers in charge, whose attention to them, as far as their means would allow, has been unremitting under the most appalling circumstances'.[28] Other narratives stress the hardships suffered by naval officers on prize voyages. James Holman described how the prize officer on board the crowded slaver *Henri-Quartre*, recently arrived at Sierra Leone in 1827, was 'confined to a small space in the after-part of the deck near the tiller. The pressure of this dense mass of human beings was suffocating.'[29] Alexander Bryson noted that prize officers were often 'worn out by excessive labour, broken rest, and exposure both by night and day upon the deck of a small vessel, probably crowded with slaves in a loathsome state of misery and disease'.[30] These adversities were heightened by the responsibility of attending to so many distressed and traumatized individuals, an intimidating and emotionally demanding task. George Giles, master of HMS *Grappler*, described the enslaved taken on board his vessel as 'very violent and frightened, and inclined to jump overboard

---

26 Christopher, *Slave Ship Sailors*, p. 165.

27 'Capture of the Spanish Slaver, *Marinerito*, by the *Black Joke*', *United Service Magazine*, part II (1832), pp. 63–65, at p. 64.

28 Quoted in *The Anti-Slavery Monthly Reporter*, 59 (April 1830), pp. 176–77.

29 Holman, *A Voyage*, vol. 1, 29 September 1827.

30 Bryson, *Report*, p. 9.

from thirst'.[31] In 1845 Lieutenant Francis Meynell described the 'ravenous' reaction of recaptives from the slaver *Albanez* to being provided with water as 'fearful' and 'a very unenticing specimen of the trouble the prize crew might expect going up to Sierra Leone'.[32]

Tense situations were exacerbated by problems of communication, made difficult by the number of different languages spoken by recaptives, often gathered from diverse communities and geographical areas along the coast. Lieutenant Philip de Sausmarez recounted a scene on a prize vessel, 'with 477 people almost all making some sort of noise, which you can scarcely call talking but which by its being unintelligible only made it the more distracting'.[33] Officers did make attempts to communicate with those on board, however. In 1831 Commodore John Hayes noted that recaptives from the Spanish slaver *Marinerito* relayed their wishes for water to the crew of the *Black Joke* by 'their noise, and signs'.[34] The logbook of the *Black Joke* while under the command of Lieutenant Henry Downes in the late 1820s reveals that this communication was developed further, and that some form of training was given to those in charge of prize vessels. It notes over twenty translations into English of the 'Accou language', words and phrases used by captive Africans from Ouidah and Badagry. These included practical phrases to assist in their everyday care, such as 'My belly is sick', 'I want to make water' and 'Go and wash'. Other disciplinary instructions such as 'Hold your tongue' and 'Silence or you'll get punished' were indicative of more difficult relations between officers and recaptives.[35]

Naval officers were ordered to manage and keep charge of prize vessels like any other ship. The evidence of disciplinary measures and methods of maintaining order suggests that some treatment of recaptives could compare to experiences of the Middle Passage, even with more supposedly sympathetic figures of authority. A parliamentary inquiry in 1827 concluded

31 NMM, MGS/42, 'Sketch of the west coast of Africa', map drawn and annotated by George Giles, master of the *Grappler*, c. 1846–49. Giles gives instructions of locations on the coast to find slave ships, and how to treat recaptives.

32 NMM, MEY/5, Meynell letters, 2 May 1845. In *Dreams of Africa*, Diouf describes the captives on board the *Clotilda* in 1860 as 'tortured by thirst' (p. 64).

33 Letter of Philip de Sausmarez from Ascension, 13 July 1832, in *Guernsey Magazine: a monthly illustrated journal* (December 1874), p. 248.

34 TNA, ADM 1/1, John Hayes to George Elliot, 6 May 1831, ff. 418–30.

35 NMM, LOG/N/41, logbook of HMS *Black Joke* by Lieutenant Henry Downes, no folios. The effort and time taken to compile this list of translations indicates the long duration of prize voyages, and the high numbers of enslaved Africans released by the crew of the *Black Joke*, the former slaver renowned for its speed and success in detaining slave vessels. Downes's logbook lists 16 captures between 1827 and 1829, and the release of 3,970 recaptives.

that officers 'have it not in their powers to alleviate ... the sufferings of the Negroes, which for a long time after capture, they are compelled to witness, and in which they too often largely participate'.[36] In November 1849 Lieutenant Henry Rogers of the steamer *Pluto* was ordered to convey the *Casco*, a Brazilian slave vessel carrying 440 recaptives, from Ambriz to St Helena, a voyage of 21 days. Rogers was engaged in suppression on both the East and West African coasts between 1843 and 1850, and this was not the first prize vessel that the young officer had conveyed – but it was the first with a human cargo.[37] Along with his small crew, the prize's captain and cook remained on the ship. In his journal, Rogers displayed sympathy for the plight of the enslaved and recognition of their emotional distress. He described how the women and children were accommodated on deck to ease crowding in the slave-hold, and that the men were brought above as often as possible. However, the daily routine of cleaning and feeding those on board the prize vessel inevitably led him to treat and write about those under his supervision in collective terms, and the demands of managing many Africans complicated Rogers's feelings towards them. He took advice from the slave captain who 'helped me to manage the slaves in the kindest way'.[38] Rogers encouraged the recaptives to dance in order to 'keep their spirits up', which was thought necessary to lessen their 'pining for their country'. This was a tradition on slave vessels, whereby slave captains enforced dancing and singing in an attempt, it was believed, to maintain calm relations on board and break melancholy. A belief in such techniques (perhaps informed by the *Casco*'s captain) clearly impacted Rogers's understanding of those under his care when he wrote that he 'made the slaves dance and sing, clapping their hands, so as to keep their blood in circulation'.[39]

Rogers was clearly distressed by the thought of an uprising among the recaptives and suffered insomnia due to 'how easily a man might have got up taken my sword, drawn and soon have killed me and given the other slaves

36 Quoted in Brown, 'Fernando Po', p. 250.

37 www.slavevoyages.org, voyage 4023 [accessed 18 May 2018]; Rogers's obituary in the *Western Morning News*, 27 November 1912.

38 Private collection, Rogers journal, 28 November 1849.

39 Private collection, Rogers journal, 28 and 29 November 1849. Accounts of captives jumping overboard or other forms of suicide were common. See Marcus Rediker, *The Slave Ship: A Human History* (London: John Murray, 2007), pp. 237–38, 288–90; David Northrup, *Africa's Discovery of Europe 1450–1850*, 2nd edn (Oxford: Oxford University Press, 2009), pp. 165–67. For an account of his experiences in command of a slave ship, which included the encouragement of dancing and singing among the enslaved, see Captain William Snelgrave, *A New Account of Some Parts of Guinea and the Slave Trade* (1734).

a chance of rising'.[40] Such fears were not misguided, with up to one in ten slave vessels experiencing an insurrection. British newspapers gave much coverage to such uprisings, which ensured that they remained in the public consciousness.[41] The likelihood of rebellion was linked to the ethnicity of those on board, and Rogers reassured himself that the recaptives under his authority were comprised of a number of different African peoples, which 'makes it more difficult for them to conspire'.[42] However, on one occasion he felt it necessary to 'proceed to punishment', due to 'a big slave having nearly throttled a small one':

> I administered a small dose to him, consisting of 2 dozen, inflicted with a rope-end … pretty severely. This must not be mistaken for cruelty, as it is a well known fact that in large communities with little intelligence, any outbreak against the laws that preserve the weak from the attacks of the strong must be punished immediately and severely. The poor slaves appear very docile, good creatures generally …[43]

Rogers's aggression towards recaptives echoes the subjugation of slaves by slave ship seamen; he also revealed paternalistic and racial assumptions reflective of his time.[44] His experiences were not unique. Lieutenant James Stoddart wrote accounts of his time in charge of the slavers *Josephine* and *Veloz* in 1836, which were later published.[45] On the *Josephine* Stoddart too consulted with the slave captain as to the best way to handle the vessel's passengers: 'they were Ac'oos, a quiet, peaceable tribe, or mostly so, very

40 Private collection, Rogers journal, 29 November 1849.

41 David Richardson, 'Shipboard revolts, African authority and the Atlantic slave trade', *William and Mary Quarterly*, 58.1 (2001), pp. 69–92; Rediker, *Slave Ship*, pp. 291–300.

42 Eltis and Richardson, *Atlas*, map 131, p. 189. For example, vessels sailing from Upper Guinea (Senegambia, Sierra Leone and the Windward Coast) were more likely to experience revolt than those from other regions, particularly West Central Africa. In 1810 Captain Edward Columbine noted that captives from the Gold Coast were 'a fierce high-spirited race of men', while those from the Congo and Angola were 'a more mild & docile race; but very melancholy in their slavery' (UIC: SLC, Columbine journals, Folder 10, ff. 136–37).

43 Private collection, Rogers journal, 29 November 1849.

44 For examples, see Rediker, *Slave Ship*, especially chs 8 and 9, and Christopher, *Slave Ship Sailors*, ch. 5. See Burroughs, 'Eyes on the prize', pp. 103–08, for the harsh treatment of recaptives by the prize crew of the *Progresso* slaver in East African waters in 1843.

45 Stoddart, 'A Cruise in a Slaver'. Stoddart was clearly unhappy with his appointment: 'to my horror and disgust I was told to take the prize up to Sierra Leone … although I had just returned the week before after an absence of three months in taking another prize up' (p. 88).

healthy and easily managed by kindness'. Nevertheless, Stoddart 'divided my men into watches, and armed each with a small cat to keep the negroes in order'.[46] On the *Veloz*, 'cats and cutlasses' were used to suppress a rebellion of captive women held below deck in which 'cats had to be used freely'.[47]

Lieutenant Philip de Sausmarez, under Captain Meredith of the *Pelorus*, was assigned prize master of the Spanish slaver *Segunda Teresa* in 1832. The slaver was arrested in the Bight of Benin with 459 enslaved Africans on board. He described the passage to Sierra Leone, with five of the Spanish crew also on board, as 'a service of certainly not the most pleasant kind', in large part due to the mutinous Spanish crew attempting to 'murder us and throw us overboard'.[48] Lieutenant de Sausmarez punished recaptives for stealing provisions and water by the 'usual method of flogging, but I found they forgot that as soon as it was over'. To set an example, when an African man was accused of 'stealing a 4lb. piece of beef', the lieutenant devised the following punishment:

> I tied him up in the rigging, with his feet, when on tip toe, just off the deck, and over his head was suspended this piece of beef, just touching his chin; in this position I kept him for one hour, and made all the slaves pass in procession around him; after this I assure you I had not one single complaint of the kind again.[49]

Such disciplinary action could be compared with the harsh punishments handed out to British seamen. Indeed, Lieutenant de Sausmarez was court martialled in 1834 for punishing Francis Brown, a seaman of his prize crew on the *Theresa Segunda*, with 24 lashes for 'neglect of duty'. Similarly, in 1829 Midshipman Edwin Hinde wrote that as punishment for 'mean and dirty tricks', one member of the *Atholl*'s crew was given 'two dozen ... with a knotted piece of rope'.[50] However, the cruelty and indignity implicit in de Sausmarez's punishment of the recaptured African suggests a different level of asserting power and control.

A lack of understanding about unknown peoples often led to imputed racial character, which had an impact on officers' treatment of recaptives.

46 Stoddart, 'A Cruise in a Slaver', pp. 188–89.

47 Quoted in Burroughs, 'Eyes on the prize', p. 102, n. 12. In contrast, on the *Josephine*, Stoddart wrote that his passengers were silent 'under terror of the uplifted cats', which were 'very seldom used'. This correlates with his assessment of the recaptives on this vessel belonging to a 'peaceable tribe'.

48 Letter of Philip de Sausmarez, p. 248.

49 Letter of Philip de Sausmarez, p. 248.

50 John Marshall, *Royal Naval Biography*, vol. 4, Part II (London, 1835), pp. 132–33; NMM, HIN/1, Hinde letters, 29 September 1829.

Stoddart claimed to be on friendly terms with the African people on his prize vessel, noting how he 'talked kindly to them through an interpreter'. His description of relations, however, also exposed racial stereotypes:

> I amused myself feeding the children on what was left from dinner. Some half-dozen of the poor things clung to me ever afterwards, watching my wants, sleeping outside my bunk, and in the morning pulling my feet out to bathe them. I gave the little bodies grand names, one Bubble & Squeak, &c., &c.; and in six weeks' time they spoke very fair English for negroes.[51]

Stoddart's narrative reveals how far emotional boundaries on a prize vessel could become blurred; the implication is that he named and 'petted' the children in a similar way to animals or domestic slaves, regarding himself as their new master.[52] Engineer John M'Kie wrote that a first lieutenant from the *Rattler* was sent in command of a prize vessel because he had 'the greatest experience in the management of slaves', and described the enslaved as 'more like tame animals than anything else'. Taken with his comments on the noxious smell on board, the implication that the captives were 'animal-like' in some way is strengthened further.[53] That the lieutenant had experience of 'management' of slaves rather than care or protection is also revealing. Others wrote with more cruelty. Alexander Bryson claimed that due to a naval surgeon's 'utter ignorance' of African languages, 'there is no possible means of treating them [recaptives] otherwise than as dumb animals'.[54]

African perspectives

Understanding West African perspectives on enslavement and recapture and giving an African voice to this story is difficult, as so few testimonies exist.[55] As Sandra Greene has noted, African narratives that do survive were

51 Stoddart, 'A Cruise in a Slaver', p. 190.

52 During the Middle Passage there are accounts of enslaved children becoming favourites of slave ship captains and crew. For example, in his *Interesting Narrative*, first published in 1789, Olaudah Equiano wrote of being favourably treated in comparison to other captives because he was a young boy at the time of his transportation. See Rediker, *Slave Ship*, pp. 121–27; Northrup, *Africa's Discovery*, p. 171.

53 NLS, MS 24634, M'Kie memoirs, ff. 34–37; Christopher, *Slave Ship Sailors*, p. 170.

54 Bryson, *Report*, pp. 256, 258.

55 Published testimonies of Africans which refer to experiences of the Middle Passage include Equiano, *Interesting Narrative*; Samuel Moore, *Biography of Mahommah G. Baquaqua, a Native of Zoogoo in the Interior of Africa* (Detroit, 1854); and Quobna Ottobah Cugoano, *Thoughts and Sentiments on the Evil of Slavery and Other Writings*

often recorded by missionaries or government officials, not to document perspectives of the enslaved necessarily, but to support abolitionist goals.[56] It is possible to create an idea of the men, women and children on slave ships, their background and the conditions of their captivity that led former slave Mahommah G. Baquaqua to declare: '[m]y wretchedness I cannot describe'.[57] In analysing the particular relationship between recaptives and the British naval officers who intercepted their ships, one concern regarding the experiences of the enslaved is whether they were aware of a favourable change in their circumstances.

The chase and boarding of slave ships was often violent. For example, in his description of the prolonged capture of the slaver *Marguerita* by the *Black Joke* in 1831, Midshipman Edwin Hinde noted that 'shots were whistling about our ears in all directions', resulting in one crew member killed and five wounded. Discussing the capture of the *Marinerito* by the *Black Joke* in the same year, Commodore Hayes noted the 'fear and consternation' which seized recaptives, 'at witnessing the conflict between the two vessels'.[58] Samuel Ajayi Crowther was aboard the Portuguese slaver *Esperanza Felix* when it was detained by HMS *Myrmidon*. After a prize voyage of nearly two and a half months, he was liberated in Freetown in 1822. Crowther's account of the slaver's capture reveals the fear and distrust inherent in such encounters. He wrote that the captives 'found ourselves in the hands of new conquerors, whom we at first very much dreaded, they being armed with long swords'.[59] Similarly, Ali Eisami, sold as a slave in Porto Novo in 1818, described the naval officer who boarded his ship as a 'war-chief', alongside other 'war-men' who came on to the vessel 'sword in hand'.[60] As Henry Rogers's narrative demonstrates, British officers would consult with the slave ship sailors as to how best control the enslaved, adding to the

(London, 1787). Cudjo Lewis described his enslavement and passage to America to Zora Neale Hurston in 'Cudjo's own story of the last African slaver', *The Journal of Negro History*, 12.4 (1927), pp. 648–63.

56 Sandra E. Greene, *West African Narratives of Slavery: Texts from Late Nineteenth- and Early Twentieth-Century Ghana* (Bloomington, IN: Indiana University Press, 2011), pp. 1–17.

57 Quoted in Diouf, *Dreams of Africa*, p. 60. See Eltis and Richardson, *Atlas*, part IV; also Diouf, *Dreams of Africa* and Fett, *Recaptured Africans*, on the West African origins of captives and the creation of shipboard communities on the slave ships *Clotilda*, *Echo*, *Wildfire*, *William* and *Bogota*, 1858–60.

58 NMM, HIN/1, Edwin Hinde to Captain Gordon, 25 May 1831; TNA, ADM 1/1, Hayes to Elliot, 6 May 1831.

59 Crowther to Revd Jowett, in Curtin (ed.), *Africa Remembered*, p. 312.

60 'Narrative of the travels of Ali Eisami', in Curtin (ed.), *Africa Remembered*, pp. 206–16, at p. 214.

confusion.[61] The lack of communication and fear of white men perpetuated the sense of anxiety and danger. Crowther believed the English sailors capable of murdering the Portuguese traders, concluding that 'parts of a hog hanging, the skin of which was white' were body parts. Indeed, many Africans believed that white men were cannibals: in his evidence before a Select Committee on the slave trade in 1849, the former slave Augustino claimed that many Africans embarked on slave ships 'jumped overboard, for fear they were being fattened to be eaten'.[62]

After initial distrust, both Crowther and Eisami had positive perceptions of the officers involved in their release. Eisami wrote that 'they took off all the fetters from our feet, and threw them into the water, and they gave us clothes that we might cover our nakedness, they opened the water casks, that we drink water to the fill, and we also ate food, till we had enough'.[63] Commodore George Ralph Collier, on describing conditions on slave ships captured by the *Thistle* and *Tartar*, wrote, 'I ventured to order the shackles of every Slave to be removed as soon after their capture as possible.'[64] This symbolic removal and discarding of restraints is found in other officers' narratives. In a letter of 1815, John Tailour's language is punctuated with racial stereotypes, but he nevertheless expressed sympathy towards the enslaved. 'Some would have us believe that these black slaves are an insensible unfeeling race', he wrote:

> I wish you had seen the effect produced on the first party which were brought on board here ... after knocking their irons off & giving each a waist cloth, I took up a pair of the shackles, showed it them all round & with indignation of countenance threw them into the sea. It had the power of an electric shock. Joy in all its forms ... in short, they showed all which can be discovered in the Human Kind of these feelings.[65]

---

61 In the case of the *Echo* in 1858, members of the slaving crew arrested by the US Africa squadron were unchained to re-exert control over the recaptives. See Fett, *Recaptured Africans*, pp. 51–52.

62 *UK Parliamentary Papers*, 1850 (9), pp. 162–63. Augustino gave evidence relating to his transportation on a slave ship from West Africa to Brazil in 1830; David Richardson, 'Through African eyes: the Middle Passage and the British slave trade', in Douglas Hamilton and Robert J. Blyth (eds), *Representing Slavery: Art, Artefacts and Archives in the Collections of the National Maritime Museum* (Aldershot: Lund Humphries, 2007), pp. 42–49, at p. 48.

63 'Ali Eisami', in Curtin (ed.), *Africa Remembered*, p. 214.

64 Report of George Collier, 27 December 1821, reproduced in *Sixteenth Report of the Directors of the African Institution* (1822), pp. 83–84.

65 NLS, MS 9879, copy letter from John Tailour to General Sir Charles William Pasley, 3 May 1815, ff. 333–35.

Lieutenant Mildmay, in charge of the *Yeanam* prize in 1823, ordered a young girl to be released from 'a thick iron chain, ten feet in length'. The irons were then placed on the slave ship's captain, so he 'should not be ignorant of the pain inflicted upon an unprotected and innocent child'.[66] The offer of clothing had similar symbolism. Commander Moresby of HMS *Sappho* noted that when recaptives from a Portuguese slave ship were taken on board his vessel, 'every exertion has been made by the officers and men of this sloop to alleviate their sufferings ... even tearing up their own clothes to cover the naked wretches'.[67]

While such examples of compassion reflect well on the officers involved, African perspectives in these accounts are secondary to positive reflections of British conduct and pride in their liberating role. Furthermore, recaptives' experiences were clearly varied. George McHenry, a surgeon and superintendent of the Liberated African Establishment at St Helena, described how many of those he witnessed disembarking from prize vessels remained 'manacled in couples ... thus chained to prevent them from inflicting punishment upon their captors'.[68] As exposed in the narratives of Midshipman Rogers and Lieutenant de Sausmarez, Africans could be poorly treated by naval officers. Joseph Wright was embarked on a Portuguese slaver in 1827 and subsequently freed by the Royal Navy. However, his experience of British guardianship was not positive:

> Next day the English vessel overtook us and they took charge of the slaves. We were very poor for water. We were only allowed one glass of water a day and we were allowed only breakfast, no dinner. Many of the slaves had died for want of water, and many men died for crowdedness ... One day as I sat by the fireside where they were cooking, boiling water was thrown on my head, and my head became all peeled and sore, and this pained me very much.[69]

Relations became difficult in other ways, too, particularly with women and children on board. Alexander Bryson recommended the removal of

---

66 *Case of the Vigilante, a Ship Employed in the Slave Trade; with Some Reflections on that Traffic* (London: Harvey, Darton & Co., 1823), p. 9.

67 'Reports from British Naval Officers Relating to the Slave Trade', *UK Parliamentary Papers*, 1857–58 (2443), correspondence between Rear-Admiral Sir F. Grey, Commodore Wise and Commander Moresby, 20 and 23 September 1857, pp. 137–38.

68 George McHenry, *Visits to Slave Ships* (British and Foreign Anti-Slavery Society, 1862), n.p.

69 'The narrative of Joseph Wright', in Curtin (ed.), *Africa Remembered*, pp. 322–33, at pp. 331–32. Curtin identified Wright's vessel as the *Velas*, captured by the *Maidstone*. Wright later became a missionary in Sierra Leone.

alcohol from prize vessels to prevent misconduct by sailors. 'Should there be female slaves on board', he wrote, 'it is utterly impossible to prevent irregularities of another kind taking place.'[70] Many naval officers exhibited feelings of sympathy and kindness, but their opinions on race, humanitarianism and the anti-slavery cause more widely varied enormously, impacting their treatment of those under their care. Even well-intentioned conduct, the encouragement of singing or dancing for example, could be inadvertently cruel. McHenry was scathing about the treatment of Africans by some prize crews. He described how:

> some jack-tar, in the exuberance of gaiety, possibly from anticipation of the pleasures awaiting him on shore, will perhaps call upon the slaves for a song. These unfortunate and degraded creatures … accustomed to implicit submission and obedience, will then strike up with loud voices a whining monotonous string of notes, accompanied with clapping of hands, repeating the same tune many a time without the least variation.[71]

Lieutenant Edwin Hinde's letters exemplify this gulf between perceptions and reality. In 1830 the *Atholl* captured a French slaver with 227 slaves on board, and Hinde was sent with the second lieutenant, William Ramsay, to convey the prize to Sierra Leone. In contrast to the many other distressing accounts of conditions on prize vessels, Hinde appeared to enjoy the excitement of the task, writing home: 'I never lived better in my life: we lost 12 slaves who died in the passage: however the slaves are not so miserable as you would suspect; in general they are merry and after when on Deck they used to sing & dance.'[72] Although Hinde implies that the Africans on board his prize danced voluntarily, there are disconcerting undertones in his description of the Africans under naval authority. That he 'never lived better' regardless of witnessing the deaths of 12 Africans is also an uncomfortable admission.

From the treatment they received from naval officers in some instances, recaptives may not have appreciated that there had been a change in the authority of their white male captors. In contrast to other idealistic representations of British liberation, elements of distrust remained. In the case of the prize voyages examined here, it is difficult to see how the concept of freedom was communicated by British officers, or was understood by those they were releasing from the slave trade.

---

70 Bryson, *Report*, p. 210. There was a long history of sexual exploitation of women captives on slaving vessels. See Christopher, *Slave Ship Sailors*, pp. 187–92.
71 McHenry, *Visits to Slave Ships*.
72 NMM, HIN/1, Hinde letters, 23 February 1830.

3 Lieutenant Henry Samuel Hawker, *The Portuguese slaver Diligenté captured by HM Sloop Pearl*, c. 1838

Visual representations

Alongside written accounts of prize voyages, there are also rare visual depictions. Lieutenant Henry Samuel Hawker produced a sketch in watercolour of the Portuguese slaver *Diligenté* captured by HM sloop *Pearl* in 1838 with 477 captives on board. The vessel was taken as prize by Hawker to Nassau in Cuba. It was a low and fast sloop of the kind introduced by slave traders to evade capture by the British patrols. This sketch is from a distance (probably from the *Pearl*) and shows many enslaved Africans on deck, although the number can be estimated as only around a third of those on board, the remainder presumably still in the hold.[73] While most of them are sitting, others are lying on the deck and appear to be sick or dying, tended to by other Africans and white men in red and blue coats, signifying British naval personnel. The sketch is revealing of overcrowding and mortality, as one African body is thrown overboard. Such eyewitness representations provide insight into conditions on prize voyages and the nature of the enslavement process: for example, the emaciated condition of the enslaved before boarding, at the point of sale.

Similar malnutrition is depicted in a sketch by Commodore Charles Wise of a group of recaptives taken on board HMS *Vesuvius* in September 1857. A slave ship, thought to be Portuguese, was driven on shore by Commander Moresby of HMS *Sappho* in the River Congo. From the 1,200 captives embarked, only 311 were removed to the *Vesuvius*; over 800 were believed to have drowned or died from exposure. Moresby described the scene on the grounded slaver as 'fearful and heartrending in the extreme'.[74] Other correspondence from Commodore Wise positioned him as staunchly abolitionist, likely impacted by his experiences on the squadron. In a report to the Admiralty in 1859, he described the slave trade as a 'cruel system … accompanied by the most terrible, most heart-rending loss of life that can well be conceived'.[75] His rough sketch depicts recaptives sitting on deck, gathered around a large bowl of food. One individual at the forefront looks skeletal, with their ribs showing, and black spots might reveal evidence of smallpox among others. Wise depicted some of the Africans with their hands crossed, perhaps as a form of prayer or ritual, and there appears to be an African ruler in a tribal headdress and beads. Some appear to be scarified or branded on their chests. That an officer took time to sketch recaptives in this way serves as a reminder of the processes of communication and

73 *War, Art, Racism & Slavery* (London: Michael Graham-Stewart, 2009), pp. 14–19.
74 'Reports from British Naval Officers', pp. 137–38.
75 TNA, FO 881/824, Commodore Charles Wise, 'Report on the Slave Trade on the West Coast of Africa', 20 July 1859, p. 5.

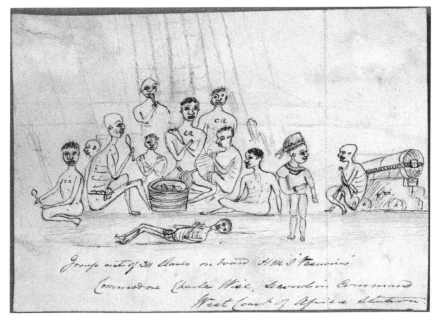

4 Commodore Charles Wise, 'Group out of 311 slaves on board
HMS *Vesuvius*', c. 1857

interpersonal relationships that may have developed between naval officers
and African shipmates while surviving together on a crowded vessel.

In March 1845 Francis Meynell was Acting Lieutenant of HM sloop
Albatross when the vessel captured the slaver *Albanez* off the River Congo.
Two hundred enslaved Africans were already embarked; there were also
three rafts alongside, formed of water-casks, crowded with Africans for
boarding.[76] Meynell was tasked with transporting the prize to Sierra Leone
under Lieutenant Elliot on a voyage that lasted six weeks. Writing about
his experiences to his father later that year, Meynell wrote: 'I boarded her
at the capture[;] she had 740 slaves, 140 of whom died on her passage up
to Sierra Leone. I went up in her and a most miserable business it was.' At
Sierra Leone, Meynell reported that '500 were landed but near 30 have died
since[,] it's a very horrible business this slave trade'.[77] Meynell produced two
watercolours of the slave ship; his depiction of recaptives in the hold below

76 The name of this slave vessel has been spelled in various ways. For consistency, the
spelling on www.slavevoyages.org, voyage 3483 is used. The capture of the *Albanez* was
detailed in a letter from Captain R. Yorke of the *Albatross* published in the *Illustrated
London News*, 10 May 1845.

77 NMM, MEY/5, Meynell letters, 2 May and 17 August 1845.

5 Lieutenant Francis Meynell, *Slaves below deck*, c. 1846

deck in particular captures the suffering and bodily trauma of the slave trade. While free of shackles or constraints, the status of the recaptives as human cargo is self-evident, and in Marcus Wood's words, 'fatigue, ennui, discomfort and sheer depression are the primary impressions'.[78] Compared to the more brutal imagery of the transatlantic slave trade publicly distributed by the abolitionist movement, Meynell's painting of the slave-hold is quiet, still and melancholic. However, while there is humanity in the painting there is also a sense of detachment, leading the watercolour to appear more as an observational sketch than a judgement on the slave trade.[79] James Smalls has written that most visualizations of the slave trade through art represented 'an inherently political act' which automatically identified the artist's views on slavery. Meynell's work sits apart in that he was an eyewitness to the slave trade, but there is no clear perception of his views on slavery and no indication that he intended his sketch to be used for abolitionist ends.[80]

78 Wood, *Blind Memory*, p. 25.

79 As evidenced by his sketchbook and illustrated logbook (NMM, MEY/1 and MEY/2), Meynell was a prolific artist. He sketched many varied landscapes and scenes from his naval service, from China to the South Atlantic, including some sympathetic depictions of other races.

80 James Smalls, 'Art and illustration', in Seymour Drescher and Stanley Engerman

One painting with which similarities can be found is *Nègres à fond de calle* (Negroes in the ship's hold) by Johann Moritz Rugendas, painted for his *Voyage pittoresque dans le Brésil* (1827–35). Like Meynell, Rugendas was an eyewitness, seeing the hold of a slave ship while on a scientific mission to the Brazilian interior. Rugendas's work was intended to be informative rather than declamatory, so a similarly objective approach is apparent.[81] The construction of both scenes is similar: Africans sit or lie beneath an opening to the hold; some sit on the beams while others lie on the floor; some look ill or emaciated and the lack of water or food is evident. One important difference, however, is that Meynell's image has no white presence.[82] His depiction of the recaptives is somewhat impersonal, with little extreme suffering represented, particularly when compared, for example, with George McHenry's description of a slave-hold on a prize vessel:

> [Recaptives] are to be seen in all stages of emaciation, and I may add, decomposition. Several absolutely rotten, already smell as intolerably as if they had been dead some days. The heavy acid odour from those who are still living, mingling with the intolerable stench from the dead ... rendered more overpowering by a suffocating atmosphere, ranging from 100 to 120 degrees Fahrenheit.[83]

Perhaps conditions on the *Albanez* were not as appalling, although the 148 African deaths during the passage to Sierra Leone suggest otherwise. The *Albanez* was also of a similar size and with a comparable number of slaves on board as the *Clara Windsor*, of which onboard conditions Richard Carr McClement gave such a distressing testimony.[84]

Meynell's sketch is often cited as an accurate representation of a slave-hold, but its veracity in this regard may be questioned. The amount of room depicted is very generous compared with other slave vessels of this period. For example, the height of the space for the stowage of slaves on the *Minerva*,

(eds), *A Historical Guide to World Slavery* (Oxford: Oxford University Press, 1998), pp. 65, 76. Most visual representations that exposed the horrors of the slave trade were instigated by the abolitionist movement and were intended to stir sympathy in the viewer. For an overview of this visual culture, see Oldfield, *Popular Politics*, ch. 6. To the best of my knowledge, Meynell's paintings were not used in contemporary literature or propaganda. The NMM catalogue suggests they were unseen until presented to the museum in 1957 by Meynell's daughter-in-law.

81 Smalls, 'Art and illustration', p. 73. See Hamilton and Blyth (eds), *Representing Slavery*, p. 272.

82 Wood, *Blind Memory*, pp. 24–25.

83 McHenry, *Visits to Slave Ships*.

84 www.slavevoyages.org, voyage 3483; voyage 4336 [accessed 15 May 2018]. The *Albanez* had a tonnage of 215 tons compared to the *Clara Windsor*'s 218 tons.

on trial in 1842, was given as 'only one foot 2 inches'; even accounting for half of the slaves being accommodated on deck, 'the remainder below were squeezed to excess all the Slaves being obliged to lay flat down'.[85] Perhaps Meynell's sketch is from memory after a visit to the hold: it is doubtful whether he could have endured the 'human dungeon', in McHenry's words, long enough to complete a watercolour sketch, or why he would wish to. Read alongside later letters from HMS *Cygnet* informing his family of further prizes and financial gain, it becomes clear that Meynell measured his success in the release of captive Africans in monetary terms:

> we took a good prize which in 2 years time I suppose will be payable, with 560 slaves ... in the last 3 months I share in 4 prizes which will give me upwards of £150[;] good work for a few months[,] it beats China even but it is active work for an officer at any rate and he deserves all he gets ... Star has still taken more prizes than any vessel on the station. £50 or 60£ more in my pocket thank God.[86]

Such observations can be read in several ways. Meynell wrote with what appears to be limited sympathy for the enslaved, instead concentrating on more mercenary motives. Alternatively, perhaps the nature of his work and what he had witnessed had caused Meynell such distress that the financial recompense was the only positive news he could report back home.

Questions of freedom

The capture and passage of a prize vessel to British territory was the first phase of an ambiguous journey to 'freedom' for recaptives. Africans released from slave vessels by the Royal Navy joined a tradition of supposedly free migrants struggling to find self-determination in the Atlantic world. The stories of African-American slaves who negotiated their freedom with the British during the American War of Independence only to find themselves sent with London's poor blacks to begin the doomed colonial experiment in Sierra Leone in 1787 marked the beginning of an elusive promise of freedom throughout the following century.[87] A common thread throughout the experiences of the formerly enslaved in British territories in the nineteenth century is how their needs were not necessarily a priority for those who released them.

85 Admiralty enclosures printed in Eltis and Richardson, *Atlas*, p. 152.
86 NMM, MEY/5, Meynell letters, 12 January 1846.
87 Byrd, *Captives and Voyagers*; Cassandra Pybus, *Epic Journeys of Freedom: Runaway Slaves of the American Revolution and Their Global Quest for Liberty* (Boston: Beacon Press, 2006); Schama, *Rough Crossings*.

The ways in which naval officers understood their role on the West African coast was impacted by this undercurrent of thinking about the nature of their interactions with recaptives, focused on their respective positions of liberator and liberated. The nature of this relationship – from capture, to conveyance, to release and 'liberation' – was constantly evolving. As Alexander Bryson wrote, after the capture of a slave vessel, 'the slaves in the meantime will begin to perceive in what relation they stand to their liberators'.[88] It was invariably the British, however, who imposed their ideas of liberty, via their own idealized view of the process. Such relations were imbued with British national pride and expectations of gratitude. Naval surgeon George Maclaren served on the brig-sloop *Serpent* on the West Indies station and was engaged in the suppression of the Spanish slave trade. Discussing in his journal the prizes taken by his vessel around Tobago and Grenada in 1836, he wrote:

> Thus in the course of eight days have three vessels been captured & 1254 human beings rescued from worse than Egyptian bondage, through the instrumentality of a single vessel – I doubt much if British naval history can afford a parallel. How deep the debt of gratitude of these sable sons of Africa to the great Being who redeemed them from slavery & brought them to a state of perfect freedom, to perform a part in the civilized world.

How pleasing, Maclaren wrote, to be 'employed in so glorious a cause'.[89] Officers clearly felt pride in their role as 'liberators'. In 1843 Captain John Foote sent a 'set of chains' to the Lordships of the Admiralty from the *Madagascar* off Ambriz. The chains were 'found on the person of one of the slaves at Cabenda; all the men are shackled together by Tens and Twenties'. Foote added: 'I feel great gratification in having been the humble instrument of delivering so many fellow beings from the accursed Slave Holder.'[90] However, the celebration of Britain's liberating role sits uneasily with officers' beliefs in how far freedom was applicable to African peoples. These ambiguities were particularly pronounced in the period that preceded the passing of the Emancipation Act of 1833, before which many Britons were slaveholders in the Caribbean.[91]

---

88 Bryson, *Report*, p. 257. The Royal Navy liberated nine out of ten of all recaptured slaves, so for the majority of the estimated nearly 200,000 Africans released on the West African coast between 1808 and 1867, their encounter with freedom was with the British. See Eltis and Richardson, *Atlas*, map 185, p. 282.

89 CUL, Add. 9528/2/1, Maclaren journals, 6 October 1836.

90 TNA ADM 1/5517, Captain John Foote to Sidney Herbert MP, 1 June 1843.

91 The Legacies of British Slave-ownership project (https://www.ucl.ac.uk/lbs/) shows that until 1833 large-scale slave ownership was common in British society, passed on by inheritance and marriage settlement.

The act of releasing captives from a slave vessel at sea did not constitute their freedom; that was not granted until the vessel was condemned at an Admiralty court, but even then ambiguities remained.[92] If the capture was declared illegal, the ship and its human cargo would be returned to the original captain (who often stayed with the prize for this reason). For those enslaved on board the *Maria de Gloria* in 1833, for example, this meant a return to enslavement and a third Atlantic crossing back to Brazil. If the capture was deemed legal, the vessel was condemned or sold, and the recaptives were registered as British citizens and maintained for a time at the expense of the British government.[93] An estimated 65,000 were emancipated in Freetown.[94] Recaptives were taken to King's Yard and thus became the responsibility of the Liberated African Department. Registers were kept with details of their name, gender, age, height and body marks to prevent their subsequent re-enslavement.[95] The theme of British self-congratulation was ever-present in this process. An inscription on the gateway to King's Yard, commissioned in 1817 by Governor Sir Charles MacCarthy, read: 'Royal Asylum and Hospital for the Africans rescued from slavery by British Valour and Philanthropy'.[96] In the abolitionist vision of an exemplary 'civilized' colony, there was little concern for reparation for the formerly enslaved. Instead, the plan of apprenticeship was devised in Sierra Leone to assimilate recaptives, in the belief that they could not be returned to their homes or left to fend for themselves. Some liberated Africans were taken into European households in Freetown as servants, 'to any resident who would pay one pound for indentures and become responsible for the maintenance, clothing, and education of the apprentice'.[97] With support from missionary societies,

92 Jake Christopher Richards has explored the difficulties in defining the legal status of newly liberated Africans in the Atlantic world in 'Anti-slave-trade law, "liberated Africans" and the state in the South Atlantic world, c. 1839–1852', *Past and Present*, 241 (2018), pp. 179–219.

93 Burroughs, 'Eyes on the prize', p. 101.

94 Bethell, 'The Mixed Commissions', p. 89. Over 10,000 Africans were emancipated in Havana and over 3,000 in Rio de Janeiro.

95 The African Origins Project (http://www.african-origins.org) and more recently, Liberated Africans (liberatedafricans.org) provide details of thousands of people emancipated under campaigns against slavery in the nineteenth century. See also Suzanne Schwarz, 'Reconstructing the life histories of liberated Africans: Sierra Leone in the early nineteenth century', *History in Africa*, 39 (2012), pp. 175–207.

96 www.sierraleoneheritage.org/sites/monuments/kingsyard/ [accessed 22 November 2017].

97 Frederick Forbes, *Six Months' Service in the African Blockade, from April to October, 1848, in Command of H.M.S. Bonetta* (London: Richard Bentley, 1849), pp. 9–10. The Abolition Act of 1807 provided that Africans unlawfully imported as slaves into British colonies were to be 'apprenticed' for not more than 14 years.

others were settled in villages around Freetown, where they learned English and took on European names and habits, including a Christian education.[98]

Idealistic rhetoric was challenged by the realities of abolitionist policies, as recaptives landed at Sierra Leone remained subject to British control.[99] Governor Thomas Perronet Thompson was one prominent critic of the early apprenticeship scheme favoured by the Sierra Leone Company, condemning it in 1809 as slavery by another name and publicly charging 'all the former governors of this colony with having been volunteers in the slave trade'.[100] Naval officers saw nothing amiss with regarding former slaves as requiring new masters. Commodore George Collier recounted meeting children in Sierra Leone who 'are removed from the loathsome holds of a slave ship, and sent to a village without any other feeling than what a slave experiences on a change of masters'.[101] Such attitudes were demonstrated in Samuel Crowther's account, who wrote that after disembarkation he and his fellow recaptives were 'assured ... of our liberty and freedom'. However, when they refused to testify against the Portuguese slave owner who had captured them, 'we were compelled to go by being whipped'.[102]

By the 1830s, liberated Africans in Sierra Leone were maintained at government expense for six months and allotted land and tools. They began trading in vegetable produce or fish in the Freetown streets, or earned money

---

98 A small number of recaptives were also sent to settle in Bathurst in the Gambia. The largest recaptive group in the colony was the Aku (as Yoruba people were generally called in Sierra Leone); the Ibo was the next largest. In 'Becoming African: identity formation among liberated slaves in nineteenth-century Sierra Leone', *Slavery and Abolition*, 27.1 (2006), pp. 1–21, David Northrup examines how recaptives preserved and adapted homeland cultures and religious practices in Sierra Leone.

99 For example, in '"A most promising field for future usefulness": the Church Missionary Society and the liberated Africans of Sierra Leone', in Mulligan and Bric (eds), *A Global History*, pp. 37–59, Maeve Ryan explores the failure of the partnership between the CMS and the Liberated African Department, 'an uncomfortable marriage of paternalistic idealism and austere practicality' (p. 38).

100 BA (Whitbread Collection), W1/4144, copy letter from George Caulker (a British official in the Secretary's office at Freetown) to Samuel Whitbread, 7 March 1809. Thompson took issue with the case of two Africans liberated from American slave vessels by Captain Frederick Parker of HMS *Derwent* in 1808, sold as apprentices for 20 dollars each. See also Cassandra Pybus, '"A less favourable specimen": the abolitionist response to self-emancipated slaves in Sierra Leone, 1763–1808', in Stephen Farrell, Melanie Unwin and James Walvin (eds), *The British Slave Trade: Abolition, Parliament and People* (Edinburgh: Edinburgh University Press, 2007), pp. 97–112; Emma Christopher, '"Tis enough that we give them liberty"? Liberated Africans at Sierra Leone in the early era of slave-trade suppression', in Burroughs and Huzzey (eds), *Suppression*, pp. 55–72.

101 MoD, MSS 45, 'Second Annual Report', ff. 217–18.

102 Crowther to Revd Jowett, in Curtin (ed.), *Africa Remembered*, p. 314.

cutting firewood. Commander George Bedford of HMS *Raven* believed that many liberated Africans in the colony 'have thus raised themselves by industry from the most lowly condition'.[103] African men were also enlisted into Britain's Royal African Corps and West India regiments, employed in the mid-century to defend West African possessions. This had the advantage of reducing the need for British personnel in unhealthy West African environments.[104] Many were employed on British naval vessels. For example, James Pinson Labulo Davies, born to recaptive Yoruba parents and 'educated at the grammar-school at Sierra Leone', was lieutenant on the *Bloodhound* steamer when the vessel was involved in the attack on Lagos in 1851.[105] James 'Kaweli' Covey joined the crew of HMS *Buzzard* in 1838 after his recapture by the Royal Navy and five years spent in the CMS mission school at Freetown.[106] Bedford wrote of the 'wise and philanthropic design' whereby liberated African boys were put 'under the charge and tuition of the various artificers onboard, that they may acquire a knowledge of these trades and be enabled to make themselves useful members of Society'.[107] This was not an opinion shared by all, however. Commodore John Hayes wrote that while the work of Krumen (West African seamen) was 'done better, and cheerfully done … the liberated African is indolent and dissatisfied'.[108] Such negative portrayals of liberated Africans were found in other officers' narratives, reflecting racial stereotypes of the period. Commander Henry Beamish wrote that they 'have nothing but a mixture of ingratitude and laziness to return for British kindness & British food'.[109]

These representations reflect tensions surrounding the ambiguities of freedom for those released from the slave trade by the Royal Navy. In the 1850s, engineer John M'Kie described how young girls were 'mostly bought

103 MoD, MSS 151, Bedford diaries, no folios; David Northrup, *Indentured Labor in the Age of Imperialism* (Cambridge: Cambridge University Press, 1995), p. 45. See Fyfe, 'Four Sierra Leone recaptives', pp. 77–85, for the business and trade opportunities available to liberated Africans.

104 S. C. Ukpabi, 'West Indian troops and the defence of British West Africa in the nineteenth century', *African Studies Review*, 17.1 (1974), pp. 133–50. See also the research outcomes of the University of Warwick's *Africa's Sons Under Arms* project (2014–18).

105 *The Times*, 'The Capture of Lagos', 17 February 1852.

106 Covey later became interpreter for the captives of *La Amistad*. See Benjamin N. Lawrance, '*La Amistad*'s "interpreter" reinterpreted: James "Kaweli" Covey's distressed Atlantic childhood and the production of knowledge about nineteenth-century Sierra Leone', in Lovejoy and Schwarz (eds), *Slavery, Abolition*, pp. 217–55.

107 MoD, MSS 151, Bedford diaries.

108 TNA, ADM 1/1, Commodore Hayes to Captain George Elliot, 9 September 1831, ff. 482–85.

109 CAC, BEAM 1/9, Beamish journals, [no date], 1863, no folios.

to be trained as domestics', while men 'are apprenticed for a certain number of years and taught to work before attaining their freedom'.[110] M'Kie clearly did not associate apprenticeship with freedom, and he thought it appropriate that Africans were 'taught to work' before they could be considered free. Similarly, naval surgeon Peter Leonard discussed recently landed recaptives at Sierra Leone in his published account:

> It struck me that on landing they expected to be allowed to go wherever they pleased, and were consequently disappointed and angry when they found themselves still under control. It was impossible to gather from their looks whether any of them were keenly alive to the miseries of the situation from which they had just been released, or whether they were capable of appreciating the advantages of emancipation.[111]

For Leonard, the 'advantages of emancipation' clearly did not involve freedom from a controlling authority.

Themes of British protection, paternalism and control remained dominant. One reason cited against repatriation was to prevent liberated Africans from being resold into slavery. In 1837 Captain W. Walkhope wrote that this concern arose 'chiefly from the want of a proper superintendent with power ... similar to that of the slave protectors sent to the colonies'.[112] Walkhope's reference to the British West Indies highlights the wider trans-Atlantic debate over apprenticeship, which had relevance for the treatment of liberated Africans in West Africa. Concepts of freedom for former slaves in the Caribbean were influenced by negative beliefs in the innate character of African peoples. Freedom, it was believed, came with certain responsibilities (industry, moral standing, and so on), the understanding of which required African people to undertake a period of guidance and education. Similarly, liberated Africans were regarded as incapable of embracing these responsibilities without British direction.[113] After much criticism, the system of apprenticeship ended in 1847, and from the 1840s the Colonial Office supported the recruitment and transportation of liberated Africans to the British West Indies as wage-labourers on the sugar plantations. This labour emigration scheme was part of the British 'mighty experiment' to replace slave labour with 'free', to fill shortfalls of labour created by the Emancipation Act of 1833.[114] Almost half

---

110 NLS, MS 24633, M'Kie memoirs, ff. 67–68.

111 Leonard, *Records of a Voyage*, p. 106.

112 UKHO, MP 90/Ca6, remarks of Captain W. Walkhope, f. 631.

113 Drescher, 'Emperors of the world', p. 144; Thomas C. Holt, *The Problem of Freedom: Race, Labor and Politics in Jamaica and Britain, 1832–1938* (Baltimore, MD: Johns Hopkins University Press, 1992).

114 Drescher, *Mighty Experiment*.

of all Africans removed from slave vessels ended up in the British Caribbean under arrangements of apprenticeship, indenture or military service.[115] The emigrants also included some Kru, whose perceived industrious character led them to be considered ideal candidates for indentured labour.[116] The scheme represented a shift in thinking by the British government, from a responsibility to support liberated Africans' freedom to an expectation that they should contribute to the post-emancipation cause. In fact, few Africans released from slave vessels volunteered to undertake a second sea voyage, leading to, in David Northrup's words, 'ethically ambivalent schemes' to force new recaptives to emigrate or enlist in the military.[117]

Those disembarked outside Sierra Leone experienced similar constraints on their freedom. The Atlantic island of St Helena was owned by the East India Company until it became a Crown colony in 1834. A Vice-Admiralty Court was established there in 1839 and the Liberated African Establishment came into operation as a receiving depot, with an estimated 26,000 recaptives landed on this isolated settlement.[118] Around one-third of those disembarked died from disease soon after and were buried in large institutional graveyards.[119] Those who survived were maintained under strict discipline by colonial authorities at the depots of Lemon and Rupert's Valley, where they were used as labourers, or more likely, transported as migrant labourers. Up until 1867, just over 17,000 recaptives were transported onwards from St Helena, representing 70 per cent of all those liberated by its Vice-Admiralty Court and virtually all who survived in the depots thereafter.[120] Lieutenant Henry Rogers disembarked the recaptives of the *Casco* at St Helena in 1849. '[O]ne in particular wanted to stay with me', Rogers wrote, 'but poor fellow he is not free and must go where he is sent. For their freedom is but nominal, they are now being prepared

---

115 Rosanne Adderley, *'New Negroes from Africa': Slave Trade Abolition and Free African Settlement in the Nineteenth-Century Caribbean* (Bloomington, IN: Indiana University Press, 2006); Johnson U. J. Asiegbu, *Slavery and the Politics of Liberation 1787–1861: A Study of Liberated African Emigration and British Anti-Slavery Policy* (Harlow: Longman, 1969).

116 Robert Burroughs, '"[T]he true sailors of Western Africa": Kru seafaring identity in British travellers' accounts of the 1830s and 1840s', *Journal of Maritime Research*, 11.1 (2009), pp. 51–67.

117 Northrup, *Indentured Labor*, pp. 46–48, 51.

118 Pearson, *Distant Freedom*.

119 Archaeological investigations in 2008 identified the remains of 325 liberated African skeletons in an unmarked cemetery. See Andrew Pearson, Ben Jeffs, Annsofie Witkin and Helen MacQuarrie, *Infernal Traffic: Excavation of a Liberated African Graveyard in Rupert's Valley, St Helena* (York: Council for British Archaeology, 2011).

120 Pearson, *Distant Freedom*, pp. 128–32, 219, ch. 6.

for <u>emigration</u> to our Colonies, as there are now three vessels waiting for slaves.'[121] Rogers did not believe that the process of British liberation made the enslaved 'free' and nor did he alter his terminology with respect to the liberated Africans, still referring to them as 'slaves', only this time in the context of British colonies.

Indeed, the emigration process met with much criticism that selected Africans would find themselves in little more than 'a new form of the slave trade'.[122] During a Select Committee hearing in 1842, Captain Joseph Denman stated his belief that the scheme would 'perpetuate their slavery':

> nor could the forcible removal of these poor creatures from an asylum containing thousands of their countrymen, and possibly many of their near kindred, be rendered justifiable by any consideration whatever. I have seen a cargo of slaves, after the completion of one voyage across the Atlantic, condemned to another for their own supposed benefit; and I can bear witness to the horror of the victims, when they found themselves once more on the 'middle passage'.[123]

Commodore Charles Hotham also expressed his dissatisfaction with the process in letters to the Admiralty in 1848. For 'slaves already diseased and suffering from a long voyage', he wrote, to send them to the West Indies 'would be to repeat all the horrors of a middle passage'.[124] Unlike Denman, however, Hotham wrote with more practicality than emotion, with concern that such action would reflect badly on the British:

> The general opinion in the colony is unfavourable to the success of the emigration scheme ... foreigners are loud in their outcry against the proceedings; the Spanish consul (a clever intelligent man) told me that they sent away mere children who were unable to explain whether they were willing or not to go. The greatest number we can expect to get per annum is 5,000 of both sexes & is it worth while [*sic*] to lose our national character for philanthropy and humanity for such a pittance?[125]

The irony of Spanish nationals accusing the British of creating conditions akin to the slave trade was clearly not lost on Hotham. However, his priority

---

121 Private collection, Rogers journal, 19 December 1949. Rogers's emphasis.

122 Anon., *African Emigration to the British Colonies* (1847), quoted in Burroughs, '[T]he true sailors', p. 58.

123 'Minutes of Evidence', in *Trial of Pedro de Zulueta*, pp. 158–59.

124 HUA, U DDHO 10/11, Charles Hotham to 'My Lord' [the Earl of Auckland], 29 August 1848.

125 HUA, U DDHO 10/11, Charles Hotham to the Earl of Auckland, 23 March 1848.

was the preservation of Britain's national character rather than the fate of liberated Africans.

The British stressed their favourable treatment of recaptives as compared to others, particularly the Brazilians, with concerns expressed about the mistreatment of those liberated at Havana and Rio de Janeiro.[126] Naval officers were keen to compare (in their eyes) favourable British conceptions of freedom with other European ideas of liberty. In order to secure labour for their West African and Caribbean colonies, in the 1840s and 1850s the French began purchasing the freedom of slaves and then binding them to contracts to work off the cost of their freedom. Over 20,000 African labourers were sent to Martinique or Guadeloupe on six-year contracts.[127] John Thompson, Master of HMS *Sharpshooter*, wrote with irony in his remark book about the treatment of 'free negro emigrants' outside a French factory in Loango Bay in 1858:

> each of whom had the badge of freedom round his neck consisting of a rope ring with a loop attached to it for the purpose of stringing them together by a rod or rope. As a matter of course this might be for ornament, so might the whips that abound in the place & for the playful amount of whipping. 600 negroes were in the barracoon on this occasion with a barque in the [anchor symbol] ready to take them away … So much for Free French Emigration. The agent gets an ounce of gold or the sum of £3.4 for every negro shipped.[128]

In his correspondence with the Admiralty Secretary, Commodore Charles Wise declared that at the French factory at Loango, 'the voluntary free emigrants are now guarded in the same manner as slaves'.[129] One perceived consequence of such practices was the undermining of Britain's suppression efforts. Commander George Burgess referred to the hypocrisy of Europeans in the eyes of African rulers:

> Nothing will persuade these Chiefs that paying a sum of money for a man is not slave dealing, and the spectacle they now see of England standing

126 Beatriz G. Mamigonian, 'In the name of freedom: slave trade abolition, the law and the Brazilian branch of the African Emigration Scheme (Brazil–British West Indies, 1830s–1850s)', *Slavery and Abolition*, 30.1 (2009), pp. 41–66.

127 Northrup, *Indentured Labor*, pp. 48–50. The Portuguese also used enslaved Africans on their plantations in the 1850s.

128 NYPL, Thompson journal, [no date] December 1858.

129 'Reports from Vice-Admiralty Courts and from British Naval Officers Relating to the Slave Trade', *UK Parliamentary Papers*, 1858–59 (2569), Commodore Wise to the Secretary of the Admiralty, 9 September 1858, pp. 189–90.

alone in her endeavours to put down the slave trade, and of other Nations indulging in it (or a close imitation) has the effect of detaching these men from their alliance with, and respect towards us.[130]

Such criticism of the French emigration scheme highlights the ambiguities surrounding definitions of slavery and freedom for Africans. This is demonstrated by the indifference shown by most Europeans to the expansion of the internal slave trade in many parts of the African continent in the nineteenth century, a growth in large part in response to the development of 'legitimate' trade and the labour demands involved in the production of crops such as palm oil.[131] Writing from Cape Coast Castle in 1862, Commander Henry Beamish wrote that government policy 'zealously upholds Domestic Slavery on the one hand, while on the other it proposes to disapprove of and to be determined to put down the export of slaves'. Beamish thought it 'a little odd' that 'one must not call a slave a "slave" and yet he can not be freed'.[132] In 1857 Commander V. G. Hickley, Senior Officer of the Southern Division, clearly questioned how far freedom was appropriate for some Africans. He hoped that Britain, 'in return for the unquestionably satisfactory results, be not quite so hard on the domestic slave system in the country'. He added, '[s]lavery is an ugly word in Europe, but does not mean so much in Africa; and that slave labour must be employed to eradicate slavery, I think any one seeing Africa must allow'.[133]

Slavery meant many things to nineteenth-century naval officers. While the transatlantic trade in Africans as slaves was unacceptable, domestic slavery was regarded as necessary by some. This was particularly the case if the 'satisfactory results' were closely tied to Britain's economic interests in West Africa. As Richard Huzzey has argued, what constituted 'liberty' in practice meant very different things to nineteenth-century observers, bound by imperial agendas, paternalism and racial attitudes.[134] A sense of displacement and uncertainty applied to the emancipation processes and resettlement of supposedly liberated Africans and *emancipados* across the

130 CAC, BEAM 1/8, Burgess journal, 1857, no folios.

131 In *Slavery in the Twentieth Century: The Evolution of a Global Problem* (Walnut Creek, CA: Altamira Press, 2003), Suzanne Miers has argued that by the end of the nineteenth century, slavery in Africa was a 'thriving and widely practiced institution' (p. 34).

132 CAC, BEAM 1/9, Beamish journal, [no date] 1862, no folios.

133 Journal of Commander Hickley, [no date] June 1857, *UK Parliamentary Papers*, 1857–58 (2443), pp. 119–20.

134 Richard Huzzey, 'Concepts of liberty: freedom, laissez-faire and the state after Britain's abolition of slavery', in Hall, Draper and McClelland (eds), *Emancipation and the Remaking*, pp. 149–71.

Atlantic world.[135] The nature of the liberation process was fraught with opportunities for exploitation, and supposedly free migrants invariably ended up in a place where coercion, rather than choice, defined their fate.

Officers' 'gift' of liberty

One final exploration of the relationship between African 'liberation' and British action relates to individual Africans taken into British guardianship by naval officers of the West Africa squadron. There are, for example, several examples of African children being taken to England under the personal protection of naval officers.[136] The print 'African Slavery' (1813) depicts a slave in the Portuguese settlement of Benguela with an iron collar fastened around his neck. The accompanying caption reports that '[t]his miserable being was purchased & made free, by a British Naval Officer, for Sixty Dollars'.[137] The officer was Captain Frederick Irby of the *Amelia*, a senior officer on the earliest formation of the West Africa squadron. Irby brought the 14-year-old boy to Norwich in 1813, where he was christened and enrolled at school under the name 'Charles Fortunatus Freeman'. A Norwich baptism register suggests that Irby in fact transported to England three African boys, stating that they were all brought from Africa 'thro[ugh] the humanity of the Hon Captain Frederic Paul Irby of Boyland Hall, Norfolk'.[138] A baptism

135 Domingues da Silva et al., 'The diaspora'; Mamigonian, 'In the name of freedom'. Fett, *Recaptured Africans*, examines the experiences of recaptured Africans seized by the US and temporarily kept in federal detention at Charleston harbour in 1858 and Key West in 1860 before being sent to Liberia. In 'Liberated Africans in Cape Colony in the first half of the nineteenth century', *The International Journal of African Historical Studies*, 18.2 (1985), pp. 223–39, Christopher Saunders argues that many liberated Africans at the Cape employed as servants or free labourers were in practice regarded as slaves.

136 The 'freedom' of these children is ambiguous, however, as the experience of Olaudah Equiano makes clear. In his *Interesting Narrative*, Equiano claimed that while a slave in Virginia he was purchased by Michael Henry Pascal, a lieutenant in the Royal Navy. Equiano wrote that Pascal 'meant me for a present to some of his friends in England' (p. 64). Pascal renamed him Gustavus Vassa, took him to London and then into service in the Royal Navy. In 1762, reneging on his promise of freedom, Pascal sold Equiano to a merchant captain.

137 'African Slavery', M. Dubourg, published by Edward Orme, 1813 (NMM, ZBA2440).

138 Norfolk Record Office, Baptisms Register for the parish of St Peter's Mancroft, Norwich, 1813. www.archives.norfolk.gov.uk/education/docs/Norfolk%20and%20the%20Abolition%20of%20Slavery.pdf [accessed 3 January 2013]. The other boys were named Paulo Loando and Edward Makenzie.

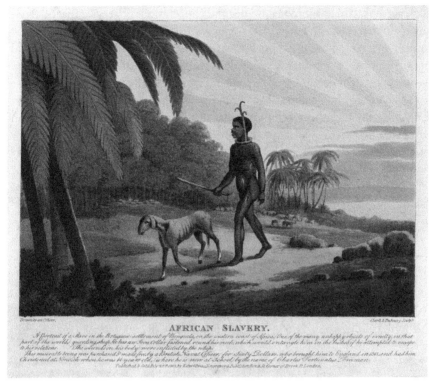

6 M. Dubourg, *African Slavery*, published by Edward Orme, 1813

register for 1813 of All Saints Church in Fawley, Hampshire, notes that a 10-year-old African boy 'from Poppoe' was also brought to England by Irby and baptized in that parish in the name of Irby Amelia Frederic, receiving his name from the captain and his ship.[139] A similar story is revealed in Suffolk parish registers from 1846, which record a black boy of 7 or 8 years old named Thomas Alert, 'recaptured from a Brazilian Brigantine by Captain Bosanquet near the River Gabon'. Charles Bosanquet served on the *Alert* in the 1840s and had a distinguished career on the anti-slave-trade patrols. Again, the boy was baptized with the name of his ship. Once in England, he was 'given over to the care of the vicar'.[140]

It is difficult to assess the motivations of Irby or Bosanquet without their own thoughts on their relationships with these boys. Both men were active in anti-slavery societies (see Chapter 6) which might play a part in explaining

139 www.stgeorgesnews.org/2004/06f11.htm [accessed 15 January 2017].
140 Noted in *Black and Asian Sources in the Suffolk Record Office*, Suffolk County Council (2011).

such actions, which went beyond normal expectations of service (particularly since, in Irby's case, he paid for a boy's freedom). The idea of rescue is prominent; so too are concepts of guardianship and the offer of educational opportunities, as another way of delivering the British viewpoint.[141] The issue of consent is problematic: with severely limited options, did these boys have any choice about leaving Africa with the officers? Their time in England may have been temporary. In 1823 Midshipman Binstead noted in his diary a reunion in Loango between an African boy, part of the crew of the *Owen Glendower*, and his father, the king's prime minister. The boy had been taken 'by force', presumably by slave traders. When the ship he was travelling on was wrecked at Princes Island, 'this boy was taken off the Island by Sir Geo[rge] Collier former commodore and taken to England where Sir Rd [Robert] Mends took him', and subsequently recruited him on the *Owen Glendower*.[142]

Ideas of 'rescuing' and 'saving' children have resonances in the age of exploration in Africa, where many stray children were 'collected' by explorers.[143] In 1850 Lieutenant Frederick Forbes brought back to Britain a young African girl intended as a 'present' for Queen Victoria from the King of Dahomey. The act of a ruler presenting enslaved children to ships' captains as gifts was part of the traditional interaction with slave ships.[144] When given responsibility for the girl, in his words an 'extraordinary present', Forbes regarded his choice as to take her with him or leave her to die. Furthermore, his conviction was that 'in consideration of the nature of the service I had performed, the government would have considered her as the property of the crown'. Forbes was aware that the girl's future lay in the context of her being property exchanged between monarchs. Beyond such impersonal considerations, however, Forbes thought the girl 'a perfect genius', who 'has won the affections, but with few exceptions, of all who have known her'. Once in England, while Queen Victoria paid for her education, Sarah Forbes Bonetta (as she was christened) lived with the Forbes family in Windsor.[145]

During their mission to Abomey (the capital of Dahomey) in 1863, Commodore Arthur Eardley-Wilmot and Captain John Proctor Luce were

141 Ray Costello, *Black Salt: Seafarers of African Descent on British Ships* (Liverpool: Liverpool University Press, 2012), pp. 17–20.

142 NMRN, 2005.76/2, Binstead diaries, 20 May 1823.

143 Kennedy, *The Last Blank Spaces*, pp. 171–72.

144 Joan Anim-Addo, 'Queen Victoria's black "daughter"', in Gretchen Holbrook Gerzina (ed.), *Black Victorians/Black Victoriana* (New Brunswick, NJ: Rutgers University Press, 2003), pp. 11–19.

145 Forbes, *Dahomey and the Dahomans*, pp. 80–81; Walter Dean Myers, *At Her Majesty's Request: An African Princess in Victorian England* (New York: Scholastic, 1999).

similarly given as 'gifts' from King Glele the lives of several of those destined for public execution in the annual 'customs'. Wilmot noted that the king declared that one man 'from henceforth belongs to you, to do as you like with him, to educate him, take him to England, or anything else you choose'.[146] Again, the transaction between naval officer and ruler had undertones of trading in people as property: the officers believed the African prisoner to be better off under British protection, but concepts of 'belonging' persisted, and they did not question the idea that in such cases those involved experienced little more than a change of masters. Other 'gifts' included two girls intended for Queen Victoria, and another girl who was dubiously 'presented to the Commodore as a wife to comfort him, & to wash his clothes & cook his meals'. Captain Luce was aware of the power held by officers in his position and how significant freedom from the king's rule could be:

> One of those presented to her Majesty objected to this transfer of her person – she was accordingly changed for another outside the gate without our seeing it & we heard that she was afterwards flogged, for speaking in the presence of the King & ordered to be sold for foreign slavery, so that the poor girl sadly missed her turn in the tide which would have led to liberty if not to fortune.[147]

The girls were left under the care of missionaries at Ouidah, including the Revd Peter Bernasko. Wilmot was later instructed by the Foreign Office to ascertain 'what character the girls severally bear, what progress they have made … & also whether the state of their health is such as to warrant one of them being sent to this country'.[148] They never arrived in England, as three years later Wilmot wrote to the head of the Slave Trade Department, William Wylde, to inform him:

> You will see that my wife is dead, and that one of the Queen's girls has had a child by Mr Dawson, whose name you may remember in Burton's Book. I have no doubt that Bernasko himself has had the best of the two girls? But what can you expect otherwise. The laws of nature must be obliged, and the people in Africa are not worse in this respect that we are in this civilized country![149]

146 Wilmot, 'Despatches', p. 9.
147 RAI, MS 280, Luce journals, vol. 4, f. 146.
148 TNA, ADM 123/183, Under Secretary of State for Foreign Affairs to the Secretary of the Admiralty, 27 October 1863.
149 DUL, WYL/30/2-5, Arthur Eardley-Wilmot to William Wylde, 3 January 1867. In Richard Burton's book *Mission to Gelele, King of Dahome* (1864), 'Mr Dawson' is noted as an 'ex-missionary and actual merchant at Whydah'.

There are suggestions of sexual exploitation here, and Wilmot appears indifferent to the plight of the girls; officers' views about African women are explored further in the following chapter.

'Freedom' was a relative term in naval officers' encounters with recaptives: the process of British 'liberation' reveals a succession of circumstances in which nominal freedom for the formerly enslaved was subject to British control. Recaptives were liberated in a prescribed image, a British conception of freedom that often focused more on a demonstration of national character than a consideration of their needs. In their varied representations of prize voyages and relationships with recaptives, individual naval officers often expressed compassion and kindness. However, in the wider context of British ideas of liberty, ideas of dependency and property persisted, offering an alternative reality to the idealism of abolitionist ideology and rhetoric.

5

Encounters with Africa

A recurrent theme of this book is how slavery and the slave trade dominated the observations of naval officers. This is clearly the case in their attitudes towards recaptives, but also applies to their relationships with other African people met on shore. What follows is an examination of cultural encounters between British naval officers and West African peoples, and the role of racial attitudes and identity therein. As Philip Curtin and others have argued, supposed knowledge and prejudices about Africans and the nature of the British relationship with them served as filters through which the observations of those working or travelling in West Africa were recorded.[1] Officers offered commentary on the different manners, customs and religious beliefs they encountered, but also their ideas for African 'improvement'. To an extent, naval officers perceived West Africans through the lens of metropolitan attitudes; many observations subscribed to common racial prejudices. Others, however, were more considered, born of experience, interaction and affiliation.

Naval officers and racial stereotypes

A set of racial assumptions existed at the beginning of the nineteenth century, fed by travel literature and historical theories on racial identity, which affirmed non-European societies as inferior to those of Europe. The expanding slave trade in the eighteenth century reinforced assumptions of racial superiority as West Africa was viewed through its dependency status as supplying slave labour. Enslavement was justified with references to the older

---

1 Curtin, *Image of Africa*, pp. 479–80; P. J. Marshall and Glyndwr Williams, *The Great Map of Mankind: British Perceptions of the World in the Age of Enlightenment* (London: Dent, 1982), p. 3.

Judaic and medieval Christian association between the origins of the black man and the curse of Ham (in which Noah's grandson from Ham, Canaan, was cursed to a life of servitude).[2] Naval surgeon Robert Flockhart repeated this association in a letter from Sierra Leone in 1838. 'There is nothing of romance out here', he wrote, 'nor anything to make one poetical, although you see the descendants of Ham coming along side in canoes in their native purity.'[3] Expressions of an ethnocentrically based dislike of the African's physical appearance were fed by moral judgement, as blackness was often associated with heathenism and bestiality. West Africans were portrayed as brutish and deviant; black skin was taken as a natural sign of inferiority, alongside other physical features such as thick lips or a protruding jaw.[4]

Published travel accounts of West Africa proliferated in the eighteenth and nineteenth centuries, many focusing on shocking or titillating features of African life. For example, the slave trader William Snelgrave published an account of the conquest of Dahomey in 1727, filling his narrative with stories of human sacrifice and cannibalism; his justification for the slave trade lay with his claim that Africans enjoyed a better standard of living when removed from Africa.[5] Implicit throughout early travel narratives was the assumption that West Africans were at an early stage of social existence, out of which they had the potential to rise, but only through the imitation of European standards and behaviour.[6] Hence slave traders and plantation owners such as Edward Long could represent black people as only suited for subservience. Pro-slavery activists promoted images of bloodshed and savagery in West Africa, based on supposedly eyewitness accounts, such as Robert Norris's *Memoirs of the Reign of Bossa Ahadee, King of Dahomey* (1789) and Archibald Dalzel's *The History of Dahomey* (1793), in which the colonial encounter in West Africa was staged as civilized European values constantly under threat from African 'anarchy'.[7]

2 Lorimer, *Colour, Class*, p. 21. See Davis, *The Problem of Slavery*, ch. 3, on the ancient legacy of slavery.

3 NRS, GD 76/458, Flockhart letters, 12 December 1838.

4 David Bindman, *Ape to Apollo: Aesthetics and the Idea of Race in the 18th Century* (Ithaca, NY: Cornell University Press, 2002), p. 32; Nancy Stepan, *The Idea of Race in Science: Great Britain 1800–1960* (Basingstoke: Macmillan, 1982), pp. xii, 8.

5 Roxann Wheeler, 'Limited visions of Africa: geographies of savagery and civility in early eighteenth-century narratives', in James Duncan and Derek Gregory (eds), *Writes of Passage: Reading Travel Writing* (London: Routledge, 1999), pp. 14–44; Marshall and Williams, *Great Map*, pp. 231, 233.

6 Marshall and Williams, *Great Map*, p. 37. Such perceptions were informed by Enlightenment theories of stadial history, which divided the history of societies into successive stages defined by the nature of subsistence.

7 Ralph A. Austen and Woodruff D. Smith, 'Images of Africa and British slave-trade

Eighteenth-century attitudes towards race were flexible to a degree. By mid-century several thousand black people – former slaves, seamen, servants, musicians, performers etc. – lived in Britain, and especially in London.[8] The counter-discourse of the noble 'savage' represented a significant challenge to the bestial stereotype, shaping the image of the slave in the sentimental literature of the period. Indeed, some black people, notably Ignatius Sancho and Olaudah Equiano, gained a kind of celebrity status in English society due to their influential position in the abolitionist movement.[9] Nor was all travel writing on West Africa offensive. The objectives and aims of the Association for Promoting the Discovery of the Interior Parts of Africa (founded 1788) and its explorers, and particularly Mungo Park (who journeyed to the Niger in 1795–97), can be regarded as part of a process of reimagining the African interior from the late eighteenth century.[10] Park wrote sympathetically that, 'whatever difference there is between the Negro and European, in the conformation of the nose and the colour of the skin, there is none in the genuine sympathies and characteristic feelings of our common nature'.[11] Works of social observation such as Thomas Bowdich's *Mission from Cape Coast Castle to Ashantee* (1819) continued the theme of dispassionate writing in relation to West Africa.[12]

Naval officers added their observations to this body of commentaries on West Africa. As David Lambert has argued, from the beginning of the nineteenth century new conceptions of exploration and geography were 'concurrent and connected' with histories of abolition and the anti-slavery mission. Officers contributed to an outpouring of accounts of Africa

abolition: the transition to an imperialist ideology, 1787–1807', *African Historical Studies*, 2.1 (1969), pp. 77–79; Curtin, *Image of Africa*, pp. 43–45. In his *History of Jamaica* (1774), Edward Long argued that the mental and moral character of Africans made them nearer to animals than to men.

8 Norma Myers, *Reconstructing the Black Past: Blacks in Britain, c. 1780–1830* (London: Frank Cass, 1996); David Olusoga, *Black and British: A Forgotten History* (Basingstoke: Pan Macmillan, 2016). In *The African Link: British Attitudes to the Negro in the Era of the Atlantic Slave Trade, 1550–1807* (London: Frank Cass, 1978), pp. 23–24, Anthony Barker has argued that before the 1770s, black people were often judged as inferior due to cultural attributes and traditional associations in Christianity rather than theories of innate racial inferiority.

9 Patrick Brantlinger, *Rule of Darkness: British Literature and Imperialism, 1830–1914* (Ithaca, NY: Cornell University Press, 1988), pp. 175–77.

10 Curtin, *Image of Africa*, p. 207; Mary Louise Pratt, *Imperial Eyes: Travel Writing and Transculturation* (London: Routledge, 1992), ch. 4.

11 Quoted in Marshall and Williams, *Great Map*, pp. 253–54.

12 Brantlinger, 'Victorians and Africans', p. 173.

and Africans which merged topographical and ethnological description with moral debates about humanitarianism.[13] Considering their frequent interactions with African peoples, naval officers were well placed to make observations. There were regular meetings at sea with African tradesmen to purchase food and stocks, or with 'women mammies' who 'came on board seeking washing'.[14] Meetings occurred in coastal settlements where officers engaged in information gathering, and 'palavers' to negotiate anti-slavery treaties with African rulers often took place on board Royal Navy vessels. William Petty Ashcroft described such a gathering in his published memoirs:

> Sometimes we would have three or four black kings on board a day, signing Treaties ... They would come off in their state canoes, some with more than forty paddles, with tom-toms beating. Each was given a Purser's No. 2 jacket with a crown and anchor badge sewn on the left breast. They were served with a bottle of rum and biscuits.[15]

But not all contact was so well-mannered, particularly when men left their ships to pursue negotiations or investigate slave trading on shore. Here naval officers often relied on a language of physical difference to describe African peoples. Early nineteenth-century sensibilities were affronted by African dress or nudity, associated with excessive physicality, immodesty and promiscuity, although as Marcus Wood has argued, a sense of voyeurism may have been just as influential.[16] The popular representations of degenerate Africans from travel literature undoubtedly influenced preconceptions, as did a fear of the unknown. Midshipman Cheesman Henry Binstead was deployed on anti-slave-trade patrols in the Cazamanza River in 1823. In his journals he described an encounter with 'ten savage looking natives' who 'told our guide that white man no good for always Roast Black Negroes and if we attempted to land at the town the Chief would murder us all'.[17] A later encounter with an inhabitant of Fernando Po revealed animalistic and fear-inducing stereotypes. Binstead was 'doubtful whether it was a human

13 Lambert, 'Taken captive', pp. 63–64.

14 NLS, MS 24633, M'Kie memoirs, ff. 54–56.

15 William Petty Ashcroft, 'Reminiscences', serialized in *The Naval Review*, part V, 53.1 (1965), p. 62. A sketch by J. T. C. Webb, c. 1850 (held by the National Maritime Museum) depicts West African chiefs on board a naval vessel, presumably as part of negotiations. See Hamilton and Blyth (eds), *Representing Slavery*, p. 240.

16 Marcus Wood, *Slavery, Empathy and Pornography* (Oxford: Oxford University Press, 2002).

17 NMRN, 2005.76/1, Binstead diaries, 5–6 March 1823. The belief that Europeans roasted and ate Africans was common among captives on slave ships.

being from its strange colour and appearance'. He termed people of the island 'a horrid wild set of savages'.[18]

Scholarship regarding British encounters with indigenous populations in the empire reveals that observations regarding Africans as fearful and debased applied to many non-European 'others'.[19] But other racial stereotypes were more particular to relations with West Africans and closely interlinked with the broader themes of the British anti-slavery cause, particularly the drive for 'civilization'. A common image of the African in the early nineteenth century – exemplified by the abolitionist medallion produced by Josiah Wedgwood – was as the suffering and respectable victim of slavery. For British abolitionists, the existence of slavery offered a symbolic test of national virtue, expressed in ideologies of benevolent paternalism, where those of 'superior' feelings were regarded as duty bound to help the less fortunate.[20] The moralizing tone of *West African Sketches*, compiled from reports written by Commodore George Collier and others, set out that the African character was 'certainly not beyond the power of habit and education to model and assimilate' through 'fostering care' from Britons.[21] Missionary activity in Sierra Leone exemplified the value of British influence in, according to Collier, 'protecting the untutored and ignorant African, and giving the most patient consideration to his most minute grievances and wants'.[22] The motives behind Thomas Fowell Buxton's Niger Expedition in 1841 were certainly presented in philanthropic terms. However, in their attempts to gain support for the conversion of West Africans, missionary groups produced propaganda which encouraged stereotypes based on racial difference. As a result, cultural divides between Europeans and Africans could transform a sense of moral and spiritual responsibility into ideas of racial superiority; a passion to improve other peoples distorted into 'cultural aggression'.[23]

Among naval officers, examples of perceived savagery were used to support the need for European influence.[24] In his surveying remarks of 1832, assistant surgeon D. G. Miller of the *Aetna* regarded the Kanyabac people of the

18 NMRN, 2005.76/2, Binstead diaries, 9 June 1823.

19 C. A. Bayly, 'The British and indigenous peoples, 1760–1860: power, perception and identity', in Daunton and Halpern (eds), *Empire and Others*, pp. 19–41.

20 Quirk and Richardson, 'Anti-slavery', pp. 87–88.

21 *West African Sketches*, pp. 3, 22.

22 MoD, MSS 45, 'Second Annual Report', f. 49.

23 Lorimer, *Colour, Class*, pp. 75–77; Christine Bolt, *Victorian Attitudes to Race* (London: Routledge, 1971), pp. 111–12; McCaskie, 'Cultural encounters', p. 673.

24 See, for example, William Fitzwilliam Owen's perceptions of the depravity and pagan culture of Chaka, King of Natal, in his *Narrative of Voyages*, p. 389.

River Grande in Guinea as 'morally isolated from the rest of mankind' and therefore incapable of 'emerging from their low and barbarous condition':

> Unfortunately their intellectual faculties are applied to objects which tend rather to alienate the mind from moral improvement ... love of contention & bloodshed, and a most inveterate spirit of revenge and retaliation, however trivial the cause of offence, are the principal sources of their feelings & passions.[25]

Those Africans regarded as 'civilized' by naval officers had often been exposed to Western culture. In letters, naval surgeon Dr McIlroy discussed the eldest son of a Loango ruler who had spent time in the United States, where he 'was put to school where he learnt to read and write'. McIlroy demonstrated the cultural arrogance that was prevalent among travellers to West Africa when he declared that, consequently, 'he was a very superior person to any of the natives in this part of the world, who are in the lowest grade of civilization'.[26] Evidence of wilful or lazy behaviour was understood in terms of African people requiring guidance and a master. As Captain William Allen wrote in his published account of the Niger expedition, white races were 'compelled to exertion' while 'with the negro, on the contrary, his climate superinduces a repugnance to exertion; he places his whole happiness in the idea of repose'.[27] In this context, officers also wrote in a patronizing manner about the perceived infantile nature of African peoples. Midshipman Rogers's account of his meeting with King Madora in the River Congo was imbued with paternalism, as he wrote, 'the king insisted on my sitting on his stool ... while I was visiting him, I was the old man and he was the little boy'.[28]

Analysis of these narratives must consider their intended readership. Letters written home often placed emphasis on aspects of African life considered most repellent – cannibalism or human sacrifice, for example – to stress the author's heroism and daring. As Midshipman Augustus Arkwright wrote to his grandfather from the schooner *Prompt* in 1842, 'I certainly have seen

---

25 UKHO, MP 90/Ca6, D. G. Miller, 'Remarks on some parts of the West Coast of Africa', 1832, ff. 34–36.

26 NMM, LBK/41, McIlroy letters, 2 July 1842.

27 Allen and Thomson, *A Narrative of the Expedition*, vol. 2, p. 420. The tradition of ecological determinism, whereby tropical climates were said to induce laziness, had a long history in shaping how Europeans described the work ethic of Africans. This theme is particularly prominent in literature from slave plantations in the Americas. For example, see Douglas Hamilton, 'Slave life in the Caribbean', in Hamilton and Blyth (eds), *Representing Slavery*, p. 56.

28 Private collection, Rogers journal, 17 April 1850.

a great deal of life amongst savages', including 'beating off cannibals when attacked by them'.[29] Some of the most sensationalist, and outwardly racist, narratives were often found in published naval reminiscences of suppression. Following the tradition of contemporary travel literature, authors often wrote of their encounters with Africans for amusement, for shock value, and to generate sales.[30] Naval surgeon Peter Leonard was particularly racist in his account of African peoples. He portrayed children in Freetown as 'naked, woolly-headed sable cherubs', describing how he watched them 'scratching up the mud, and wallowing in it like as many black suckling pigs'.[31] There were, however, significant variations in officers' representations of African peoples, and others wrote with more neutrality and sensitivity.

Positive observations

Many naval officers took time to write positively about the different African peoples they met. This was particularly the case with West African seamen, notably the Kru (also known as Kroo or Krew), originating from the coast northward of Cape Palmas, who were employed to assist on HM vessels with navigation, interpreting, transporting men between ship and shore, and other subservient positions.[32] Black men had for many years played a significant part in Britain's maritime world, particularly in the multiracial crews of British slave ships in the eighteenth century.[33] The number of black sailors in English port towns was significant enough in 1816 for the African Institution to apply for provision and maintenance charges to be made for those 'lately discharged from his Majesty's ships ... to take care of them till they can safely be sent back to Africa'.[34] Favourable accounts of Kru as outstanding seafarers and as personifying strength and reliability are common. Commander James Dacres of the sloop *Nimrod* wrote that Krumen 'will be found of most inestimable service in watering, wooding, and all duties not requiring seamanship'. He found them 'a hard working

---

29 DRO, D5991/10/74, Augustus Arkwright to his grandfather, 7 November 1842.

30 Curtin, *Image of Africa*, p. 324. For example, F. Harrison Rankin's *The White Man's Grave: A Visit to Sierra Leone in 1834* was widely read in the 1830s. Rankin gave an impression of Africans as an amusing but childlike people.

31 Leonard, *Records of a Voyage*, pp. 48–51.

32 John Rankin, 'Nineteenth-century Royal Navy sailors from Africa and the African diaspora: research methodology', *African Diaspora*, 6 (2013), pp. 179–95; Burroughs, '[T]he true sailors', pp. 51–67.

33 Christopher, *Slave Ship Sailors*, ch. 2. Costello, *Black Salt*, traces the history of seafarers of African descent over several centuries. In *Colonial Naval Culture*, Daniel Spence challenges the perceived 'whiteness' of the Royal Navy in later colonial contexts.

34 *Tenth Report of the Directors of the African Institution* (1816), p. 37.

and well behaved set'.[35] Due to their perceived masculinity and physical strength, Kru were employed in British settlements 'performing domestic duties, and acting as body-guard ... being looked upon with dread by the other natives'.[36]

Krumen were regarded as an integral part of the ship's crew, and were given generic names – 'Seabreeze, Tom Piston, Jack Galley, John Rudder' – or named with royal connections such as 'King George' or 'Prince of Wales'.[37] The alleged loyalty of the Kru and their quasi-British identification, often termed the 'Irishmen' or 'Scotchmen of Africa', seemingly secured their place on board.[38] They were also valued for their theatrical and musical talents. Commander Thomas Boteler alluded to amiable relations on board the *Hecla* as the Kru performed 'a theatrical representation' of a 'bush fight' for the ship's crew:

> On taking a prisoner a consultation was held as to what they should do with him, when after a most safe and mature deliberation, it was determined not to give offence to their friends the English by selling him as a slave ... they sentenced him to have his throat cut, which was accordingly with all due form, gravity & dispatch immediately performed. Johnny Krooman fully understands flattery ... an English audience turned the scale.[39]

Commodore George Collier wrote extensively about the Kru in his reports to the Admiralty, declaring them 'in all respects so superior to every class of the natives of Africa', and 'much attached to the naval service of Great Britain'. As Boteler noted, the Kru were admired for their abstinence from slave trading. Collier believed that exposure to European culture elevated the Kru from the savagery that characterized other African peoples: '[t]he wealth or riches, the krew people acquire by their constant intercourse with the English, unfits them however in some degree for the savage life of their neighbours north and south'.[40] Officers' good relations with the Kru earned them consideration. In 1830, Commodore John Hayes learned that several Krumen at Sierra Leone were owed a proportion of the bounty awarded for captured slavers. In their defence he wrote to the Admiralty Secretary: 'it appears that those poor creatures have been used

35 UKHO, CRB 1846, remark book of James Dacres, 1845–46, f. 5.
36 MoD, MSS 151, Bedford diaries.
37 NLS, MS 24633, M'Kie memoirs, ff. 54–56.
38 Burroughs, '[T]he true sailors'.
39 MoD, MSS 73/1, Boteler journal, ff. 20–22; Costello, *Black Salt*, pp. 44–46.
40 NMM, WEL/10, 'Report of the Forts'; MoD, MSS 45, 'Second Annual Report', ff. 120–21, 137–38.

for many years to do all the <u>deadly</u> work of the Squadron, and there can be no doubt of their labours having saved many valuable European lives'.[41] An engraved powder horn (used for carrying gunpowder) belonging to 'Ben Freeman' describes the seaman as 'A Sober Honest Man [who] has sailed in HM Ship *Thais* from Sierra Leone to Ambriz to the satisfaction of the officers'. Ben Freeman was one of four African seamen taken on board the *Thais*, active on the squadron in 1812–13. They were not, however, treated as equals and while on board received only two-thirds allowance.[42] The status of the Kru as surrogate Britons was also limited by the presence of a master–servant relationship. Collier wrote that the Kru were often treated in a severe way to 'insure their faithful services'.[43]

Positive observations of African peoples extended to encounters on shore. Officers often offered affirmative sentiments with surprise, suggesting that their preconceptions of Africans were challenged by those they met. Attempts to make distinctions between different African societies were related to the surveying roles of the nineteenth-century navy in West Africa. Alongside traditional topographical aims, naval surveys also set out to increase knowledge of indigenous peoples, and frequently offered commentary on the slave trade and its suppression.[44] Assistant surgeon D. G. Miller travelled the West African coast in the surveying vessel *Aetna* between 1830 and 1832 and took care in his reports to distinguish the different peoples he encountered. He declared 'the aborigines up the [River] Nunez' as 'a mild inoffensive race; their countenances are open and regular, expressive of ingenuousness and benignity'.[45] The Foulahs, a largely Muslim people who traded in slaves and other goods from the African interior, were described by Miller with respect as 'intrepid, cool, and indefatigable, and at the same time acute and ingenious'.[46] Such a favourable portrayal was repeated by Captain Edward Belcher of the same vessel. He declared the Foulahs 'a shrewd intelligent people' who were said to 'possess great bravery

41 TNA, ADM 1/1, Commodore Hayes to J. W. Croker, 4 December 1830, ff. 177–80. Hayes's emphasis.

42 Powder horn held by the National Maritime Museum (ZBA2465); see Hamilton and Blyth (eds), *Representing Slavery*, p. 172. The National Museum of the Royal Navy holds an inscribed scrimshaw (carved or etched bones traditionally created by whalers) belonging to 'Jim Freeman, Head Krouman of HMS Sybille Comdre [Francis] Collier 1827 ... [and] HMS Owen Glendower Sir Robert Mends Comdre 1823'.

43 MoD, MSS 45, 'Second Annual Report', ff. 128–29.

44 Bayly, 'British and indigenous peoples', p. 32.

45 TNA, ADM 105/92, D. G. Miller, 'Remarks on some parts of the West Coast of Africa, in 1830 & 1831', ff. 16–18.

46 TNA, ADM 105/92, Miller, 'Remarks', f. 15. See Curtin, *Image of Africa*, p. 156, n. 15, for the confusion over the terminology of these people.

and perseverance, and to be inured to hard labour'.[47] In a similar way to the Kru, the Foulahs were admired for masculine characteristics of strength, bravery and intelligence, and although slave traders, were respected for their hard-working nature.

Commander B. Marwood Kelly of the surveying vessel *Pheasant* visited Fernando Po in 1823. The island was a popular point of reference for naval officers on the squadron; bases were leased there, and naval vessels stopped frequently for supplies. In his report to the Admiralty, Kelly described the locals of the island, called Bubi, with impartiality: 'the eye is quick and piercing, and upon the whole their countenances bespeak good humour and kindness'.[48] Kelly's narrative provides an informative counterpoint to the views of some of his contemporaries, such as Midshipman Binstead, or Lieutenant George Courtenay, who described 'vile stinking carcases smeared with palm oil and clay'.[49] In a desire to learn more about the Bubi character, Kelly gained their confidence by 'allowing them to examine the surface of the skin of my hands, legs & bosom, which they did with great curiosity'. He concluded, 'upon the whole I think them an extremely unoffensive, cheerful people; neither cruel, treacherous, nor revengeful'. Importantly, Kelly believed them superior to other African races because, like the Kru, 'Slavery, that curse of the human race, is perfectly unknown among them.'[50]

Officers' perceptions were influenced by a variety of social and cultural conditions which affected racial attitudes, as explored later in this chapter. Personal interactions also played a part in forming opinions. In his published account of his service, Commander Henry James Matson defended African peoples against popular stereotypes:

An African chief is not, as is generally supposed in this country, a kind of 'King of the Cannibal Islands', delighting in human sacrifices, and all that sort of thing; he is, generally speaking, a humane, shrewd and intelligent man. I have visited King Boy in the Nun, King Peppel in the Bonny, Duke Ephraim in the Old Calabar and the Chief of Benin, whose name I forget; and I could but admire, in most cases, the propriety of their conduct.[51]

47 Captain Belcher, 'Extracts from Observations on Various Points of the West Coast of Africa, Surveyed by His Majesty's Ship *Aetna* in 1830–32', *Journal of the Royal Geographical Society of London*, 2 (1832), p. 283.
48 UKHO, MP 107, 'A Survey of a Bay in the Island of Fernando Po, together with remarks on the NW Coast of that island by Commander B. Marwood Kelly', no folios.
49 UIC: SLC, Series V, Folder 16, Courtenay journal, no folios. Their primitive appearance, in officers' eyes, was attributable to a thick layer of clay that covered their bodies. See Brown, 'Fernando Po', p. 255.
50 UKHO, MP 107, 'A Survey of a Bay'.
51 Matson, *Remarks on the Slave Trade*, p. 48.

Describing a dinner with one king, Matson remarked that 'we sat down like men, and not like monkeys'.[52] Commander John Tudor of the *Firefly* reported the following favourable impressions of the African character to the Admiralty in 1850:

> I should say that they are fully as quick, and intelligent as any Europeans I have ever met with, and I do not hesitate to say Sir that should at the Great Industrial Meeting of 1857 specimens of mankind be exhibited the sons of Africa for quickness, intelligence and all the better feelings of the heart would in no way be behind the sons of Europe.[53]

The West Africans that Tudor had met in his two years on the squadron had clearly influenced his views. His opinion that Europeans and Africans were equal in some respects was fair and tolerant, although the assumption that Africans might be publicly 'exhibited' serves as a reminder of the hierarchy of nations and races in this period.[54] Many encounters between officers and Africans were little more than observational: fear, prejudice or indifference may have prevented meaningful interaction. Other officers appeared genuinely interested in the different African cultures they encountered.

Engagement with African cultures

While West African societies differed considerably along the coast, nineteenth-century cultural exchanges between naval officers and African peoples were particularly influenced by practices and ways of life regarded by Europeans as irrefutably 'African'. For instance, it was a commonly held opinion that African people were, in the words of one naval officer, 'slaves to the grossest superstitions'.[55] This tied with the Enlightenment belief that humankind had progressed from barbarism in part due to freedom from superstitious forms of religion, seen to lack morality and humanity and create a 'kingdom of darkness', in Thomas Fowell Buxton's words.[56] Naval

52 Matson, *Remarks on the Slave Trade*, pp. 48–49.

53 TNA, ADM 123/173, 'Best means', reply of John Tudor, 12 July 1850.

54 Sadiah Qureshi, *Peoples on Parade: Exhibitions, Empire, and Anthropology in Nineteenth-Century Britain* (Chicago: University of Chicago Press, 2011), examines the popularity and profitability of the public exhibition of foreign peoples in the nineteenth century.

55 NMM, AGC/N/33, Cornelius T. A. Noddall, Master of HMS *Wolverine*, 'A short account of the presentation of a gold medal from Queen Victoria to a native chief …', f. 14.

56 Ali Rattansi, *Racism: A Very Short Introduction* (Oxford: Oxford University Press, 2007), pp. 24–25. Buxton quoted in Brantlinger, 'Victorians and Africans', pp. 173–74.

accounts reflected the messages of the missionary cause, in which 'humanity and pity must be strongly excited' by the 'distress and moral turpitude which superstition and its concomitants occasion'.[57] Nineteenth-century missionary propaganda stressed the polarizing cultural barriers between Christianity and indigenous 'heathen' religions which were seen to encourage cruelty and domination. Examples commonly cited from other areas of the world included polygamy among Native Americans, the killing of twins in Nigeria, Chinese foot-binding or cannibalism in New Guinea.[58] British travellers in West Africa rarely made attempts to understand African cultures, and to an extent naval officers can be included in this generalization: there was little need for them to acknowledge the place of religious deities in African life.[59] Naval officers were cautious about the potentially dangerous influence of West African traditions, regarding the worship of idols, or 'fetishes', as a curiosity, but also as an example of barbarism. For example, George Courtenay condemned the veneration of the alligator by the local population of Dix Cove in Ghana, 'so much so that a mother would rejoice to see her child devoured by one of these voracious animals'.[60] Courtenay denounced such rituals as an example of immorality.

One officer who expressed an interest in the veneration of religious curiosities was Captain John Proctor Luce, Senior Officer in the Bights in the early 1860s. Luce accompanied Commodore Arthur Eardley-Wilmot to Abomey to negotiate terms of abolition with the King of Dahomey in 1862–63. In his journal of the mission, Luce engaged in long descriptive passages on the nature of the religious 'fetishes' he witnessed. For example:

> we observed about 20 priests & priestesses – they were bare to the waist but had handsome fetish country cloths from waist to knee. There were a few small flags about the trees & a couple of small mats with sacrificed cocks hanging against them. The priests and priestesses four abreast were dancing & singing round the place.

While clearly baffled by such practices, Luce offered few judgements. He also attempted analysis of their place in African life, remarking that 'some of the fetish figures here are rather indelicate which strikes me as singular because the people are remarkably decent in their personal appearance &

---

57 *West African Sketches*, p. 24.

58 Hugh McLeod, 'Protestantism and British national identity, 1815–1945', in Peter van der Veer and Hartmut Lehmann (eds), *Nation and Religion: Perspectives on Europe and Asia* (Princeton, NJ: Princeton University Press, 1999), pp. 44–70, at p. 47; Bayly, 'British and indigenous peoples', p. 33.

59 Temperley, *White Dreams*, pp. 81–82; Davis, *Problem of Slavery*, pp. 501–02.

60 UIC: SLC, Series V, Folder 16, Courtenay journal.

7 Portrait of J. P. Luce, taken Melbourne 1865, unknown photographer

habits'.[61] Officers expressed more concern about the practice of 'customs' – religious celebrations given by an African ruler for his subjects – which often involved human sacrifice. Anti-slavery treaties increasingly included stipulations for the abolition of the practice, regarded as 'fostered by the ignorance and superstition of the "fetish" priests'.[62] Lieutenant Frederick Forbes visited the King of Dahomey in 1850 and witnessed the 'horrible and ridiculous' annual customs financed by the king's 'slave-hunt' in a neighbouring country. In his published journal he declared 'what follows is almost too revolting to be recorded':

> the mob now armed with clubs and branches, yelled furiously, calling upon the King to 'feed them – they were hungry' ... a demoniac yelling caused us to look back. The King was showing the immolations to his people ... a descent of twelve feet stunned the victim, and before animation could return, the head was off; the body, beaten by the mob, was dragged by the heels to a pit at a little distance, and there left a prey to wolves and vultures.

Forbes's description of the display in the king's palace of 'six newly-cut-off human heads ... the blood still oozing', as a demonstration of the king's authority, echoed the travel writing of Archibald Dalzel and others of the previous century.[63] The publication of such shocking content – 'the first description ever given to the world' – may be regarded as evidence of Forbes's desire to gain fame and respect for the account of his travels.[64] However, Forbes was notable in offering little judgement in his accounts of West Africa and its peoples; his tone was largely neutral, and he wrote about African religions and beliefs with genuine interest and curiosity, rather than in explicitly racist terms. He certainly wrestled with his disgust at the exhibition of violence and bloodshed, which sat uncomfortably with his respect for other elements of West African societies. 'Many of their customs

---

61 RAI, MS 280, Luce journals, vol. 4, ff. 46–48, 169.

62 Wilmot, 'Despatches', p. 11.

63 Frederick Forbes to Commodore Fanshawe, 5 November 1849; journal of Lieutenant Forbes, 25, 30, 31 May 1850, in Coates (ed.), *King Guezo*, pp. 35, 53, 60, 64–66. See also Captain Henry Huntley's dramatic descriptions of 'native customs' in his *Seven Years' Service on the Slave Coast of Western Africa*, 2 vols (London: Thomas Cautley Newby), for example, vol. 1, pp. 396–99.

64 Forbes, *Dahomey and the Dahomans*, p. 6. Forbes had also previously published *Five Years in China; from 1842 to 1847* (1848), an account of his service there. His memoirs were read by others on the squadron: in 1862 Captain Luce noted that the explorer Richard Burton had given him a copy of *Dahomey and the Dahomans* to read (RAI, Luce journals, vol. 3, f. 207).

are strangely at variance with the horrors of others', he wrote about the Dahomans. 'The forms and ceremonies of polite society contrast oddly with the sacrifices of their unoffending prisoners of war.'[65] Furthermore, Forbes offered unusual insight into other causes of 'immoral' behaviour, rather than relying solely on the innate character of African peoples:

> Most travellers are forcibly struck with the rapid improvement in morality, which, in barbarous equally with civilised countries, characterises the interior of the country as compared with its seaports ... the habits of seafaring men of all nations and classes in the main tend to demoralise the society into which for a time chance throws them ... idolatrous though they be, and barbarous in the extreme, the people of the interior are generally far more moral than the semi-civilised and nominally Christianised inhabitants of the sea coasts.[66]

Like Forbes, Captain Luce wrote with disgust about the human sacrifices he witnessed, although also with a fascinated interest in the sensationalism of the event. While Commodore Wilmot was 'made fierce' in explaining to their Dahoman hosts that it was 'feelings of humanity ... that made such spectacles distasteful to the English', Luce appeared captivated, describing how he and Dr Haran (also accompanying the mission) 'nerved ourselves to look steadily & calmly at all that might happen'. Luce watched as a victim had his head removed, 'sawed, hewed & hacked' with 'dreadful clumsiness'. He made an additional note in his journal's margin, describing this as 'butcher's work' and 'horrible'. Luce then recorded the 'savage mutilations' as 'two other savages rushed in & cut pieces off the buttock & hips & heart – the hands were also hacked off & with the pieces, were stuck on sticks & carried about in triumph'. Seemingly enthralled by the violence and unruliness of the king, his warriors and the excitement of the crowd, Luce portrayed the scene as 'very wild & striking'.[67]

Captain Luce and Commodore Wilmot also wrote with a degree of affection for the Dahomans they stayed with on the mission, supporting the idea that those officers who spent time on shore were more inclined to view the Africans they met sympathetically. On expeditions and anti-slavery missions, naval officers were dependent on their hosts for subsistence and safety. They were also reliant on multilingual African intermediaries such as Samuel Ajayi Crowther, William Pascoe (a former slave who

65 Forbes, *Dahomey and the Dahomans*, p. 2.

66 Forbes, *Dahomey and the Dahomans*, p. 5. This was also an argument of eighteenth-century abolitionists, who asserted that the slave trade had degraded coastal societies (Curtin, *Image of Africa*, p. 255).

67 RAI, MS 280, Luce journals, vol. 4, ff. 110, 120–29.

accompanied Captain Hugh Clapperton and other British expeditions in the 1820s and 1830s), or the African missionary Peter Bernasko, who assisted Commodore Wilmot on his expedition.[68] In a long and detailed journal of his trip, Luce detailed the stops on the journey, the many processions and displays witnessed and presents given and received. He also revealed respect for his hosts: when invited, he and the Commodore 'performed a very respectable war dance', for which the 'applause was tremendous'. They also participated in athletic races with the Dahomans; Luce recorded how 'all this caused a good laugh', dispelling the notion that all encounters with Africans were based on fear and stereotype.[69] Wilmot reported that 'at all the villages where we slept, comfortable quarters had been provided, and water furnished. Nothing could exceed the civility of every one.' In setting out his intentions behind the mission, Wilmot tied notions of British identity and moral character to ideas of racial tolerance and sympathy. 'My policy was to be friendly with every one', he wrote, 'and endeavour to show the character and disposition of an Englishman towards the nations of this country – that we could treat them with forbearance, and have some sympathy with a black man!'[70] The Revd Peter Bernasko wrote to Wilmot after the expedition to inform him that the people of Dahomey 'love you very much with their heart. From the least to the greatest all cry out for to see your lovely, masterly and fatherly face.'[71] However, the practice of human sacrifice remained incompatible with British ideals. Wilmot acknowledged that in a country where 'war, war, war is alone thought of', such customs were too powerful to be surrendered.[72]

An eagerness to learn and explore other elements of different African cultures is evident in officers' narratives. For example, several officers made attempts to communicate and study local languages. George Augustus Bedford, on surveying work on the *Raven* in the 1830s, described how in the River Gallinas he 'became such good friends with the natives' and took time to learn local words from the 'village school master': 'I did much in this way by figuring the shape of objects, such as the moon, stars &c upon the ground, or in my book.' He included in his diaries 'a list of native words, spelt so as to represent the sounds as close as I could imitate them, with their English meaning attached'.[73] Lieutenant Frederick Forbes

---

68 Kennedy, *The Last Blank Spaces*, pp. 168–69.

69 RAI, MS 280, Luce journals, vol. 4, ff. 38–39, 87–88.

70 Wilmot, 'Despatches', pp. 2, 4–5, 12–13.

71 DUL, WYL/26/68, translation of letter from Peter Bernasko at Whydah to Commodore Wilmot, 27 November 1863.

72 Wilmot, 'Despatches', pp. 2, 4–5, 12–13.

73 MoD, MSS 151, Bedford diaries. Similarly, assistant surgeon D. G. Miller included

believed he had made a 'discovery of such importance to the civilization of Africa' in his rediscovery of the vocabulary of the 'Vahie' or Vei language at Bohmar, near Liberia. He wrote to the secretary of the British Museum in 1849 to acquaint him with 'an alphabetical arrangement of the characters of a phonetic African language discovered by me a few months since and acknowledged by all in Sierra Leone & Liberia to be a novelty'. It is likely that Forbes sought fame and notability for his linguistic discoveries, although he was also 'anxious my own profession should bear the honour that it may deserve'.[74] Accompanying correspondence suggests that Forbes's discovery led to a subsequent expedition by the missionary the Revd Sigismund Koelle, who discussed the vocabulary in depth in his *Polyglotta Africana* (1854).[75]

Attempts to facilitate conversations and gather knowledge were part of a wider tradition of cultural exchange in West Africa in this period, emanating from the work of missionaries and explorers.[76] Naval surgeon William Balfour Baikie became heavily immersed in local life during his posting as unofficial British consul at Lokoja (at the confluence of the Niger and Benue rivers). He married an African woman, mastered the Hausa and Fuldi languages, and translated parts of the Bible and prayer book.[77] Other officers engaged with the objectives of the Royal Geographical Society, founded in 1830 to promote geographical science. Captain John Washington was a founder member and appointed secretary in 1836. Washington took up the cause of Mohammedu-Siseï, an African Muslim living in Britain in the late 1830s. Originally from the Gambia, Siseï was sold into slavery as a prisoner of war but was released by a British frigate and carried to Antigua, where he became a soldier in the West India regiment. Continuing the theme of African people perceived to be uplifted by the British example, Siseï was to return to Africa, where in Washington's words, he would

vocabulary from the peoples of the rivers Nunez and Grande in his 'Remarks' (UKHO), ff. 39–40.

74 Lieutenant F. E. Forbes, 'Despatch communicating the discovery of a Native Written Character at Bohmar, on the Western Coast of Africa, near Liberia, accompanied by a Vocabulary of the Vahie or Vei Tongue', *Journal of the Royal Geographical Society*, 20 (1850) pp. 89–113; BL, Add 17817, Frederick Forbes to the Secretary of the British Museum, [no date] January 1849. The title-page of the 1851 edition of *Dahomey and the Dahomans* identified the author as 'Discoverer of the Vahie Phonetic'.

75 Forbes, 'Despatch', p. 101. On Koelle, see https://www.bl.uk/collection-items/polyglotta-africana [accessed 20 January 2018].

76 For example, while leading the Abeokuta mission in the 1840s, Samuel Crowther translated the Bible into the Yoruba language and compiled a Yoruba–English dictionary.

77 Blake, *Religion*, p. 158. The Bible Society later published his edition of the Psalms in Hausa.

'impart to his countrymen some few of the blessings of civilisation which he may have acquired', which will 'raise their countrymen from their present degraded state'.[78]

Cultural encounters were also linked to the importance of eyewitnessing and committing to paper a memorable scene. Daily duties for some on board naval vessels included the production of topographical sketches of the seas and coastlines in journals, logbooks and inventories.[79] Commander Henry Need of HMS *Linnet* took this task further and painted the landscapes he saw and the people he met while serving on the West Africa squadron for his own personal record.[80] Officers were certainly struck by the exotic and attractive natural geography of the continent. In his letters of 1842, naval surgeon Dr McIlroy described the scenery on the River Benin as 'very extraordinary', comparable 'to some of those imaginary Fairy Islands described in the Arabian Nights'.[81] Some of the imagery produced was utilized in the anti-slavery cause. Captain William Allen was official naval observer to the Niger Expedition of 1834 under Liverpool businessman Macgregor Laird. Allen's landscape view showing the *Confluence of Rivers Niger and Tchudda* was displayed at the Royal Academy and featured in his *Picturesque Views of the River Niger Sketched During Lander's Last Visit 1832–33* (1840), published in support of Sir Thomas Fowell Buxton's Society for the Extinction of the Slave Trade. *The Friend of Africa* declared Allen's sketches as 'one of the most pleasing additions ... to our knowledge of the interior of Africa'.[82]

An interest in African cultures is also revealed in officers' collection of material objects from the West African coast. In doing so they became part of an existing network of trade and travel in this period which sourced museum specimens (such as metals or weaponry), flora, live animals and human

78 Captain Washington, 'Some Account of Mohammedu-Siseï, a Mandingo, of Nyáni-Marú on the Gambia', *Journal of the Royal Geographical Society of London*, 8 (1838), pp. 448–54. Washington later became an eminent surveyor and hydrographer.

79 See, for example, Luciana Martins and Felix Driver, 'John Septimus Roe and the art of navigation, c. 1815–30', in Tim Barringer, Douglas Fordham and Geoff Quilley (eds), *Art and the British Empire* (Manchester: Manchester University Press, 2007), pp. 53–66.

80 NMM, volume of 143 watercolours by Commander Henry Need of HMS *Linnet*, on anti-slave-trade patrols 1852–56 (ART/10). Need was acquainted with David Livingstone, and some of his pictures became incorporated into illustrations for Livingstone's *Missionary Travels* (1857) and *Narrative of an Expedition to the Zambesi* (1867). See Leila Koivunen, *Visualizing Africa in Nineteenth-century British Travel Accounts* (London: Routledge, 2009), pp. 151–52, 301.

81 NMM, LBK/41, McIlroy letters, 20 December 1841.

82 *The Friend of Africa* (1841), p. 92.

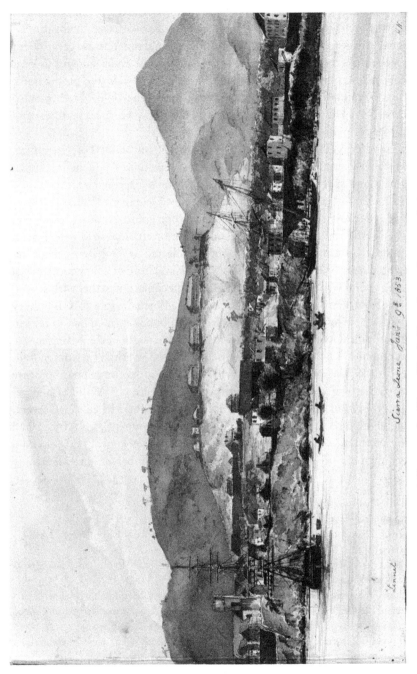

8 Commander Henry Need, *Sierra Leone, January 9th 1853*

commodities for a mass market in Victorian Britain, where exhibitions were profitable and collecting was a popular pastime.[83] Inspired by accounts of exploration, the practice of classifying, naming and drawing specimens became the concern of ordinary people as well as scientists.[84] Midshipman Augustus Arkwright noted how his cousins in England 'possess great talent in collecting Natural Curiosities'. As a result, 'I am endeavouring to pick up a few here and there. Ivory and gold are the most valuable productions: rings and chains are made by the natives from the gold.' He was also interested in specimens of 'skins of wild animals, savage creatures and musical instruments'.[85]

Commodore Wilmot sent items to William Wylde at the Foreign Office, to add to his personal 'collection of "African curiosities"', including birds, arrow-root and specimens of palm leaf from which 'excellent rope' could be derived.[86] A number of objects were collected by Lieutenant William Bent of the *Vengeance* during his service at Lagos, including gourd drinking vessels and a wooden staff.[87] Many pieces of material culture were deposited with British institutions. Commander Thomas Boteler collected several items while on surveying duty in West Africa, including a tusk and head of a hippopotamus, a tooth of a sperm whale and various geological specimens, together with several weapons from Fernando Po and Sierra Leone. Boteler wrote to Canterbury Museum, where he had recently been elected an honorary member, to inform the philosophical institution about his findings. He wrote, 'I shall ever feel the greatest interest' in the work of the museum, and hoped that 'the voyage I am about to undertake in all probability will afford many opportunities to procure other articles, worthy of being added to your collection'.[88] William Stanger sailed on the *Albert* on the Niger Expedition in 1841, where he collected several objects including a large calabash (a percussion instrument), an African idol and an ivory bracelet. Stanger was a fellow of the Geological Society and a founder member of Wisbech Museum, where a number of these items are

---

83 Qureshi, *Peoples on Parade*, p. 108.

84 Koivunen, *Visualizing Africa*, pp. 32–33.

85 DRO, D5991/10/74, Augustus Arkwright to his grandfather from Sierra Leone, 7 November 1842.

86 DUL, WYL/27/8-9, Commodore Wilmot to William Wylde, 20 March 1864; WYL/27/12, Wilmot to Wylde, 2 April 1864.

87 These items are currently held by the Royal Albert Memorial Museum & Art Gallery in Exeter. Some are mentioned in Len Pole, *Iwa L'Ewa: Yoruba and Benin Collections in the Royal Albert Memorial Museum* (Exeter Museums, 1999).

88 Thomas Boteler to Canterbury Museums, 2 January 1828. With thanks to Canterbury Literary and Philosophical Institution Museum for the information on their holdings. Boteler's *Narrative of a Voyage*, vol. II, p. 299, describes the discovery of a hippopotamus head.

now held.[89] Similarly Captain C. Bowen of HMS *Driver* donated several items to the Bristol Institution, a branch of the Philosophical & Literary Society. Its donations book for 1825 includes note of 'spears used by the natives of Fernando Po in the Bight of Biafra. Model of a canoe used by the natives of the River Camauron [*sic*] in the same Bight. The latter was a present from King Agua to the Commander of HM Ship Driver.'[90]

Some items of material culture brought back to Britain were gifts, part of the exchange of presents during meetings or treaty negotiations. Others may have been acquired in more dubious circumstances of financial interest, as the spoils of battle or taken with little concern for ownership. In their donations to institutions, there is also a sense that naval officers wished to contribute to the tradition of information gathering about other cultures, or to demonstrate the commercial potential of raw materials found in West Africa.[91] Some surviving material culture collected from the African coast is specifically connected to the slave trade, which arguably reveals officers' pride in anti-slave-trade service. For example, a hand-sewn flag from a slave ship captured by Commodore Wilmot was sent to William Wylde in the 1860s.[92] Captain Lionel de Sausmarez was engaged in the suppression of the slave trade in South East Africa in the 1870s as Senior Lieutenant of HMS *London*. He brought home chains taken from a slave-gang on the West African coast, and a slave ankle fetter 'cut from a stolen female slave'.[93]

Many naval officers articulated informed reflections about the West African societies in which they spent time. On the one hand this was part of officers' official responsibilities; on the other, personal experiences, bound

89 Wisbech and Fenland Museum holds other material of interest. A carved wooden figure was, according to the museum catalogue, 'captured by HMS *Arrogant* during the suppression of the slave trade in 1861'. The figure is thought to be an African 'fetish' from Porto Novo (the settlement was destroyed by *Arrogant* and other British vessels in 1861).

90 With thanks to Bristol City Museum and Art Gallery Ethnography Collection (where some of these items are held) for this information. Other items include an Asante stool collected 'West Coast of Africa 1827' by naval officer William Henry Brereton [or Breton]. A fellow of the Royal Geographical Society, Brereton described himself as an 'explorer and writer'. He was later employed as police magistrate in Van Diemen's Land and wrote *Excursions in New South Wales, West Australia and Van Dieman's Land during the years 1830, 1831, 1832 and 1833*.

91 Koivunen, *Visualizing Africa*, pp. 138–39.

92 The flag is held by the National Maritime Museum. See Hamilton and Blyth (eds), *Representing Slavery*, pp. 172–73.

93 With thanks to Guernsey Museum for this information from their catalogue records. Similarly, Ulster Museum holds a shell leg ornament collected from a recaptive by the Ulster traveller Gordon Augustus Thompson. Thompson was invited to cruise on the British ship HMS *Pelorus* by its Captain, Richard Meredith. The *Pelorus* captured the Spanish slaver *Segunda Theresa* in 1832.

to an engagement with African landscapes and peoples, meant that for some officers their further involvement in the British presence in West Africa was inevitable. Commodore Arthur Eardley-Wilmot was passionate about his role in the diffusion of Christianity and 'civilization' on the West African coast. Before sailing there in 1861, he wrote to Wylde about a dream he had of erecting a lighthouse at Lagos, which 'would be <u>prophetic</u> of that gospel light which is destined to spread its rays over the benighted millions of Africa'.[94] This belief in the anti-slavery cause was undoubtedly encouraged by his family connections: he was the fourth son of the colonial administrator Sir John Eardley Eardley-Wilmot, who as an MP in the 1830s and 1840s had been an active campaigner for abolition and emancipation.[95] Commodore Wilmot's belief in African potential is revealed in his involvement in the 'First Industrial Exhibition', held in Freetown in 1865. Local people were asked to exhibit agricultural and manufacturing products for sale, after an idea conceived at the Young Men's Institute in Freetown (established by the Colonial Chaplain to enable young men to 'improve themselves').[96] In the accompanying catalogue, Sierra Leone Governor Samuel Blackall summarized the links between the exhibition and the anti-slavery mission: 'If we trace the history of any nation emerging from barbarism to civili-zation', he wrote, 'we shall find that, though the first move was effected through foreign conquest or occupation, the remainder has been achieved by the people themselves.'[97] As vice-president of the Officers of the Exhibition, Wilmot 'warmly supported the idea', contributing £10 to the fund and 'promising all his assistance not only in collecting articles … but by applying to those who were considered the powerful friends of African civilization in England'. Blackall spoke of Wilmot as 'so true and generous a friend, and so liberal a contributor to all useful institutions in Africa'.[98] The Royal Navy featured prominently at the opening of the exhibition; the streets of Freetown were 'lined by blue jackets and marines' from the *Rattlesnake* and other naval vessels, alongside Sierra Leone dignitaries. A class on 'Naval Architecture and Ships' Tackle' included a model of the *Rattlesnake* and the

94 DUL, WYL/24/36, Commodore Wilmot to William Wylde, 8 November 1861. Wilmot's emphasis.

95 Peter Chapman, 'Wilmot, Sir John Eardley Eardley-, first baronet (1783–1847)', *Oxford Dictionary of National Biography*, Oxford University Press, 2004, www.oxforddnb.com/view/article/52438 [acccessed 15 March 2016].

96 *Industrial Exhibition at Sierra Leone 1865: Its History, French and British Catalogues, Appointment of Jurors, Their Reports, and Lists of Their Awards* (London: Hatchard and Co., 1866); *A Brief Statement of the Services of Vice-Admiral Eardley-Wilmot, C.B.* (Totnes, 1878), p. 14.

97 *Industrial Exhibition*, pp. 10–11.

98 *Industrial Exhibition*, pp. 1, 5, 9.

Ranger, and Wilmot won a medal for the 'best collection of ropes and ships' tackle, made chiefly from African fibres'.[99]

The exhibition was not particularly well received outside the colony, however. Not only did 'English philanthropists' regard the exhibition 'with coldness and indifference', the Admiralty, too, was unimpressed. 'The exhibition at Sierra Leone may be useful but it is not a naval affair', Wilmot was informed. While 'admitting African youths into their messes' would be 'useful in the colony', the Admiralty 'never contemplated educating young gentlemen!'[100] To a degree, then, officers' engagement with African cultures remained limited by their profession. As Frederick Forbes wrote about his linguistic discoveries, 'from the opposite nature of the duties of a naval officer, I could neither spare time, nor hope for the opportunity, of faithfully arranging a grammar or making translations'.[101]

Official duties could coexist with personal interests and concerns, however. Wilmot had ties with the Royal Geographical Society, which continued after his service on the West African coast. In 1867 he was asked to submit his opinion to the society as a reviewer of two papers on African exploration.[102] He gifted to the society a 'war fetish', seized during a clash in 1865 between sailors of the *Archer* and pirates who attacked British commercial shipping in the River Congo. Wilmot also commissioned a painting by Thomas Baines to commemorate the action.[103] His experiences in West Africa clearly had an influence on his personal interests and pursuits beyond his official capacity as a naval officer. Wilmot's self-perception as a man engaged with increasing knowledge about the African continent must have been gratified when *The Times* reported that his mission to Dahomey 'will bear a place even by the side of the more brilliant achievements of the heroes of the Nile'.[104]

---

99 *Industrial Exhibition*, pp. 7, 30, 68.

100 Governor Blackall, quoted in *Industrial Exhibition*, p. 10; DUL, WYL/27/10-11, Frederick William Grey at the Admiralty to Commodore Wilmot, 23 March 1864.

101 Forbes, 'Despatch', p. 101.

102 The papers were by R. B. Walker: 'Letters from the River Ogowé' and 'Visit to the Samba and Agoshe falls Western Equatorial Africa', both dated 7 June 1867. With thanks to the Royal Geographical Society Archive for information on their holdings.

103 The 'war fetish' is now identified as the remains of a Kongo *nkisi nkondi*. The unfinished painting is held by the Royal Geographical Society. In 'Commodore Wilmot encounters Kongo Art, 1865', *African Arts* (summer 2010), pp. 52–53, Wyatt MacGaffey argues that most of the detail of the painting 'belongs to the nineteenth century imaginary of barbaric Africa'.

104 *The Times*, 26 June 1863. This was not an opinion shared by all, however. *The Leeds Times* expressed 'amazement at the simplicity with which an Englishman … suffered himself to be hood-winked and humbugged by the bloodthirsty miscreant who now wields the sceptre of Dahomey' (27 June 1863).

African women

A further avenue for the examination of cultural encounters is the attitudes of naval officers towards African women. As social class played a part in racial classification in British society, the same was true of gender.[105] It was often claimed that a woman's inferior intellect was a result of her biology and deficient brain structure, with similarities to those of lower classes and races. The separation of women in the domestic sphere with men as household heads was regarded as essential for the maintenance of social order, and so British middle-class women were characterized by virtuousness and submissiveness.[106] In contrast, Asian and African women were regarded as 'savage' yet simultaneously exotic, and were often romanticized by early nineteenth-century explorers and travellers (the majority of whom were men). While the domestic ideal of the Western woman was integral to the civilizing mission, the perception of the sexualized 'savage' was also exciting, representing, in Joanna de Groot's words, 'the blending of conquest and enjoyment, of power and pleasure, of desire and domination'.[107]

Naval officers often positively distinguished African women from men. In part, this was perhaps influenced by an awareness of the black woman's alleged unbridled sexuality, as exemplified by the public display and sexual objectification of Sara Baartman, the 'Hottentot Venus', in Britain in 1815.[108] Several naval narratives of encounters with African women are full of appreciative comments on their exotic beauty. However, race remained an

---

105 Historians have linked the ways in which domination and subordination crossed gender, race and class in the nineteenth century. For example, Midgley, *Women against Slavery*; Anne McClintock, *Imperial Leather: Race, Gender and Sexuality in the Colonial Context* (London: Routledge, 1995); Ann Laura Stoler, *Race and the Education of Desire: Foucault's 'History of Sexuality' and the Colonial Order of Things* (Durham, NC: Duke University Press, 1995).

106 Joanna de Groot, 'Sex and race: the construction of language and image in the nineteenth century', in Susan Mendus and Jane Rendall (eds), *Sexuality and Subordination: Interdisciplinary Studies of Gender in the Nineteenth Century* (London: Routledge, 1989), pp. 89–128, at pp. 93–97; Catherine Hall, 'Going a-trolloping: imperial man travels the Empire', in Clare Midgley (ed.), *Gender and Imperialism* (Manchester: Manchester University Press, 1998), pp. 180–99, at pp. 191–92.

107 See de Groot, 'Sex and race', quoted at p. 111; Curtin, *Image of Africa*, pp. 218–19.

108 Yvette Abrahams, 'Images of Sara Bartman: sexuality, race, and gender in early-nineteenth-century Britain', in Ruth Roach Pierson and Nupur Chaudhuri (eds), *Nation, Empire, Colony: Historicizing Gender and Race* (Bloomington, IN: Indiana University Press, 1998), pp. 220–36. Baartman was brought to England by naval surgeon Alexander Dunlop, who traded as an exporter of museum specimens from the Cape of Good Hope. See Qureshi, *Peoples on Parade*, pp. 2–3, 108–09.

important qualification in their descriptions, and those women thought of most favourably often conformed to Western standards. For example, in 1826 naval surgeon Richard Jackson wrote of the women of the River Cameroon: 'their heads & necks would bear a comparison (remove but their sable complexion) with many of our English Beauties, having high & commanding foreheads, sparkling & expressive eyes, lips not overthick, and teeth that would rival the pearl in whiteness'.[109] For Jackson, thick lips and dark skin were signs that detracted from physical beauty, although he remained charmed by the females' exoticism. In 1858 an unidentified naval officer wrote of 'Mrs Lightburne' of Falengia in similar terms. 'Her colour, although very dark, had a depth and richness that cannot be understood by those who have never seen an African beauty', he wrote, 'her hands and feet would be a study for the most imaginative sculptor.'[110] Commander Henry Need of the *Linnet* made several sketches of the women he met on the West African coast and appeared to be similarly enamoured.[111]

Naval men spent years away from their wives and families while serving at sea, and if inclined, sexual relations occurred when possible: the popular image of Jack Tar as a sexual troublemaker had a long history.[112] This was alluded to by Lieutenant Francis Meynell, writing to his father from St Helena in 1846 that '[m]any of our officers loose [*sic*] their hearts here'.[113] For example, despite the Admiralty's warning to the crew of the River Congo expedition of 1816 that liaisons with local women were a 'great cause of the disputes' with local people, one officer described how a 'little black venus' arrived in camp to stir 'an amorous flame in the breasts of several of our gentlemen'.[114] In 1836 an officer of the *Thalia* wrote of forbidden relations between the women of Fernando Po and European visitors. Adultery was punished by the amputation of a hand, and 'two women were observed by our watering party to have lost a hand each'.[115] James Holman observed relations on a British boat, where a woman from the island 'began to ingratiate herself into the favour of an honest tar, who, nothing loath, seated her near him, with an arm around her neck'.[116]

A sketch of 'Officers of HM Brig *Bonetta* on board a hulk in Sierra Leone, Africa in '37' was likely drawn by a crew member of the *Bonetta*,

109 Jackson, *Journal of a Voyage*, p. 109.
110 'Journal of a Naval Officer', p. 257.
111 NMM, ART/10.
112 Lincoln, *Representing the Royal Navy*, p. 32.
113 NMM, MEY/5, Francis Meynell to his father, 12 January 1846.
114 Quoted in Kennedy, *The Last Blank Spaces*, pp. 223–24.
115 UKHO, MP 90/Ca6, remark book of HM sloop *Thalia*, 1836, ff. 652–54.
116 Holman, *A Voyage*, 24 November 1827.

and a number of his colleagues are named and appear on the *Bonetta's* muster roll. The hulk referred to was probably the *Conflict*, allegedly used as a floating brothel for crews of British vessels visiting Sierra Leone during this period.[117] That it was a place for frivolities is signified by smoking and drinking. The pose of the African woman depicted suggests she is a prostitute, and her interlinked arms with the sailor identified as 'Robertson' implies sexual relations. In his journals naval surgeon Fleetwood Buckle referred to the sexually transmitted diseases present among the crew of the *Bristol*, including syphilis and gonorrhoea.[118]

It is very difficult to learn more about these sexual encounters, whether they were consensual or exploitative, or whether meaningful relationships developed. Notions of respectability would have prevented most officers from including such details; bound by Victorian standards of decency, it was rare for explorers or travellers to admit to emotional relationships with 'other' peoples.[119] However, in his journals of 1862–63, Captain John Proctor Luce showed little restraint in his frequent references to his affections for the West African women he met. In Accra he found the women 'pretty' and 'becoming', while in Bathurst he reported on 'excellent figures & handsome faces'. At Fernando Po, Luce declared 'the women are really worth seeing', with 'exquisite figures'. Luce described the tattoos of these women, 'from the breast to the navel', and claimed that they 'did not at all mind my tracing these quaint cuts with my finger, or my admiring their beautifully small hands & brilliant white teeth'.[120] Luce enjoyed the explorative and adventurous elements of anti-slavery service. Sailing for Lagos from Accra, he noted: 'I half blush as I record the fact of passing by another place without landing to expose its wonders.'[121] At one point in his narrative, he breaks off from describing the beauty of the coastline and quotes at length a section of the poem 'Locksley Hall' by Lord Alfred Tennyson, first published in 1842. Luce wrote that amidst 'mellow moons & happy skies' and 'knots of Paradise':

> Barely comes the trader, rarely floats a European flag.
>
> ...

117 NMM (ZBA4579); http://collections.rmg.co.uk/collections/objects/531534.html [accessed 5 May 2018].

118 WC, MS 1395, Fleetwood Buckle diaries, 12 June and 15 July 1866.

119 Kennedy, *The Last Blank Spaces*, p. 198. One writer who did acknowledge intimate relations was John Hanning Speke. During his expedition to find the source of the While Nile in 1860–61, Speke spent months in residence at the court of the ruler of Buganda. He admitted his love for one of the girls he met there, and likely fathered her child.

120 RAI, MS 280, Luce journals, vol. 3, ff. 150, 177, 209–10.

121 RAI, MS 280, Luce journals, vol. 3, f. 160.

9 'Officers of HM Brig *Bonetta* on board a hulk in Sierra Leone, Africa in '37', unknown artist, c. 1837

There the passions cramped no longer, shall have scope & breathing space,
I will take some savage woman, she shall rear my dusky race.
Iron jointed, supple-sinewed, they shall dive & then shall run,
Catch the wild goat by the hair, & hurl their lances in the sun,
Whistle back the parrots call, & leap the rainbows of the nooks
Not with blinded eye sight poring over miserable books.[122]

Here his enjoyment of what he regarded as the untamed nature of West Africa extended to his perceptions of African women. The escapism of this verse is telling: Luce longed for his 'passions cramped no longer', and his favoured outlet for such release was in the perceived wildness and romanticized savagery of relations with an African woman. Thousands of miles from the domestic constraints of home, Luce was clearly attracted to the sexual freedom of Tennyson's utopian vision. Luce was married, mentioning how he 'sent home a long letter to the wife', but his sexual frustrations are clear in other journal passages from his mission to Dahomey. Commodore Eardley-Wilmot was asked if he wished to 'receive the personal attentions' of one of the king's daughters during his stay at Abomey. The offer was declined but, in Luce's opinion, 'the good St Anthony never had to withstand more seductive temptations'. Later, three princesses paid the officers a 'long visit', during which Wilmot 'called them our wives, whereupon the one he chose for himself sat down on his knee'. On a further visit, the princesses 'recognised their husbands … They sat a long time, smoked a little, drank a little, & quietly accepted the trifles [gifts] we gave them.'[123] Whether sexual relations took place is left ambiguous, but Luce and Wilmot clearly enjoyed the company of these women in intimate surroundings.

Luce and Wilmot both showed particular affection for the Amazons, the female warriors of Dahomey. Commodore Wilmot, for example, took issue with Richard Burton's derogatory depiction of a female warrior in his 1864 publication, calling the portrait 'ridiculous, they are very good looking if not handsome, well made and active'.[124] Luce condescendingly wrote that while the Amazons 'tried to look fierce … there was no mistaking their sex & as a whole they were certainly as fine & (after their colour) as pretty a collection of able-bodied, clean-limbed, light, strapping, jolly girls as one could wish to see'.[125] Luce wrote with both racial and gendered prejudice, but there is genuine warmth in his commentary. After one of the warriors injured her hand, she was tended to by Luce and Dr Haran. Luce wrote of the present (an earthenware basin) sent to them both to express her gratitude:

122 RAI, MS 280, Luce journals, vol. 3, f. 188.
123 RAI, MS 280, Luce journals, vol. 3, f. 153; vol. 4, ff. 63, 77–78, 105–06.
124 DUL, WYL/28/21-26, Arthur Eardley-Wilmot to William Wylde, 14 May 1865.
125 RAI, MS 280, Luce journals, vol. 4, ff. 51, 134–35.

I shall value it more than a china one from a shop. It will be a pleasing reminder of that woman, however low in the scale of humanity, however deeply sunk in barbarism, tho' diverted from her proper sphere & following a bloody & cruel career, can be soft & gentle, kind & grateful, a woman still.[126]

Although Luce subscribed to offensive stereotypes of barbarism and a woman's 'proper sphere', he recognized the woman's generous character. In Catherine Hall's words, the opportunity for Englishmen to travel the empire 'with impunity' offered 'forms of authority which they might not be able to achieve at home, visions of "native" sexuality'.[127] Luce's narrative in particular was imbued with a sense of independence and excitement, less one of geographical discovery or observation, and more focused on personal experience and adventure. His narratives reflect the impact of travel literature and the emergence of biographical writing in the nineteenth century, the practice of subjectively exploring one's own experiences and engaging with different landscapes and peoples.[128] His encounters with African women conform to racial and gendered stereotypes, but nonetheless exemplify his personal conceptions of freedom and exploration.

Changing racial attitudes

The racial attitudes of naval officers towards West Africans were rarely either overtly racist or liberal for their time, but often existed in a space somewhere in between, as the realities of their experiences in the interior intertwined with the popular vision of Africa they might have had before leaving Britain. From the mid-century, however, perceptions were increasingly influenced by a more racist and derogatory body of thinking which encouraged beliefs in immutable racial difference, supported by the development of new scientific and evolutionary understandings of race.[129] This represented an abandonment of an earlier consensus around monogenism: the idea, with roots in Christian theology, that all humans belonged to a single biological species and humans were united by their common humanity.[130] For example, scientists increasingly

---

126 RAI, MS 280, Luce journals, vol. 4, f. 113.

127 Hall, 'Going a-trolloping', p. 180.

128 Pratt, *Imperial Eyes*, p. 75; Regina Gagnier, *Subjectivities: A History of Self-representation in Britain, 1832–1920* (Oxford: Oxford University Press, 1991).

129 Bolt, *Victorian Attitudes*, ch. 1.

130 Up to the end of the eighteenth century, natural scientists attempted classifications of nature and living things (see the work of, for example, Carl Linnaeus), but there was little speculation about the biology behind racial differences. Curtin, *Image of Africa*, p. 37; Stepan, *Idea of Race*, pp. 1–2.

brought typological orientation to their studies: the theory that every individual belonged to a certain type. Fashionable in the 1820s and 1830s, phrenology popularized the belief that skull shape provided an indication of racial temperament, intelligence and character. From this emerged the idea that behaviour was determined by the different organs of the brain, which differed between races.[131] Assistant surgeon D. G. Miller was clearly influenced by such theories when he wrote a commentary on a group of Krumen on HMS *Aetna* in 1830. He found them 'superior to the natives in intelligence and moral influence'. This assertion was supported by the Kru's 'cerebral developments' which 'indicated considerable mental endowments':

> Benevolence, Veneration, Firmness, & Cautiousness were conspicuous: Imagination, with 2 or 3 exceptions, was deficient: Philoprogenitiveness was, in general, rather large. The Kroomen are divested of those Slavish fears which the natives feel, and approach strangers with freedom and confidence.[132]

By mid-century, racial science and the methods for its scholarly study had evolved. Polygenism was the belief that certain human groups were intrinsically morally and physically inferior to others. This shift included new pessimism about the unchangeability of racial 'natures'.[133] The scientific community also looked to anthropological and evolutionary explanations of racial make-up, notably Charles Darwin's *On the Origin of Species by Means of Natural Selection* (1859). Darwin regarded species as continually adapting by natural selection; the implication was that humans were part of the process of evolution and therefore had animal ancestry. Darwin was a staunch abolitionist, but the so-called 'lower' races were seen to fill the gap between animals and humans.[134]

These broader theories of immutable racial difference had an impact on the attitudes of British society and filtered into the cultural perceptions of

131 Desmond and Moore, *Darwin's Sacred Cause*, pp. 31–43; Stepan, *Idea of Race*, pp. 21–27, 45–46. The relationship between physiognomy, particularly skull shape, and the racial aesthetic was widely discussed among eighteenth-century scholars: see Bindman, *Ape to Apollo*, esp. pp. 92–123 and ch. 4. See Doulton, 'The Royal Navy's anti-slavery campaign', pp. 60–64 for examples of racial 'typing' in the later period of suppression in the western Indian Ocean.

132 TNA, ADM 105/92, Miller, 'Remarks', ff. 6–7.

133 Porter, 'Introduction', in Porter (ed.), *Oxford History*, pp. 23–24. These ideas were exemplified in the work of the Scottish anatomist Dr Robert Knox, who in 1850 declared 'race or hereditary descent is everything; it stamps the man' (quoted in Stepan, *Idea of Race*, pp. 3–4).

134 See Desmond and Moore, *Darwin's Sacred Cause*, for an examination of how Darwin's humanitarian roots drove his work on human ancestry.

the men of the West Africa squadron.[135] Racial arguments which asserted the innate inferiority of black people were seen to explain the 'failure' of emancipation and philanthropic hopes for the moral and social improvement of African peoples, as explored in Chapter 3. Other stereotypes emerging from 'middle-class' cultures of respectability increasingly intertwined Victorian racial and class prejudices. The immigrant poor, particularly the Irish, were often portrayed as 'savages': both black people and the lower classes were perceived as irrational, superstitious, childlike or excessively sexual.[136] The unsympathetic description of a 'wretched' village on the River Pongas in 1858 by an officer of the West Africa squadron could as easily refer to a poverty-stricken British community: '[African villages] resemble one another in the quantity of naked children that run about, the number of men that lounge about, and the hard-worked, miserable women that straggle in the streets.'[137]

Popular culture of the mid-nineteenth century (increasingly influenced by the United States) reinforced existing stereotypes and created new ones. In theatre, by the late 1840s the comic Jim Crow role for black actors was pervasive, reinforcing the image of black people as irresponsible and indolent.[138] An officer subscribed to such stereotypes while ostensibly praising the Foulahs of the Gambia: 'The idea conveyed by pictures of Negroes, or by meeting some woolly-headed, blubber-lipped black in the streets of Liverpool, or lounging about the London Docks, is quite dispelled on meeting these people.'[139] The philanthropic image of blacks in print changed from an object of pity to a figure of fun. A proliferation of cheap sensational fiction reinforced popular racial stereotypes, such as the comic figure of Topsy in *Uncle Tom's Cabin*.[140] Black minstrels were also popular in the second half of the century, presenting a comic derogatory stereotype

---

135 Philip Curtin has argued that the change in racial attitudes on the West African coast was relatively slow in comparison with the more rapid rise of racism at home (Curtin, *Image of Africa*, p. 383). Scientific racism arguably had a greater impact on those serving in the Indian Ocean in later decades. See Doulton, 'The Royal Navy's anti-slavery campaign', especially pp. 88–96.

136 Tim Barringer, 'Images of otherness and the visual production of difference: race and labour in illustrated texts, 1850–1865', in Shearer West (ed.), *The Victorians and Race* (Aldershot: Scolar Press, 1996), pp. 34–53; Christine Bolt, 'Race and the Victorians', in C. C. Eldridge (ed.), *British Imperialism in the Nineteenth Century* (London: Macmillan, 1984), pp. 126–47, at pp. 140, 142.

137 'Journal of a Naval Officer', p. 250.

138 Hazel Waters, *Racism on the Victorian Stage: Representation of Slavery and the Black Character* (Cambridge: Cambridge University Press, 2007), pp. 4–5, 130, 187.

139 'Journal of a Naval Officer', pp. 257, 260.

140 Wood, *Blind Memory*, ch. 4.

of black men.[141] Such portrayals emerge in naval narratives. Engineer John M'Kie wrote that the King of Bonny visited the *Rattler* in 1850, 'wearing an ill fitting dress suit and high hat which gave him the identical appearance of a Christy Minstrel'. He mockingly wrote that the king 'thought by coming in the style he did would impress us with his high state of civilisation whereas it only exposed him to derision'.[142]

New knowledge of Africa, influenced by a wave of exploration from the 1850s, appeared to support new racial sciences. The search for the source of the White Nile – expeditions were led by Richard Burton, John Speke, James Grant, Samuel White Baker, David Livingstone and Henry Stanley – raised popular interest, and explorers' accounts were best-sellers.[143] Livingstone believed that Africa could not 'raise itself' without 'contact with superior races'. Other explorers asserted that the continent was beyond salvation: Burton believed abolitionist philanthropy was misguided because Africans were irredeemably inferior, characterized by 'stagnation of mind, indolence of body, moral deficiency, superstition, and childish passion'.[144] Captain Luce met Burton in 1862 and thought him 'very clever & entertaining ... his descriptions of what he has seen & done & what he proposes to do keep one either roaring with laughter, or staring with amazement at the manner of man he must be'. Luce believed 'he will be a benefactor to the African trade & people'.[145] This new popular image of primitive African societies was used to justify imperialism, and racial superiority encouraged hostile assertions of difference from naval officers.[146] In his diary for 1858, surgeon Richard Carr McClement placed the inhabitants of Sharks Point on the River Congo at the bottom of the racial hierarchy, incapable of moral improvement. '[O]ne is struck with the impression that human beings could not be reduced to such a degraded scale', he wrote. 'If they are a specimen of their "benighted"

---

141 Sarah Meer, *Uncle Tom Mania: Slavery, Minstrelsy and Transatlantic Culture in the 1850s* (Athens, GA: University of Georgia Press, 2005); Lorimer, *Colour, Class*, pp. 82–91.

142 NLS, MS 24634, M'Kie memoirs, ff. 12–13, 16–18.

143 Brantlinger, *Rule of Darkness*, pp. 179–81. For example, Samuel White Baker, *The Albert N'yanza, Great Basin of the Nile, and Exploration of the Nile Sources*, 2 vols (London: Macmillan, 1866); Richard F. Burton, *The Lake Regions of Central Africa*, 2 vols (London: Longman, 1860).

144 Livingstone, quoted in Brantlinger, *Rule of Darkness*, p. 181; Burton, quoted in Brantlinger, 'Victorians and Africans', pp. 179, 181.

145 RAI, MS 280, Luce journals, vol. 3, ff. 164, 176, 208. In 1863 Richard Burton was asked by the Foreign Office to undertake an anti-slavery mission to Dahomey, following Commodore Wilmot's promise to make a return visit to the king.

146 Brantlinger, *Rule of Darkness*, ch. 6. For an overview of the new pessimism surrounding non-European capacity, see Porter, 'Trusteeship', in Porter (ed.), *Oxford History*, pp. 198–221.

country people I doubt whether civilisation will ever make great progress amongst them.'[147]

Naval surgeon Fleetwood Buckle served on the *Bristol* on the West Africa squadron in the 1860s. He was sensationalist, stressing a brutal and savage stereotype of Africans in his journals. He wrote of the threat of violence to Europeans 'off Kabenda', describing how the 'worst cruelties are practiced here. They caught a Portuguese they disliked, cut off his penis made him eat it, tied him to a tree cut off finger after finger then toes then hands & feet & peeled skin off his neck & lastly danced round him cutting him to bits with tomahawks.'[148] Buckle believed that slavery was the natural state for black sailors on board, who 'must be <u>made</u> to work'.[149] Buckle's comments are in stark contrast to some of the more dispassionate and sympathetic narratives written earlier in the century, particularly those relating to amiable relations with West African seamen who assisted the squadron. His journals help to exemplify the new imperialism of the final decades of the century, leading to the 'scramble for Africa', and representations of Africa focusing on barbarism, cannibalism and racial subordination.[150]

Ideas of race, nation and empire were interlinked in this period.[151] While knowledge of Africa increased through the accounts of travellers, missionaries and explorers, the popular image remained influenced by 'cultural chauvinism', and a desire to impose British ideals of civilization and culture.[152] The period of naval suppression in the Atlantic Ocean witnessed complex changes in metropolitan racial attitudes, affected by slavery, abolition, emancipation and the development of scientific racism. These changes were in part reflected in the outlooks of naval officers towards the African people they met: few had a distinct idea of different societies and cultures beyond the catch-all term of 'African'. Perceptions differed according to the observer, as is made clear by the number of descriptive

147 SCA, GB 0240 FA/67/3, McClement diary, 16 October 1858, www.scottish-catholicarchives.org.uk/Learning/DiaryofRichardCarrMcClement/DiaryExtracts/Landscape/tabid/157/Default.aspx [accessed 20 June 2018].
148 WC, MS 1397, Fleetwood Buckle diaries, 29 September 1867.
149 WC, MS 1395-6, Fleetwood Buckle diaries, 8 July and 6 August 1866. Buckle's emphasis.
150 Brantlinger, *Rule of Darkness*, ch. 6. See Doulton, 'The Royal Navy's anti-slavery campaign', pp. 106–14, for racist portrayals of African crew members on anti-slave-trade patrols in the Indian Ocean.
151 Catherine Hall, 'Introduction: thinking the postcolonial, thinking the empire', in Catherine Hall (ed.), *Cultures of Empire: Colonizers in Britain and the Empire in the Nineteenth and Twentieth Centuries* (Manchester: Manchester University Press, 2000), pp. 2, 19; Edward Said, *Culture and Imperialism* (London: Chatto & Windus, 1993).
152 Curtin, *Image of Africa*, pp. xii, 341–42, 479; McCaskie, 'Cultural encounters', p. 672.

terms used by naval officers to portray West Africans. 'Fellow', 'black' or 'native' suggested that African people were no more or less human than any other; 'savage', 'animal', 'creature' or 'specimen' implied an entirely separate species.[153] Generalizations are difficult, but the assumption of British superiority and paternalism is clear, as is a shift in attitudes from mid-century, as the tendency towards more benign observational reporting in earlier decades was increasingly replaced by the application of fixed stereotypes.[154]

However, the opinions of naval men did not simply reflect those of British society more generally. The paradox of a sailor's identity was that he was of necessity excluded from society when sent out to sea; as N. A. M. Rodger has written, 'the seaman remained to his contemporaries profoundly strange'.[155] There were also class and racial differences within the naval hierarchy, and at some point during their careers many sailors had been part of a multilingual and ethnically mixed lower-deck community.[156] Compared to most Britons, those serving in the Royal Navy were exposed to an array of cultures, and the West African coast was by no means the only site of cultural exchange in the nineteenth century.[157] As a result, their opinions about African peoples were varied and complex: while racial stereotypes and the legacy of slavery are pervasive, there are enough reflective and considered accounts of officers' African experiences to challenge blanket ideas of racial superiority.

153 For example, both discussing African rulers in the early 1850s, Lieutenant Henry Rogers wrote that the king at Sharks Point was a 'fellow who called himself King Jem' (31 July 1850); Midshipman Arthur Onslow described the king at Anna Bona as 'a most extraordinary looking animal' (no date, 1851–52).

154 Richard Price discusses this shift in relation to encounters with the Xhosa of southern Africa in *Making Empire: Colonial Encounters and the Creation of Imperial Rule in Nineteenth-Century Africa* (Cambridge: Cambridge University Press, 2008).

155 N. A. M. Rodger, *The Wooden World: An Anatomy of the Georgian Navy* (London: Fontana Press, 1988), p. 15.

156 Rediker, *Between the Devil*, pp. 154–55.

157 Examples of accounts of late eighteenth- and nineteenth-century encounters between naval men and indigenous peoples include Anne Salmond, *Bligh: William Bligh in the South Seas* (Berkeley, CA: University of California Press, 2011); Inga Clendinnen, *Dancing with Strangers: The True History of the Meeting of the British First Fleet and the Aboriginal Australians, 1788* (Edinburgh: Canongate, 2003); Jordan Goodman, *The Rattlesnake: A Voyage of Discovery to the Coral Sea* (London: Faber and Faber, 2005).

6

Officers' contributions
to Britain's anti-slavery culture

This study of the personal experiences of naval officers has thus far been mainly situated in West Africa and its coastline. The focus now switches to Britain, and officers' contributions to the metropolitan discourses about slavery and abolition taking place there in the early to mid-nineteenth century. While the history of the British anti-slavery movement is the subject of much scholarship, less clear are the connections between the Royal Navy and the various anti-slavery networks in existence. Indeed, in many ways the work of the West Africa squadron represented, in Robert Burroughs's words, 'an unlikely union' between the inherently conservative navy and the socially progressive anti-slavery societies.[1] Yet militarism and humanitarianism combined in this British enterprise, and the Royal Navy was at the operational frontline of Britain's anti-slavery cause. Building on the theme of naval officers playing an important part in the social and cultural history of the West African campaign, this chapter will look at the extent to which abolitionist societies and interest groups operating in Britain during the first half of the nineteenth century forged relationships with naval officers in the field, and why they regarded it as prudent and necessary to do so. After the Abolition Act of 1807, anti-slavery societies regrouped, and extra-parliamentary efforts in support of abolitionism that were prevalent in the late eighteenth century – such as petitioning, public meetings and membership of societies – continued.[2] The aspirations of British abolitionists changed alongside the understandings of 'abolitionism' and 'anti-slavery',

1 Robert Burroughs, 'Suppression of the Atlantic slave trade: abolition from ship to shore', in Burroughs and Huzzey (eds), *Suppression*, pp. 1–16, at p. 6.

2 Seymour Drescher, 'Public opinion and the destruction of British colonial slavery', in J. Walvin (ed.), *Slavery and British Society 1776–1846* (London: Macmillan, 1982), pp. 22–48.

particularly given the impact of the Emancipation Act of 1833. Naval officers of the West Africa squadron contributed to this ever-evolving anti-slavery culture: through support of societies and by providing key testimonies and evidence about the unrelenting transatlantic slave trade.

Relationships with anti-slavery societies

British naval officers were involved in abolitionist networks before 1807. Lieutenant John Clarkson, for example, brother of the abolitionist Thomas, was influential in the founding of Freetown in 1788, acted as an agent of the Sierra Leone Company, and until 1792 served as the colony's first Governor. Clarkson was also tasked with securing and transporting volunteers from black communities in Nova Scotia to settle in the area in 1791–92.[3] Lieutenant Philip Beaver was part of a group of six British naval and military men of radical political beliefs who in 1792 formed the Bolama Assocation, with a desire to establish themselves as colonists on the West African coast. The island of Bolama (today the nation of Guinea-Bissau) was chosen for the colonizing enterprise, and their goals included a proposal, in Beaver's words, 'to cultivate the western coast of Africa, without interfering with the freedoms of the natives'. Beaver's overriding belief in 'civilization' and self-improvement 'as a means of gradually abolishing African slavery' was a driving force in the mission. Although the scheme was abandoned after 18 months due to epidemics of fever, the mission was regarded as an informative first step in Britain's early incursions into West Africa.[4]

After 1807, and the declaration of Sierra Leone as a Crown colony, the newly established African Institution dominated anti-slavery discourse in Britain. The Institution relied on evangelical personal politics to achieve considerable influence over Sierra Leone's administration and the British government's abolitionist agenda in West Africa.[5] Eight former Sierra Leone Company directors sat on its committee. Captain Edward Columbine acknowledged that 'His Majesty's government in general, were very liberally

---

3 Ellen Gibson Wilson, *John Clarkson and the African Adventure* (London: Macmillan, 1980); Roger Powell, *Why Here? Why Then? The Roles of John and Thomas Clarkson in the Abolition of the Slave Trade 1807* (Wisbech and Fenland Museum, 2007). Clarkson was anxious that the 52-day voyage from Nova Scotia should in no way resemble the slave trade for the passengers on board. He issued a printed list of rules for all ship masters detailing generous room and food allowances, and daily cleaning.

4 Billy G. Smith, *Ship of Death: A Voyage that Changed the Atlantic World* (New Haven, CT: Yale University Press, 2013), pp. 6–7, 48–49, 247. One of the few survivors, Beaver wrote a book detailing the expedition, *African Memoranda: Relative to an attempt to establish a British settlement on the island of Bulama* (London: C. and R. Baldwin, 1805).

5 Ackerson, *African Institution*; Eltis, *Economic Growth*, p. 105.

disposed to attend to the requests & suggestions of the leading members of that company in all such matters as relate to the welfare of Africa.'[6] Proof of the effectiveness of the African Institution campaign in influencing the Admiralty can be seen in some of the key appointments of senior officers on the West Africa squadron. Columbine alluded to the idea that he was the preferred choice of Wilberforce and his allies. He dined at Wilberforce's residence in Kensington Gore in February 1809 and 'met with Lord Teignmouth, Mr Grant MP, William Smith MP, James Stephen MP, Lord Calthorpe & Mr Macaulay', all members of the African Institution. Before sailing to Sierra Leone, Columbine noted that 'Mr Z Macaulay & his brother Alex came on board to call on me before my departure', and later letters reveal that Macaulay exerted considerable leverage on appointments in the colony.[7]

Columbine appeared overwhelmed by his position as Governor: he was disturbed by a 'mutinous spirit' and 'repeated impertinences' from political challengers.[8] His insecurities may also have arisen from the influence of the African Institution, which permeated his governorship. In letters to Lord Liverpool (Secretary of State for War and the Colonies), Wilberforce suggested measures on Columbine's behalf, such as a nomination for the command of the militia in Sierra Leone. He also encouraged 'expressions of appropriation and confidence with which your Lordship may honor him'. Wilberforce thanked Liverpool for listening to 'the suggestions of my friends and myself', in order to 'unite with us in promoting the civilization and improvement of that vast continent'.[9] After six months in post, blighted by family bereavement and bouts of illness, Columbine informed Lord Liverpool and the Admiralty that he wished to return to Britain, keen to stress that his appointment was 'a temporary concern'. With his requests for a replacement apparently fruitless, he left the colony on his own authority in May 1811, and later died at sea.[10]

Captain Frederick Paul Irby, appointed to command the squadron between 1811 and 1814, was 'a man of our own choice', according to Zachary

6 UIC: SLC, Series III, Folder 9, Columbine journals, 4 February 1809, ff. 1, 3.

7 UIC: SLC, Series III, Folder 10, Columbine journals, 13 January 1810, f. 3; Folder 9, Columbine journals, 4 February 1809, f. 5; Ackerson, *African Institution*, p. 69.

8 TNA, CO 267/27, Columbine to Lord Liverpool, 13 April 1810; CO 267/28, Columbine to Lord Liverpool, 8 September 1810.

9 TNA, CO 267/28, William Wilberforce to Lord Liverpool, 26 June 1810. In a later letter to Columbine, Liverpool praised his 'zeal, judgement and firmness' (TNA, CO 267/27, 20 July 1810).

10 TNA, CO 267/28, 22 September 1810, 8 October 1810; TNA, CO 267/28, 1 November 1810. Columbine's wife and daughter both died from fever in Sierra Leone and his young son was invalided home. On 15 October 1810 he wrote in his journal that he had 'a heart broke down with grief'.

Macaulay.[11] Irby was a director of the African Institution and paid the highest subscription rate to the organization. At a meeting of abolitionists at the Freemason's Tavern, London, in June 1814, Wilberforce celebrated Irby's achievements 'in nobly maintaining the cause of his country', which included 'rooting out a nest of vipers, who supported slave factories on the coast'.[12] The *Report of the Directors* in 1813 noted Irby's 'spirit, energy and activity' as Commodore, and his 'praise-worthy exertions to promote the objects of the Institution'.[13] Indeed, the African Institution regarded the Royal Navy as key to its West African campaign. The directors petitioned the government to increase the strength of the squadron and sought relationships with officers in the field, eager to 'excite the attention of naval officers on the subject of the Slave Trade'. In this endeavour they were 'most ably and zealously seconded by the Honorable Commissioner Grey at Portsmouth'.[14] George Grey served in the West Indies in the 1780s and 1790s and was Commissioner at Portsmouth Dockyard from 1806 until his death in 1828. He had an illustrious anti-slavery pedigree. He was the younger brother of MP Sir Charles Grey, who introduced the Abolition Act of 1807 and who as Prime Minister (1830–34) oversaw the abolition of slavery in the Caribbean.[15] Grey's cousin was the agriculturalist and abolitionist John Grey, and his wife was Mary Whitbread, daughter of the brewer and anti-slavery supporter Samuel Whitbread.[16] George and Mary were committed evangelical Christians and numbered among their friends William Wilberforce, Charles Simeon and other leaders of the evangelical party. In his memoirs Grey's character was said to be built on 'deeply religious feeling and high moral principle'. His Portsmouth residence was a meeting place for evangelical allies and a 'centre of benevolent activity', providing, for example, charitable ministrations to sick sailors and orphan children.[17] Naval officers such as Grey personified a period of 'maritime evangelisation', in Richard Blake's words, within intersecting networks of interest between the Royal Navy and anti-slavery

---

11 Quoted in Southam, *Jane Austen*, p. 195.

12 *The Morning Post*, 18 June 1814. In June 1813 at Cape Mesurado, an extensive slave factory belonging to British slave traders John Bostock and Thomas Macquin was destroyed by ships under Irby's command. Subsequently tried and convicted under the Felony Act of 1811 (which transformed slave trading by Britons into a felony), Bostock and Macquin were sentenced to transportation.

13 *Seventh Report of the Directors of the African Institution* (1813), pp. 1–3.

14 *Fifth Report of the Directors of the African Institution* (1811), pp. 40–41; Ackerson, *African Institution*, p. 84.

15 See http://www.historyofparliamentonline.org/volume/1790-1820/member/grey-charles-1764-1845 [accessed 20 March 2018]

16 Captain Grey's sister, Lady Elizabeth, married the only son of Samuel Whitbread.

17 Creighton, *Memoir*, pp. 9–12; Blake, *Religion*, p. 57.

and religious societies.[18] In 1812 Grey was elected honorary life governor of the African Institution, 'having manifested a very ardent zeal to promote its objects'.[19]

This promotion included the circulation of abolitionist propaganda among naval officers and calling attention to the provisions of the legislature regarding abolition. For example, the *Fourth Report of the Directors* of 1810 included 37 pages of instructions for naval officers, including interpretation of the Acts, the suggested treatment of liberated Africans, and the pecuniary advantages of suppression.[20] There was clearly some cooperation or crossover in responsibility between the Institution and the Admiralty for informing officers in the field. The *Fifth Report of the Directors* of 1811, for example, stated that two important judgements (of Sir William Grant in the case of the *Amedie* and of Sir William Scott in the case of the *Fortuna*) 'have been separately printed and widely circulated in the Navy' by the Institution. Furthermore, 'the whole of these ... have been adopted by the Lords of the Admiralty and transmitted under their orders to all the naval stations'.[21] These communications were a two-way process, with the directors regularly exchanging information with officers to push for a more rigorous enforcement of abolition laws.[22]

A number of naval officers were subscribers to the Institution.[23] Published reports of the Institution highlight deeds of officers personifying 'distinguished services in the cause of humanity', and regularly featured correspondence with naval officers relating to the slave trade and discussions of the best methods to end it.[24] Captain John B. Curran of the *Tyne* wrote to Thomas Harrison, secretary of the African Institution, on his own initiative after intercepting slave traffic around the island of Mauritius in 1816. He also

18 Blake, *Religion*, pp. 27, 34. For example, supporters of the Naval and Military Bible Society, influential in the early decades of the nineteenth century, included members of the Clapham Sect – including Henry Thornton and William Wilberforce – and prominent members of the Admiralty, including Lord Gambier, Lord Northesk, Admiral Pellew and Admiral Saumarez.

19 *Sixth Report of the Directors of the African Institution* (1812).

20 *Fourth Report of the Directors of the African Institution* (1810), p. 4.

21 *Fifth Report of the Directors of the African Institution* (1811), pp. 40–41.

22 Ackerson, *African Institution*, p. 45.

23 Subscribers paid an annual fee to the organization. Officers listed included Captain Columbine, Lord Gambier, Captain Bones, Captain Irby, surgeon David Rowlands, Lieutenant Sabine, Captain Thornton, Captain Ross, Sir George Collier, Captain Kelly, Captain Campbell and Captain Constantine Moorsom. Captain C. M. Fabian, who became well-known for evangelical zeal and prominence in seamen's missions, was also a subscriber.

24 *Eighteenth Report of the Directors of the African Institution* (1824), p. 47. The Report was referring to Sir Robert Mends and Sir George Collier.

corresponded with Earl Grey and Zachary Macaulay. Curran was, he wrote, 'extremely desirous to lose no time in submitting for the information of the Directors & numbers of the African Institution any intelligence connected with the objects of the Society which can prove at all interesting'.[25] His account of the slave ship *Elenore*, captured en route from Tamatave in Madagascar with a cargo of 'wretched beings' in 'a state of extreme debility and emaciation', was addressed to the Governor of Mauritius and published by the African Institution to illuminate the cruelty of the trade. Curran also stressed his hopes that his account would assist the abolitionist cause:

> The transhipping this cargo of human wretchedness I could, Sir, cordially have wished had been witnessed by the Philanthropic Founders of the Institution in England for carrying into effect the acts of Abolition: and by those who have conferred such honor upon themselves and upon the Nation, by their perseverance through every obstacle through which they carried that measure.[26]

The African Institution also acted as a go-between for naval officers in their relations with the Admiralty, with officers recognizing the influence of the directors at times when support from the Admiralty was not forthcoming. Commander G. M. Guise wrote to William Wilberforce in 1814 to ask for assistance in negotiating his expenses relating to the capture of the slave brig *Falcon*, intercepted by the *Liberty* while bound to Havana in 1811. The enslaved Africans were confined on the ship at the harbour of St Thomas for 14 months in conditions, Guise wrote, 'shocking to the feelings of any one possessed of the smallest particle of humanity'. Guise solicited the judge of the Vice-Admiralty Court at Tortola to direct the enslaved to be landed, 'as I was convinced it was not the intention of our Government, in directing their officers to exert themselves to put a stop to the trade, that their situation should become worse than slavery'. However, the ship was acquitted by the judge, leaving Guise with the 'whole of the expenses … a very considerable sum'.[27] Similarly, in 1815 the Commander of the *Pique* wrote for advice as to how to recover the sum of £2,500 'paid by me for the maintenance and medical assistance afforded to the Africans captured by this ship in the Spanish brig *Carlos*', after the Governor of Guadaloupe

25 DUL, GRE/B52/9/1-5, Captain John B. Curran to Thomas Harrison, 28 December 1816.

26 DUL, GRE/B52/9/1-5, Captain John B. Curran to Governor Farquhar, 8 September 1816. This letter was also published in *Eleventh Report of the Directors of the African Institution* (1817), pp. 7–8.

27 G. M. Guise to William Wilberforce, 2 July 1814, published in the Appendix to *Ninth Report of the Directors of the African Institution* (1815), pp. 128–31.

refused to pay the bills of subsistence. The directors observed that the Commander's conduct exemplified 'the disinterestedness and generosity of the naval officers who have had to perform the arduous duty of executing the Abolition Acts'.[28] A letter published by the African Institution from Commodore Bullen to Admiralty Secretary J. W. Croker on HMS *Maidstone* near Martinique highlights the relationships of influence between the Institution, the Admiralty and officers in the field. Bullen expressed 'reluctant regret' that he felt 'necessitated to be so continually trespassing on their Lordships' time' in pointing out 'the glaring and increasing extent to which the Slave Trade is carried on by the French in this quarter'.[29] Here an officer's informed perspective was utilized by the Institution to add weight to its attempts to influence Admiralty policy in relation to the continuing French slave trade.

Relationships between naval officers and British anti-slavery groups continued to develop as new societies emerged throughout the 1820s and 1830s advocating the abolition of slavery throughout British territories. Captain Constantine Moorsom was involved in the bombardment of Algiers in 1816 to liberate enslaved Christians, and in the 1820s served to suppress the slave trade in East African waters in the *Ariadne*.[30] Moorsom was a subscriber to the Society for the Mitigation and Gradual Abolition of Slavery Throughout the British Dominions (established 1823), and, later, the Agency Committee, a more radical group within the society led by abolitionists Joseph Sturge and George Stephen.[31] In 1828 Moorsom published a pamphlet condemning slavery in the West Indies in partnership with the Whitby Anti-Slavery Society. The authorship of a naval officer who had witnessed first-hand the 'horrors of British colonial slavery' gave the pamphlet authority and legitimacy. In a review in *Whitby Panorama: And Monthly Chronicle*, Moorsom was said to be 'touched with the feelings of Christian compassion, and of that manly generosity which dwells in the breast of a true British Officer'. The pamphlet, it was suggested, 'has since been reprinted in other places, and extensively circulated'.[32] In April 1839 Moorsom, now a vice-admiral,

28 Extract of a letter from the Commander of the *Pique* published in *Ninth Report of the Directors of the African Institution* (1815), pp. 46–47.

29 Commodore Bullen to J. W. Croker, from Princes Island, 5 September 1825, published in *Twentieth Report of the Directors of the African Institution* (1826), pp. 163–64.

30 *The Royal Gazette, and Sierra Leone Advertiser*, 27 December 1823, p. 205.

31 *Account of the Receipts & Disbursements of the Anti-Slavery Society* (1823–26).

32 *How do we procure sugar? A question proposed for the consideration of the people of Great Britain. By a Naval Officer. Printed for the Whitby Anti-Slavery Society* (1828); *Whitby Panorama: And Monthly Chronicle*, vol. 2 (1828), pp. 220–22. The Moorsom family were prominent in the anti-slavery community of the small northern coastal town of Whitby. Richard Moorsom, Jr (Constantine's uncle) wrote *Address (An) to the Inhabitants of*

was appointed chair at 'a meeting of delegates and friends to the anti-slavery cause', held in London to consider 'the propriety' of forming a new society to succeed the British and Foreign Society for the Universal Abolition of Slavery and the Slave Trade (established 1834). Moorsom was elected a corresponding member of the society and was noted in the minutes as a regular contributor.[33]

The newly named British and Foreign Anti-Slavery Society (BFASS) was instrumental in framing Britain's promotion of anti-slavery policy on the international stage.[34] The society organized the first World Anti-Slavery Convention at Exeter Hall in London in 1840 to encourage alliance with like-minded societies abroad (and particularly the United States). Admiral Moorsom delivered a paper to the Convention on 'international intercourse', and several other naval officers were also present, including Lieutenant Charles Fitzgerald, recently invalided home from service on the West African coast in HMB *Buzzard*.[35] Fitzgerald was introduced in relation to his role in the capture of two American slavers, making him, the abolitionist Richard Madden declared: 'the first man who has ventured to go out of the routine of duty, seize vessels hoisting the American flag, and carry them into an American port'. Fitzgerald's zealous commitment to naval suppression appeared to secure his place at the Convention; the lieutenant also debated with Thomas Fowell Buxton and others over abolition in Spanish colonies, revealing an interest in the anti-slavery cause outside his official role on the West African coast.[36] Also present was Lieutenant Charles Horace Lapidge of HMS *Stag*, formerly of *Scout* in the West Indies, and later in command of the *Pantaloon* on the coast of Africa between 1841 and 1844. He was well known among his crews for his bravery and ardent dedication to the task of the West Africa squadron. In 1842 Lapidge took formal possession of the island of Bulama (first attempted by Philip Beaver), provoking a diplomatic incident with the Portuguese.[37]

Whitby and Its Vicinity on the State of the Slaves in the British Colonies (1826) urging the election of Members of Parliament who would not be 'tools of the West India interest'.

33 BL, MFR 2883, minute books of the BFASS, Reel 1.

34 James Heartfield, *The British And Foreign Anti-Slavery Society, 1838–1956: A History* (Oxford: Oxford University Press, 2016). The Aborigines' Protection Society, founded in 1837, similarly had origins in debates about the relationship between foreign policy and British philanthropy. The Society focused on ensuring the rights and well-being of enslaved and colonized peoples.

35 *Proceedings of the General Anti-Slavery Convention* (1840), vol. 1, p. 203.

36 *Proceedings*, vol. 1, pp. 239–40, 245–46. Fitzgerald was later appointed Lieutenant-Governor of British settlements on the Gambia, and from 1848 served as Governor of Western Australia.

37 TNA, ADM 1/5517, Lapidge to Captain John Foote, 27 May 1842 and 28 February

Officers' accounts of service served to frame the debate at the Convention. Captain Robert Wauchope was a subscriber of the BFASS and active in the proceedings; he declared himself qualified to contribute as someone 'well acquainted with the slave-trade'.[38] Wauchope served for three years at the Cape and St Helena in 1816–19, and then in the *Thalia*, 1834–38, as flag captain to Sir Patrick Campbell at the Cape of Good Hope (who was also his brother-in-law). He retired an Admiral of the Blue in 1838. Mid-career, Wauchope became a devout born-again Christian, and his memoirs, *A Short Narrative of God's Merciful Dealings*, were published by his family after his death in 1862.[39] His opinions on the slave trade as an anti-Christian enterprise are clear:

> It is, indeed, an accursed trade … that men calling themselves Christian should uphold and carry on the slave-trade is far worse, and nothing can show the depravity of unregenerated human natures more than the whole history of the slave-trade from first to last.[40]

Wauchope was respected by the Convention organizers as an expert on the subject of the slave trade: he was proposed as an ideal candidate for a committee 'to consider the subject of the slave-trade in Brazil' and contributed evidence on 'the condition of the liberated Africans' in response to a resolution that a committee of the BFASS take steps to investigate West African settlements.[41] Naval officers had a unique position of influence in anti-slavery circles from their rare first-hand experiences of witnessing the barbarities of the slave trade. As Wauchope passionately declared to the Convention: 'I cannot describe, the awful enormities of slavery. I have heard it said in this country that we too highly colour the picture. I contend that this is utterly imprac-ticable; imagination itself cannot portray the awful misery.'[42]

1842. The island of Bolama later became a Portuguese possession. Lapidge's dedication to the cause was not always respected. His lieutenant on the *Pantaloon*, Augustus Arkwright, declared 'if he behaved to his white friends in the manner he does to the blacks, I should feel obliged' (DRO, D5991/10/72-73, Augustus Arkwright to his mother, 19 June 1842).

38 *Proceedings*, vol. 1, p. 483.

39 Wauchope's evangelical beliefs led to disagreements with the Admiralty, for example about whether prostitutes should be allowed on HM ships. Wauchope wrote: 'My religion, at the Admiralty, stood so much in my way.' Wauchope, *A Short Narrative*, pp. 98–99.

40 Wauchope, *A Short Narrative*, p. 120.

41 *Proceedings*, vol. 1, pp. 483, 505.

42 *Proceedings*, vol. 1, p. 483. Wauchope's commitment to the anti-slavery cause continued in his retirement; he contributed to *Autograph Contributions (kindly written or furnished in aid of the anti-slavery cause)* in 1850.

Where the BFASS diverged from the Royal Navy, however, was in its opposition to the use of force by the West Africa squadron. Lieutenant Fitzgerald's testimony, for example, raised the concerns of Joseph Sturge, who felt it necessary to assert that 'this Convention is based upon the principle, that we are confined to moral, religious, and pacific means in carrying out our object'. Contrary to the practice of the squadron, he continued, 'the word "pacific" prohibits us from either directly or indirectly sanctioning a resort to arms even against the slave-trader while he holds his victim in his hands'.[43] However, organizations such as the BFASS represented only a portion of anti-slavery opinion: in Richard Huzzey's words, this was an age of 'anti-slavery pluralism'.[44] Different concerns shaped the BFASS and another new abolitionist society of the 1830s: the Society for the Extinction of the Slave Trade and the Civilization of Africa (or the African Civilization Society, as it became known), led by the abolitionist Thomas Fowell Buxton. Between 1839 and 1843, Buxton and his supporters focused primarily on the extinction of the slave trade via the government-sponsored Niger Expedition of 1841 and the broader mission of introducing commerce, Christianity and civilization into Africa. While Buxton had raised doubts about the efficacy of the squadron in his publications *The African Slave Trade* and *The Remedy*, the African Civilization Society (ACS) was more supportive of the squadron's aims and tactics than the BFASS. The society expressed pride that 'already the name of "Englishman" is honourably distinguished along the coast of Africa, as the friend of Africans'.[45]

Like the African Institution before it, naval officers were involved in and engaged with the pursuits of the ACS, reflecting their experiences in West Africa and their ability to provide perspective and information to assist in the society's mission.[46] Several naval officers were personally invited to join the provisional committee of the ACS, including Captain Charles

43 *Proceedings*, vol. 1, pp. 239–40. This opposition, it was claimed, arose from the pacifism of the Quakers (who made up a large proportion of BFASS membership). However, the Society stressed practical rather than dogmatic grounds for opposing the tactics of the squadron. See Heartfield, *British and Foreign*, pp. 84–89.

44 Huzzey, *Freedom Burning*, p. 8.

45 *Report of the Committee of the African Civilization Society to the Public Meeting of the Society* [held at Exeter Hall, 21 June 1842] (London: John Murray, 1842), p. 75.

46 Honorary members of the ACS included Rear-Admiral Sir James Hillyar, Admiral R. Dudley Oliver and Captain Taylor. Captain Sir Robert Hagan (who had served with Sir George Collier on the *Tartar*) was a colonial corresponding member. At least 22 naval officers are named in the list of subscribers, including James Brown (late Engineer of HMSV *Albert*) and Lieutenant H. C. Harston (late of HMSV *Wilberforce*) and 12 others 'collected by Lieut Harston' including Lieutenant Egerton. At a public meeting held on 21 June 1842, the chair Lord Ashley was 'supported by' Captain Joseph Denman

Bosanquet.[47] Despite his family connections to plantation slavery in the West Indies, Bosanquet had a distinguished career on the anti-slave-trade patrols.[48] As lieutenant on the *Black Joke* in 1831, he was highly praised for his action in the capture of the slave ship *Marinerito*. He later served on the *Leveret*, which saw action against slave ships around Freetown, and as Commander on the *Alert* between 1839 and 1846. While serving off Simon's Bay in 1836 (joining the *Pelican* and *Thalia* under the command of Rear-Admiral Sir Patrick Campbell), Bosanquet became involved in a diplomatic incident with the Portuguese at Mozambique, in which he was accused of breaching international law by blockading the port against Admiralty orders. Rear-Admiral Elliot looked unfavourably on Bosanquet's 'sub-imperial ventures', in Patrick Harries's words.[49] Bosanquet's forcefulness was clearly attractive to the ACS, however, and his experiences were used to exemplify the adoption of new, assertive strategies.

Captain Henry Dundas Trotter volunteered to lead Buxton's ambitious Niger Expedition of 1841. Trotter was regarded as a man of 'Christian confidence', noted for 'his humane and gallant exertions' in the anti-slavery cause as Commander of the *Curlew*. Religion played a large role on the ships

(also a subscriber), Captain Francis Maude, Captain Sir Edward Parry and Captain Beaufort (all honorary members). See *Report of the Committee* (1842).

47 The provisional committee at the Prospectus of the Society for the Extinction of the Slave Trade and for the Civilization of Africa in 1839 included Captain Henry Dundas Trotter, Captain Bird Allen, Captain William Allen, Captain Charles Bosanquet, Captain B. Marwood Kelly, Captain John Washington, Captain Fitz Roy and Captain Francis Maude.

48 Charles Bosanquet's father was Samuel Bosanquet (1768–1843), a wealthy London banker. According to the Legacies of British Slave-ownership database, the partners in his bank – Bosanquet, Beechroft and Reeves of Lombard Street – were awarded compensation for 358 enslaved people on three estates in Nevis. Charles's brother, the banker James Whatman Bosanquet, was awarded in the same claim. Captain Bosanquet's uncle was the London West India merchant Charles Bosanquet (awarded compensation for over 400 slaves on St Kitts), who wrote several economic pamphlets in support of the sugar and rum trade of the British Caribbean, see http://www.ucl.ac.uk/lbs/person/view/25287; http://www.ucl.ac.uk/lbs/person/view/2146630296 [accessed 20 March 2018]. That Captain Bosanquet could be employed to act against the slave trade while his family simultaneously made considerable profits from slave labour in the Caribbean is demonstrative of the tensions and complexities regarding anti-slavery in British society at this time.

49 Patrick Harries, 'The hobgoblins of the Middle Passage: the Cape of Good Hope and the trans-Atlantic slave trade', in Ulrike Schmieder, Katja Fullbery-Stolberg and Michael Zeuske (eds), *The End of Slavery in Africa and the Americas: A Comparative Approach* (Berlin: Global, 2011), pp. 33–42. Bosanquet was involved in the blockade and detention of the slave vessel *Diogenes*.

of the expedition, and in Trotter's own motivations.[50] Speaking at a meeting of the ACS held in Plymouth in April 1841 (before leaving for West Africa), Trotter considered his involvement in the expedition to be 'a privilege and an honour'. He asked, '[w]ho would not be proud to see the British flag, the emblem of liberty, flying at the masthead in the heart of Africa? Who would not be proud in being instrumental in contributing to the preaching of the gospel, in a land where it had never before been heard?'[51] Both Trotter and his expedition colleague, Captain William Allen, expressed a desire to address members of the ACS, to impart eyewitness experiences and assert their ideas for the West African mission in the future. Allen spoke of his feelings of 'duty' to address an ACS meeting in Devonport in April 1841 to 'confirm' the accounts of the slave trade, 'since he had been an eye-witness of what preceding speakers had so feelingly described'. Trotter made the distinction between naval officers and abolitionists – the latter articulating policy while the former enacted directives at the frontline – declaring at the Plymouth meeting that he and his naval colleagues 'were no speakers; they were more accustomed to act than to speak'. Nevertheless, both Allen and Trotter expressed their hopes for the future of the continent, imbued with paternalism. Allen believed 'there was still so much good' in the African people, and that he was 'convinced for the effort they were about to make for their regeneration would not prove in vain'.[52]

After the failure of the expedition, Trotter suffered bouts of severe ill health which prevented his active service, but he remained a prominent and active member of the ACS in tandem with his support for the missionary cause. 'I am sure you will believe that no one is more interested than I am in the welfare of the Society', he wrote to the ACS in 1842. 'I am convinced there never was a time more propitious for Africa than the present, nor one calling more for strenuous exertion on our part.'[53] Trotter served as an annual governor of the Church Missionary Society for Africa and the

---

50 At the first public meeting of the ACS at Exeter Hall in June 1840, the Lord Bishop of Chichester stated that Trotter deserved 'an honourable and well-merited eulogium for his humane and gallant exertions'; *Proceedings at the First Public Meeting of the Society for the Extinction of the Slave Trade and for the Civilization of Africa Held at Exeter Hall, on Monday, 1st June, 1840* (London: W. Clowes and Sons, 1840), pp. 27–28. The Revd Theodor Muller, CMS missionary and chaplain, gave a sermon on board the steam vessel *Albert* which was later published, in which he spoke of the expedition's mission to bring 'light and life, civilization and liberty, into the dark and deadly regions of Africa'. Trotter's colleague was the idealistic Christian officer Edmund Fishbourne, formerly Captain Wauchope's lieutenant on the *Thalia*. See Blake, *Religion*, pp. 216–19.

51 *The Friend of Africa* (1841), pp. 143–44.

52 *The Friend of Africa* (1841), pp. 142–44.

53 *Report of the Committee* (1842), pp. 94–95.

East in 1844–45 and maintained a correspondence with the Revd Samuel Crowther after the Niger Expedition. 'I still have hope that a time will come that great work shall be accomplished', Crowther wrote to Trotter in 1850, 'and the Niger will yet become a highway to bear the messengers of the glad tidings of salvation on its waters to the interior of this continent.'[54] Trotter wrote introductory remarks for a published defence of naval suppression written by the American missionary, the Revd J. Leighton Wilson, in 1851, in which he expressed his belief in the connection between anti-slavery, the British presence and the spiritual revival of the continent: 'the social and moral condition of a vast continent, and the diffusion of light and knowledge amongst the people of Africa are staked, to all human appearance, on the future conduct of this country in respect to the Slave Trade'.[55]

Captain Trotter personified the relationship between the Royal Navy, anti-slavery networks and the religious drive to advance British Christian values in Africa. Captain John Washington was similarly engaged in the efforts of British anti-slavery and religious societies.[56] Washington was present at the World Anti-Slavery Convention in 1840 and was described by Buxton as 'an energetic member of the committee' of the ACS, having established the society's periodical, *The Friend of Africa*.[57] Washington's role and responsibilities in the ACS went beyond his professional capacity as a naval officer. In 1840 he was instructed to tour Germany, 'to make the objects of the Society generally known' among scientists, leaders and 'estimable men'. He wrote to Buxton from Bohemia where he met with Prince Metternich 'on the subject of African Civilisation', having travelled to other European cities and reported on a 'very cordial reception' for the society's proposals.[58] That Buxton chose a naval officer for this diplomatic mission is revealing of his respect for the profession in matters relating to Africa and the suppression of the slave trade. Officers' involvement in anti-slavery societies uncovers both the beliefs of individuals employed on the squadron and the importance that societies placed on reaching out and including officers in their networks.

54 *Report of the Committee* (1842), pp. 94–95; Samuel Crowther to Henry Trotter, 4 July 1850, published in *The Colonial Magazine* (December 1850), pp. 1–15.

55 Captain H. D. Trotter, 'Introduction' to Revd J. Leighton Wilson, *The British Squadron on the Coast of Africa* (London: James Ridgway, 1851), p. iv.

56 For example, members of the Naval Prayer Union, formed in December 1851, included Washington, Trotter, Francis Maude and Claude Buckle (Blake, *Religion*, pp. 134–35).

57 Charles Buxton, *Memoirs of Sir Thomas Fowell Buxton, Baronet, with Selections from his Correspondence* (London: John Murray, 1848), p. 521.

58 *The Friend of Africa* (1841), pp. 13–16.

The influence of officers' testimonies

Naval officers of the West Africa squadron also shaped the wider public debates in Britain about transatlantic slavery through the publication of their testimonies of service from the West African coast. Officers' rare first-hand experiences of the brutality of the slave trade voiced in newspapers, periodicals, pamphlets and published memoirs generated public interest for the work of the squadron, and many narratives became key sources for debates about anti-slavery in the press, Parliament and other public arenas.[59] As such, officers' experiences can be added to the body of nineteenth-century travel narratives which offered a source of eyewitness evidence for the transfer of ideas and the development of anti-slavery culture.[60] Their unique position at the frontline of naval suppression was key: as one Commander was keen to stress, 'any idea one could form of the horrors of the Slave Trade would fall short of what I saw'.[61]

Squadron colleagues Commodore Sir George Ralph Collier and Commander Benedictus Marwood Kelly were both keen to influence the public debate around abolitionism. In 1820 Collier was unanimously elected an honorary life member of the African Institution for his commitment to the squadron. The directors declared that he had 'entitled himself to the cordial esteem and gratitude of this Institution, and of every friend of Africa, by the zeal, intelligence, and humanity which he has displayed throughout the whole period of his arduous command'.[62] Collier wrote passionately and articulately about his experiences of the slave trade in his official reports to the Admiralty. He concluded one of his reports with an account of a captured slaver, in which he expressed deep humanity towards the enslaved, alongside his own emotional anguish:

> On this distressing subject, so revolting to every well regulated mind, I will add that such is the merciless treatment of the slaves by the persons engaged in the traffic that no fancy can picture the horror of the voyage – crowded together so as not to give the power to move – linked one to the

59 Robert Burroughs, 'Slave-trade suppression and the culture of anti-slavery in nineteenth-century Britain', in Burroughs and Huzzey (eds), *Suppression*, pp. 125–45.
60 Kate Hodgson, 'Slave trades, slavery and emancipation in nineteenth-century European travel narratives', EURESCL: European political cultures of anti-slavery, www.eurescl.eu/images/stories/essays_wp1/Slave%20trades%20slavery%20and%20emancipation%20in%20travel%20onarratives.pdf [accessed 27 January 2018].
61 Extract of a letter from the Commander of the *Pique* in *Ninth Report of the Directors of the African Institution* (1815), pp. 46–47.
62 *The Missionary Register, for 1822* (London: C. B. Seeley, 1822), p. 319; John Marshall, *Royal Naval Biography*, vol. 4 (London, 1825), pp. 539–40.

other by the leg – never unfettered whilst life remains, or till the iron shall have fretted the flesh almost to the bone … It is to me a matter of extreme wonder that any of these miserable people live the voyage through; many of them indeed perish on the passage, and those who remain to meet the shore, present a picture of wretchedness language cannot express.[63]

The idea that the slave trade represented horrors beyond the power of words to convey is clear; the emotion of his language is striking, and somewhat unexpected for an official report to his superiors. His fervour explains why his reports were widely read and consulted outside the Admiralty. This particular passage was quoted in numerous newspapers of the period, serving to generate public awareness and support for the work of the squadron.[64] Details from Collier's reports published in *The Royal Gazette; and Sierra Leone Advertiser* (and republished in *The Times*) were intended to 'command a deep and melancholy attention from every humane reader'. The newspaper noted that Collier's words 'brought to light what the public had hardly been prepared for – the immense magnitude of this terrible traffic'.[65]

Commander Kelly was also a subscriber to the African Institution and similarly committed to the abolitionist cause. He commanded the *Pheasant* on anti-slave-trade patrols between 1818 and 1822 and was at one time in command of the squadron while Commodore Collier was invalided home. The *Pheasant* captured the Portuguese slaver *Novo Felicidade* in July 1819, and its crew discovered 71 enslaved Africans on board a small vessel. Kelly gave the following judicial evidence to the Admiralty Court at Sierra Leone regarding the conditions on board:

the state in which these unfortunate creatures were found is shocking to every principle of humanity; – seventeen men shackled together in pairs by the legs, and twenty boys, one on the other, in the main hold … One of these unfortunate creatures was in the last stage of dysentery, whose natural evacuations ran involuntarily from him amongst the yams, creating effluvia too shocking for description. The appearance of the Slaves, when released from their irons, was most distressing; scarcely any of them could stand on their legs, from cramp and evident starvation.

Kelly's evidence was widely reproduced by the African Institution and by journals in Britain and the United States.[66] Twenty years later his words

---

63 MoD, MSS 45, 'Second Annual Report', ff. 13, 241–42.

64 For example, *The Morning Chronicle*, 2 October 1821; *Glasgow Herald*, 19 October 1821; *The Bath Chronicle*, 4 October 1821.

65 *The Royal Gazette; and Sierra Leone Advertiser*, 16 February 1822, p. 25.

66 *Fourteenth Report of the Directors of the African Institution* (1820), p. 11; *The British*

featured in the 1840 Prospectus for the African Civilization Society, of which he was also a committee member. Reflective of his links to these societies, Kelly also engaged with Britain's wider anti-slavery mission on the West African coast. In his report to the Admiralty in 1823 on Fernando Po as a potential anti-slavery base, Kelly regarded the island in an 'eligible situation for giving effect to the laudable exertions, of ... the African Institution, who are straining every nerve to extend the blessings of civilization & Christianity to the wilds of Africa'.[67] Kelly's legacy of anti-slavery service has framed how he is remembered. A blue plaque dedicated to him at his former home in Saltford, Somerset, reads: 'naval officer, liberator of slaves, benefactor'.[68]

The idea that the brutality and cruelty of the slave trade needed to be seen to be believed was an influential message to disseminate to the British public at a time when pro-slavery sentiment was still a potent force in British society. As Commodore Robert Mends wrote in a report to the Admiralty in 1822 (which was also published by the African Institution), no description 'has been too animated: it is impossible it could be so. It is necessary to visit a slave-ship, to know what the trade is.'[69] Naval officers were considered as best placed to transmit their experiences to audiences back in Britain, and a key source of information from the African coast. Commander Henry James Matson made public his experiences of the slave trade to generate publicity for the abolitionist cause. His evidence of the conditions on board slave ships was used at a meeting of the BFASS in Bury St Edmunds in 1849, to 'afford information respecting the present extent and atrocities of the Slave Trade'. BFASS secretary Mr Scoble described 'harrowing' details of overcrowding and disease. 'It would be doubted', the report of the meeting continued, 'whether, even on the ground of self-interest, those engaged in this traffic would thus pack the slaves.' The evidence of Captain Matson, however, 'threw a flood of light on the whole subject' and 'questioned if the history of our race gave anything so terrible as this'.[70]

Following on from the influential body of abolitionist literature about the horrors of the slave trade circulated in the late eighteenth century, published

Review and London Critical Journal (London, 1821), p. 51; *The Missionary Register* (London, 1820), pp. 470–71; *A View of the Present State of the African Slave Trade Published by Direction of a Meeting Representing the Religious Society of Friends in Pennsylvania, New Jersey* (Philadelphia, 1824), pp. 59–60.

67 UKHO, MP 107, 'Remarks and observations'.

68 See http://www.saltfordenvironmentgroup.org.uk/history/history010.html [accessed 20 January 2018].

69 Robert Mends, 'Report on the state of the Slave Trade on the Western Coast of Africa', 26 June 1822, *British and Foreign State Papers, 1822–1823*, published in *Eighteenth Report of the Directors of the African Institution* (1824), pp. 33–34.

70 *The Bury and Norwich Post, and East Anglian*, 26 December 1849.

narratives from the West African coast were intended to have an impact on readers' consciences and sensitivities.[71] The following account relating to the scene at the capture of the Portuguese slaver *Dous Fevereiro* in 1841 by the *Fawn* under Lieutenant J. Foote of the South American station was originally extracted from the ship's log:

> the living, the dying, and the dead, huddled together in one mass. Some unfortunates in the most disgusting state of small-pox ... others, living skeletons, with difficulty crawled from below, unable to bear the weight of their own bodies; mothers with young infants hanging to their breasts, unable to given them a drop of nourishment. How they had brought them thus far appeared astonishing; all were perfectly naked – their limbs much excoriated from lying on the hard plank for so long a period. On going below the stench was insupportable. How beings could breathe such an atmosphere and live, appeared incredible. Several were under the loose planks which were called the deck, dying – one dead.[72]

This harrowing report featured in *The Friend of Africa* in 1841; it also appeared four years later in a publication in support of the Church Missionary Society. According to the accompanying commentary, this case served to exemplify the 'sufferings' and 'mental agony' of the Middle Passage, and, importantly, to highlight that the slave trade (despite British efforts) was in 'full operation' and hence keep the issue in the public eye.[73] The piece went on to compare the influence of this narrative with that of naval surgeon Alexander Falconbridge's *An Account of the Slave Trade on the Coast of Africa* (1788), which had such an impact on public opinion in the late eighteenth century in favour of the abolition of the slave trade.

As seen in Chapter 1, officers' eyewitness accounts in the public realm were also used to provide evidence of the shortcomings of abolitionist policies; during the debates over the squadron's efficacy, for example, anti-coercionists used officers' testimonies to support the argument that the enslaved suffered more as a result of naval suppression.[74] Captain Joseph Denman was particularly vocal in defence of the squadron when the navy's campaign was increasingly criticized. Alongside his membership of the ACS, Denman

71 William Wilberforce, for example, noted that 'so much misery condensed in so little room is more than the human imagination had ever before conceived'. Quoted in Rediker, *Slave Ship*, p. 327. See also the published accounts of Olaudah Equiano and the Revd John Newton.

72 *The Friend of Africa* (1841), pp. 160–61.

73 Revd Samuel Abraham Walker, *Missions in Western Africa, among the Soosoos, Bulloms &c, being the First Undertaken by The Church Missionary Society for Africa and the East* (Dublin: William Curry, Jun., and Co., 1845), pp. 45–47.

74 Burroughs, 'Eyes on the prize', pp. 99–115.

was part of another abolitionist network – that of familial connection – as his father, Lord Chief Justice Denman, was an outspoken abolitionist.[75] Denman corresponded with his father on the subject throughout the 1830s and 1840s, supplying him with information about slave traders' practices and naval strategies. Lord Denman was very proud of Joseph's actions in the blockade of the River Gallinas, writing to his other sons, '[t]here is something very noble in Joe's conduct'.[76]

In their published accounts some naval officers addressed contemporary debates about the immorality of the institution of slavery. For example, an account published in *The Amulet. A Christian and Literary Remembrancer* was taken from the journal of 'a gallant and distinguished naval officer who passed three years on the African coast'. His piece was reproduced in other journals.[77] Published one year before the Emancipation Act, the author wrote: 'we must extinguish slavery in our own colonies … [a]s long as that foul blot is permitted to stain our national character, our influence is weakened, and we cannot, with any justice or consistency, prescribe to others that they shall not make slaves'.[78] Similarly, naval surgeon Thomas Nelson published his long and considered account concerning slavery in the Brazils to provide 'information, however humble, which may either serve to confirm the opinions already entertained, or further the great and philanthropic end to which those opinions are struggling to attain'.[79]

Such accounts were thoughtful, perceptive and intended to have influence. The work of the West Africa squadron was also central to the anti-slavery narrative in British popular culture in the early to mid-nineteenth century, finding representation in art, theatre and popular fiction. As Richard Huzzey has argued, 'wherever there was money to be made in popular culture, slavery could be adopted as a theme'.[80] The presentation of the navy's role here, however, was not without its tensions, reflecting a diversity of perspectives. The passion and emotion of officers' narratives often contrasted with more sanitized and simplified interpretations of their work found in popular culture. There were, for example, many paintings

75 Gareth H. Jones and Vivienne Jones, 'Denman, Thomas, first Baron Denman (1779–1854)', *Oxford Dictionary of National Biography*, Oxford University Press, 2004, www.oxforddnb.com/view/article/7495 [accessed 4 October 2015]. In 1848 Lord Denman made speeches in the House of Commons which significantly contributed to the decision not to withdraw the West Africa squadron.

76 Quoted in Mitchell and Turano, 'Burón v Denman', pp. 45–50.

77 For example, *The African Repository, and Colonial Journal*, vol. 8 (1832).

78 *The Amulet: A Christian and Literary Remembrancer*, ed. S. C. Hall (London: Frederick Westley and A. H. Davis, 1832), p. 250.

79 Nelson, *Remarks*, pp. 2–4, 40.

80 Huzzey, *Freedom Burning*, pp. 17–18.

produced for a wide audience depicting the navy's dramatic engagements with slave ships on the West African coast. The *Black Joke*'s celebrated actions, for example against the *El Amirante* in 1830, were historicized in paintings and prints and reproduced in newspapers.[81] The primary focus of these paintings was the heroism of the navy and the thrill of the chase; any representation of the enslaved and their suffering was sacrificed to the drama of battle.[82] Some published reminiscences of naval suppression similarly set the story in a narrow naval context; naval surgeon Peter Leonard's account, for example, spent much time detailing the pursuit of slave ships while offering only racist stereotypes about the Africans he encountered.[83]

A spirit of national self-congratulation for naval achievements was also promoted in popular fiction and children's games, where the Royal Navy represented British virtue and Christian salvation in granting freedom to the enslaved.[84] Theatrical dramas celebrated the anti-slave-trade patrols as a heroic endeavour, whereby the English were portrayed as gifting liberty to Africans. In plays such as *My Poll and my Partner Joe* (1833) the honest Jack Tar hero, Harry Halyard, invokes the belief that England is synonymous with freedom and justice: 'Dance, you black angels, no more captivity, the British flag flies over your head, and the very rustling of its folds knocks every fetter from the limbs of the poor slave.' The liberated Africans are portrayed as helpless, suffering victims, dependent on the British for their freedom.[85] This 'trope of white rescue', in Sharla M. Fett's words, extended to new styles of pictorial news reporting which emerged mid-century, in particular the *Illustrated London News*, in which stories tended to frame recaptives as passive, joyful recipients of British rescue and guardianship.[86]

81 Robert J. Blyth, 'Britain, the Royal Navy and the suppression of the slave trades in the nineteenth century', in Hamilton and Blyth (eds), *Representing Slavery*, pp. 81–83, 308–11. This idealization of heroic naval action in art had a long tradition. See Quilley, *Empire to Nation*, chs 8 and 9.

82 See Wood, *Blind Memory*, ch. 2, for a wider discussion of the limitations of visual representations of the Middle Passage in popular culture.

83 Leonard, *Records of a Voyage*; Richard Huzzey and John McAleer, 'History, memory and commemoration', in Burroughs and Huzzey (eds), *Suppression*, p. 169.

84 Burroughs, 'Slave-trade suppression', pp. 127–30; Catherine Gallagher, 'Floating signifiers of Britishness in the novels of the anti-slave-trade squadron', in Wendy S. Jacobson (ed.), *Dickens and the Children of Empire* (Basingstoke: Palgrave Macmillan, 2000), pp. 78–93.

85 Waters, *Racism on the Victorian Stage*, pp. 53–56; J. S. Bratton, *Acts of Supremacy: The British Empire and the Stage, 1790–1930* (Manchester: Manchester University Press, 1991), ch. 1.

86 Fett, *Recaptured Africans*, pp. 37, 51–52, 90–92. See, for example, 'Capture of a Slaver', *Illustrated London News*, 11 May 1857.

There were, however, a range of opinions regarding the value of the West Africa squadron, which were reflected in other popular representations of naval suppression that opposed such heroic depictions. For example, the 'sea yarn' *Tom Cringle's Log* by Michael Scott began to appear serially in *Blackwood's Magazine* from 1829, depicting slavery in the Caribbean and defending the West Indian planters' way of life.[87]

As in the eighteenth century, visual culture remained a key method of championing the abolitionist cause, and naval officers produced or informed visual representations of conditions on slave vessels to sway public opinion. Arguably these representations contrasted with other popular portrayals of naval suppression in their depiction of the horrors of the slave trade and, importantly, the impact on its captives. For example, the 1823 print of the French slaver *Vigilante* was inspired by the account of its capture by Lieutenant Mildmay in the River Bonny in 1822, with 345 Africans on board.[88] The drawing was taken 'by an able draftsman at Portsmouth, whilst the vessel was detained there', and the corresponding narrative was published by a committee of the Religious Society of Friends in London. The committee wished to stress that the enslaved 'were found in the wretched condition as exhibited in this plate'. Circumstances intended to shock readers and elicit public support included the discovery of thumb screws, and evidence that the enslaved 'vented their grief upon such as were next them, by biting and tearing their flesh'.[89] The recaptives are shown in cramped conditions, restrained in pairs by handcuffs, iron collars and leg irons in an ordered, depersonalized fashion. The print's similarities to the diagrammatic representation of the Liverpool slave ship *Brooks* (first published in 1788) suggests that the British public responded to this common abolitionist imagery of 'silent, supine, suffering' slaves, in Marcus Wood's words.[90] Lieutenant Mildmay's involvement in penning this narrative is unclear (so too is why the *Vigilante* was transported to England), but what is significant is how accounts from naval officers were a legitimizing and contextualizing element to visual materials produced for abolitionist ends. Similarly, a print of the Spanish schooner *Josefa Maracayera* was produced

---

87 Burroughs, 'Slave-trade suppression', pp. 133–34.

88 Print by S. Croad and J. Hawksworth, 1823 (NMM, PAH7370). Mildmay also detained the *Yeanam* (Spanish, with 380 recaptives), the *Vicua* (Spanish, with 325 recaptives), the *Petite Betsey* (French, 218 recaptives) and *Ursule* (French, 347 recaptives).

89 *Case of the Vigilante, a ship employed in the slave trade; with some reflections on that traffic* (London: Harvey, Darton & Co., 1823), pp. 9–10.

90 Marcus Wood, 'Popular graphic images of slavery and emancipation in nineteenth-century England', in Hamilton and Blyth (eds), *Representing Slavery*, pp. 148–49. The *Brooks* famously showed how slaves were packed into slave ships, but disempowered Africans by depicting them as passive and depersonalized victims.

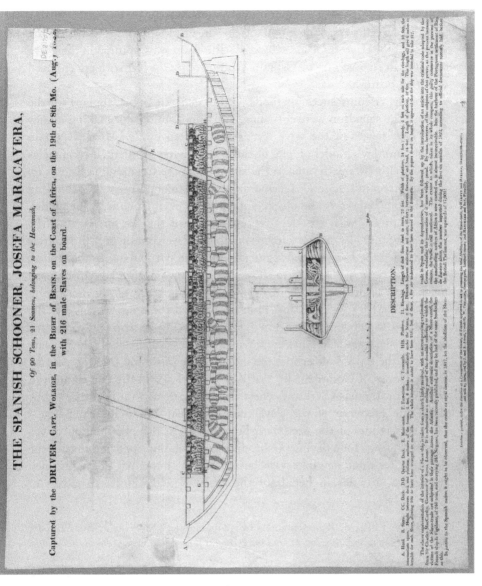

10 'The Spanish schooner *Josefa Maracayera*', 1822

'under the direction of a Committee of the Society of Friends' and was intended to offer 'striking proof of the dreadful sufferings to which the victims of the slave-trade are subjected'. The slaver was captured in the Bight of Benin in August 1822 by Captain Wolrige of the *Driver* with 216 enslaved males on board.

In some circumstances, methods used to generate public support for the work of the squadron were entwined with opportunities for making money from experiences of the slave trade. As reported by *The Mirror*, Captain Henry Huntley's model of 'one of those horrid and pestilential receptacles – a slave ship!' was exhibited in the late 1830s at the Cosmorama Rooms on Regent Street in London.[91] Cosmorama was a 'street peep-show', exhibiting representational views and objects for a curious paying public.[92] The model, it was claimed, was 'a perfect representation' of the *Semiramis*, alias the *Regulo*, captured by the *Fair Rosamond* in the River Bonny in 1831. Huntley commanded the *Fair Rosamond* and provided the 'particulars' for the replica, which had detachable decks to show the Africans imprisoned within, used to display, according to *The Mirror*, 'a frightful scene of the horrors to which the African is a victim'. Huntley utilized the press coverage of the exhibition to condemn the United States as being 'extensively connected with the slave trade'.[93] This employment of physical evidence to recreate scenes of the slave trade echoes the model of the slave ship *Brooks* presented to the House of Commons by William Wilberforce in the late eighteenth century, or Thomas Clarkson's chest displaying items to inform the public about the existence of the slave trade, a visual aid to his campaign.[94] Huntley's model of the *Semiramis* provided a visual representation of the Middle Passage for a paying public, and the exhibition appeared to have the desired effect, one newspaper declaring, '[i]f the humanity of Englishmen requires a stimulus in behalf of the enslaved and murdered natives of

91 NMM, PBP5470, 'Representation of Captain Huntley's Model of a Slave Ship', *The Mirror – of Literature, Amusement, and Instruction*, 1 June 1839; Huzzey, *Freedom Burning*, pp. 17–18.

92 Richard Altick, *The Shows of London* (Cambridge, MA: Harvard University Press, 1978), pp. 392–97. Other exhibitions included topographical models, panoramas and theatrical spectacles; representations of the battles of Trafalgar and Waterloo were particularly popular.

93 Huntley, quoted in *Devizes and Wiltshire Gazette*, 30 May 1839. Huntley later published his account of the anti-slave-trade patrols in *Seven Years' Service*, in which he described the capture of the *Regulo* and *Rapido* slave ships by the *Fair Rosamund* and *Black Joke* (chapter IV). Interestingly, Huntley did not write in the first person and termed himself 'the journalist' (p. 6).

94 Models of the *Brooks* and of Clarkson's chest are currently held by the Wilberforce House Museum in Hull.

Africa, they cannot do better than inspect this "model of a slave ship".[95] However, there is also a sense that the distressing details were included to sensationalize the slave trade.

Other naval officers acknowledged the earning potential of their experiences on the West Africa squadron. Captain Edward Butterfield of the *Fantome* intercepted a slave ship in 1841, 'containing, packed together like bales of cotton, one hundred and five little children'. After providing details of the 'fearful particulars' to *The Friend of Africa*, Butterfield added, 'If I could send my prize to England, I should make my fortune in a month, by publicly exhibiting her.'[96] Butterfield's idea was well received. A letter to the Editor saluted this 'effectual method of rousing up public feeling':

> Let one of these 'floating hells' of the horrors of which we hear and read so much, be brought to England, as nearly as possible in the condition in which it was captured. Let models of the human cargo be constructed, and put on board ... together with the whips and manacles used in confining and coercing them. Thus equipped, let the horrid vessel be brought up the Thames, and moored at London bridge ... and let the people of England see with their own eyes what is the true character of that bane and curse of Africa.[97]

These varied representations of the transatlantic slave trade are illustrative of the ways in which naval officers themselves shaped visual and material culture around naval suppression. Slavery remained a profoundly contested concept in the nineteenth century and the sites of naval suppression – naval vessels, slave ships, African settlements – can be regarded as further spaces in which the 'war of representation' over slavery and the slave trade were fought, a contest that took place in the press, in publications and in metropolitan discourses.[98] Naval officers added significant and unique contributions to these debates and dialogues. Their experiences of witnessing the slave trade were key sources of evidence for the anti-slavery movement in Britain, adding authenticity and legitimacy to claims that the transatlantic slave trade remained a formidable force, fuelling outrage about conditions

95 *Maidstone Journal and Kentish Advertiser*, 28 May 1839.

96 *The Friend of Africa* (1841), p. 207.

97 *The Friend of Africa* (1841), p. 222. In 2007, the bicentenary of the abolition of the slave trade, a model of the slave ship *Zong* sailed up the River Thames and was exhibited at London Bridge. Several projects active today have 'resurrected' slave ships as a way to engage the public with this difficult history, such as Amistad America or The Dos Amigos/Fair Rosamond Slave Ship Replica Project based in Miami.

98 Lambert, 'Sierra Leone and other sites', pp. 103–04. See also Hall, *Civilising Subjects*, pp. 106–08.

on slave ships, providing evidence of the success (or otherwise) of the anti-slavery mission, or reinforcing Britain's perceived place on the international stage. Officers' involvement in and support for anti-slavery societies bears witness to the flow of publications and correspondence between Britain and West Africa, and the formal, informal and personal networks through which information was exchanged between anti-slavery, religious and colonial interest groups. Many officers of the West Africa squadron acted beyond their official capacity in their engagement with the anti-slavery cause in both West Africa and Britain, and some seized the opportunity to contribute to change.

Conclusion

We, as Englishmen, may pride ourselves that this country gloriously vindicated the slur which for generations lay upon the fair page of its history by the noble part our Navy played in the work of suppression. Britannia never ruled the waves more triumphantly than when her sons accomplished their mission of achieving for the defenceless blacks that most priceless of God's gifts – freedom.[1]

This was one analysis of the Royal Navy's campaign to suppress the transatlantic slave trade, written in 1896. Such partisan sentiments would be thoroughly questioned now, but the inclusion of key terms – 'vindicated', 'noble', 'freedom' – says much about how the squadron's legacy was perceived in the short term. A more current assessment of the significance of the West Africa squadron might start with facts and figures. In this context, the contribution of naval forces in enforcing abolition was extensive and expensive; scholars have termed the naval effort 'costly international moral action', and moreover, the 'most expensive example recorded in modern history'.[2] One contemporary poster claimed that 'The African Slave Trade in 1862 costs

---

1 *The Story of the Sea, Edited by Q* (London: Cassell and Co., 1896), p. 446.

2 A phrase used by Chaim D. Kaufmann and Robert A. Pape in 'Explaining costly international moral action: Britain's sixty-year campaign against the Atlantic slave trade', *International Organization*, 53 (1999), pp. 631–68, at p. 631. These are cases where states, motivated by morality, absorb short-term costs even if the long-run benefits are uncertain. The commitment of British forces to this policy of intervention was remarkable. In a typical year, the system represented somewhere between 1 and 2 per cent of the total expenditure of British central government. This figure is difficult to estimate accurately because alongside the 'official' spending related to the naval budget, costs also included high associated expenditure such as treaty payments, bribes, compensation claims for wrongfully seized ships etc. See Eltis, *Economic Growth*, pp. 92–94; Huzzey, *Freedom Burning*, pp. 42–43.

British tax payers 1,000,000 a year'.[3] The campaign also incurred the loss of around 5,000 British lives, and the death of a significant number of recaptives, mostly through disease. Furthermore, the squadron's 'success' – in terms of the proportion of slave ships captured and captives released – is debatable. Estimates of nearly 200,000 African men, women and children released by the navy represent a relatively small share of the estimated 3.2 million embarked as slaves between 1808 and 1863.[4] The Atlantic slave trade was by and large at an end by the late 1860s, although there is some debate as to whether political changes within nations that continued to trade in enslaved Africans were more influential in its demise than the British naval effort.[5] The accession of the Lincoln administration in the United States in 1861 (and the acceptance of the reciprocal 'right of search') was certainly highly influential, as was Cuba's decision to end participation in the slave trade in 1867. Nevertheless, the work of the West Africa squadron was the first chapter in a long history of British naval campaigns directed against international slavery, including the Indian Ocean slave trade from the 1860s; against 'black-birding' (coercion through trickery or kidnapping) in the Western Pacific; and numerous naval campaigns against slave trades across the Red Sea and Persian Gulf in the 1920s and 1930s.[6] Because so much illegal transportation takes place at sea, British naval forces continue to police anti-trafficking campaigns, the war against drugs and other illegal trades.[7]

Envoys of Abolition has argued that the influence of the West Africa squadron was more nuanced than can be gauged by a measurement of numbers of ships detained, treaties signed, or individuals released from the transatlantic slave trade. This book has been concerned primarily with the individuality and independence of naval officers working within a professional, military framework. Naval officers engaged in the suppression of the

---

3 'Poster against the shipping of slaves to Cuba' (1862) as shown in *Towards Liberty: Slavery, the Slave Trade, Abolition and Emancipation: Study Sources Available at Sheffield Local Studies Library and Sheffield Archives* (Sheffield City Council, 2007), p. 15. Compare this sum, however, to the £20 million granted to Britain's slave owners as 'compensation' for the abolition of slavery in 1833, equivalent to 40 per cent of state expenditure.

4 Eltis and Richardson, *Atlas*, p. 274.

5 John Macmillan, 'Myths and lessons of liberal intervention: the British campaign for the abolition of the Atlantic slave trade to Brazil', *Global Responsibility to Protect*, 4 (2012), pp. 98–124.

6 Miers, *Slavery in the Twentieth Century*; Emma Christopher, Cassandra Pybus and Marcus Rediker (eds), *Many Middle Passages: Forced Migration and the Making of the Modern World* (Berkeley, CA: University of California Press, 2007); Doulton, 'The Royal Navy's anti-slavery campaign'.

7 See, for example, the work of the charities Human Rights at Sea and Slave Free Seas, focusing on human rights ambiguities at sea.

slave trade in West Africa were expected to fulfil an array of responsibilities. Alongside the official duties of law enforcement, capture and coercion, there were other roles that dominated officers' experiences of anti-slavery service: as humanitarians, explorers, negotiators, innovators, guardians, 'liberators'. These different constituent parts of anti-slave-trade service – many of which were unfamiliar roles for British naval officers – are infused with themes that run throughout the collective of individual stories in this book: religious imperatives, morality, philanthropy, duty, racial identity, arrogance, coercion, indifference, continuity and change.

The squadron operated for sixty years, during which many societal and cultural shifts took place that affected Britain's place in the world. Many of these changes had significant impacts on the life of a naval officer. However, while certain notions of naval professionalism were transformed by 1867 as compared to 1807, a universal element of naval duty was born of patriotism and pride in one's work. As Michael Lewis has asserted, the overriding motivations of naval personnel were 'Predilection, the inborn love of such a life, Patriotism, the inborn love of Country, and Ambition, the urge to better oneself'.[8] The nineteenth-century British naval officer was expected to set an example for society to follow: the navy, it was believed, provided 'the tone of moral feeling and conduct to a large proportion of our population'.[9] Professionalism and attachment to 'manly, seamanlike' notions of duty are therefore constantly cited in officers' narratives from the West African coast.[10] Lieutenant Clerkson, according to Commodore Bullen, boarded and disarmed a Spanish slave vessel at anchor off Lagos in 1825 because 'he was solely actuated by that zeal, and indefatigable exertion in the performance of his duty'.[11] In this sense, anti-slavery service was no different to any other naval commission, in that the desire to do the best job possible, to impress superiors and advance one's career outweighed all else. Before his return to England in the *Sybille*, with his crew much depleted by sickness, Commodore Francis Collier wrote to the Admiralty: 'It becomes a proud satisfaction for me to add that in 32 months this ship and tender have captured 6,575 slaves and that the Squadron since I have had the honor of being entrusted with the command have captured 11,914.'[12]

8 Lewis, *Navy in Transition*, p. 209.

9 Lincoln, *Representing the Royal Navy*, p. 194, quoting a retired naval surgeon in a pamphlet published in 1824.

10 Phrase used by Henry Dundas Trotter to describe Lieutenant Webb's 1843 despatch to the Admiralty regarding the Niger Expedition (NMM, BGY/W/2).

11 Commodore Charles Bullen to J. W. Croker, 28 February 1825, *Twentieth Report of the Directors of the African Institution* (1826), p. 124.

12 TNA, ADM 1/1, incomplete letter from Francis Collier, no date [c. 1830], ff. 475–78.

Collier's calculation of his success in numerical terms depersonalizes the captives released under his command, but he was stressing his achievements directly in relation to the task he was given: to intercept slave ships and transport recaptives to British territory.

The notion of duty was at the core of officers' understanding of their work. Commander Hugh Dunlop wrote to his sister with pride to report, 'I have now liberated about 600 poor slaves men, women and children.' This achievement, however, required personal sacrifice as Dunlop contracted fever three times as a result of spending time on the mainland. 'I could not have done what has been done without going on shore', Dunlop wrote, 'duty called me, and of course such being the case I could not think of myself.'[13] In a letter home, Midshipman Augustus Arkwright wrote about his understanding of the nature of duty in these terms: 'Our country has the first demand for our services, and private convenience, or happiness, must ever give way to the public good. Duty, is the great business of a sea officer ... all private considerations, must give way to it, however painful.'[14] Arkwright pragmatically separated professionalism and duty from 'private considerations' and personal experiences. However, life on the West African coast was so unlike any other commission as to make Arkwright's detachment of professional from personal motivations impossible for others.

The extraordinary nature of anti-slavery service meant that understandings of professional duty, of fighting and bearing arms, often converged with an individual's spiritual obligation and religious imperative to bring about the end of the slave trade. Commodore John Hayes believed that conflicts with slavers 'operate in an extraordinary way to keep alive that Warlike Spirit in the officers and men'.[15] Commodore George Ralph Collier's reports and correspondence exemplify these complex relations between naval professionalism and moral idealism, whereby his passionate abolitionist beliefs dominated his official reports and the manner in which he discharged his duty as Commodore. Naval officers were undeniably affected by the human trauma and dislocation of what they witnessed, experiences that transcended their normal workload. Abolitionist rhetoric of the eighteenth century is echoed in their narratives. For example, in 1822 William Hall, master of the *Morgiana*, described the enslaved as 'unfortunate fellow creatures', and wrote with disgust about 'horrable [*sic*] dealers in human flesh'.[16] Officers such

---

13 NMM, MSS/87/002/1, Hugh Dunlop to his sister Fanny, 14 January 1850.

14 DRO, D5991/10/54, Augustus Arkwright to his mother from Bathurst, 21 March 1842.

15 TNA, ADM 1/1, John Hayes to Captain George Elliot, 6 May 1831, ff. 418–30.

16 CRL, MS 27, Hall journal (1822), no folios. Hall's language recalls the 'inhumanity

as Collier or Denman contributed their own testimonies to metropolitan public discourses surrounding abolition. As naval men trained to witness the brutalities of war and to an extent hardened to inhumanity, the profound emotion in their narratives of their encounters with the slave trade is striking. Their sense of high moral purpose contrasted with later writing, however, influenced by shifting racial attitudes and Victorian concepts of masculinity, in which sentiment assumed a less positive sense.

Indeed, not all officers were, or aspired to be, humanitarians motivated by the moral imperative to end the slave trade. Other narratives present an alternative reality of indifference, self-interest and concerns for survival. Conditions of service were frequently tedious, pestilent and dangerous. Debates surrounding the moral necessity of acting on behalf of the enslaved were set against instances of disease, high mortality and poor conditions, to the extent that officers' anxieties for their own welfare and security often outweighed humanitarian concern for African lives. With plummeting morale, many questioned their commitment to the abolitionist cause and were concerned solely with material rewards: a normalized incentive structure based around prize money thus existed to facilitate extraordinary work. When naval surgeon Dr McIlroy referred to a captured slave ship as a 'valuable prize', he was assessing its potential financial reward for the British crew rather than the prospect of release from slavery for the 450 captives on board.[17] Some men asserted that disgust at the nature of life and work on the West African coast overrode all else. Such disillusionment led to instances of officers orchestrating abolitionist policy at the frontline while also harbouring resentment towards it, and at times publicly and privately expressing opposition to both the naval campaign and the fundamental beliefs at the heart of the anti-slavery cause.

The men who engaged most profoundly with the dynamics of anti-slavery were invariably those who had designated roles on shore, attempting to eradicate slave trading from West African societies. It might have seemed that 'the Royal Navy had gained an empire and lost a role' after the end of the Napoleonic Wars, but the humanitarian cause provided many new responsibilities for naval personnel.[18] Post-1807, abolitionism evolved from

of dealers in human flesh' depicted in Isaac Cruikshank's 1792 satire *The Abolition of the Slave Trade*, revealing the influence of such abolitionist sentiment in popular culture. Cruikshank referred to the notorious case of Captain John Kimber of the merchant ship *Recovery*, who murdered an enslaved African woman after she refused his demand that she dance on deck.

17 NMM, LBK/41, McIlroy letters, 3 October 1841. McIlroy was referring to a slaver detained by HMS *Fantome* near St Helena.

18 N. A. M. Rodger, quoted in Samson, 'Too zealous guardians?', p. 71. This was not only the case in West Africa as Samson's *Imperial Benevolence*, pp. 7–41, makes clear.

a social and political crusade to become state policy. Britain's military institutions may have had a non-political status, but naval officers of the West Africa squadron could not ignore the principled implications of their new position, facilitating humanitarian intervention on the international stage.[19] Through its suppression efforts, Britain, declared Commodore Charles Hotham, had earned a 'national character for philanthropy and humanity'.[20] However, humanitarianism in this context often had undertones of cultural arrogance. Anti-slavery was perceived as a standard for civilized nations, and as its prime proponent, the British believed it their duty to fight the moral crusade to save non-Europeans from slavery. Naval officers absorbed these principles in their dealings with West African societies. As Commander Wilmot wrote in his published defence of the squadron in 1853:

> England alone is determined to maintain the principles she has so long professed to the world, and not to flinch in the setting forth of her strength and power, until this glorious object shall have been accomplished. We stand alone, the Champions of this Exalted Cause. If Africa is ever to be free and happy, England must be the Apostle of that freedom.[21]

The sense of superiority and arrogance of British influence in instructing Africans – in Wilmot's words, 'how you can make your country the richest upon earth' – was a constant throughout the period of naval suppression. Captain Columbine's letter to the rulers at Sherbro in 1810 extolled the same faith in the British enterprise as Wilmot's letter to the Commander-in-Chief at Abeokuta over forty years later.[22] In its broader context this message could lead to coercion and pressure, increasingly regarded as justification for increased naval intervention and British imperial expansion.[23] Negotiations with African rulers represented another mode

19 See Ryan, 'The price of legitimacy'.

20 HUA, U DDHO 10/11, Charles Hotham to the Earl of Auckland, 23 March 1848.

21 Arthur Parry Eardley-Wilmot, *A Letter to The Right Honorable Viscount Palmerston on the Present State of the African Slave Trade and on the Necessity of Increasing the African Squadron* (London: James Ridgway, 1853), p. 15.

22 UIC: SLC, Series III, Folder 11, Columbine papers, [no date] August 1810, ff. 103–05; CRL, Church Missionary Society Archive, CA2/08/04, Arthur Eardley-Wilmot to 'Obba Shoron', 3 April 1852.

23 That by the later decades of the nineteenth century the ideology of anti-slavery was used to bolster British imperial ambitions has been asserted by several scholars. See, for example, Joel Quirk, 'Uncomfortable silences: contemporary slavery and the "lessons" of history', in Alison Brysk and Austin Choi-Fitzpatrick (eds), *From Human Trafficking to Human Rights: Reframing Contemporary Slavery* (Philadelphia, PA: University of Pennsylvania Press, 2011), pp. 25–43.

of exerting imperial power, to achieve abolition and end cultural practices deemed unacceptable by the British. However, the officers tasked with the navigation of these relationships were often confronted with the resistance and independence of African rulers, and the moral ambiguities inherent in societies that placed a high importance on war and enslavement.

These relationships were part of naval officers' involvement in wider personal, trade and religious networks of communication concerning anti-slavery in West Africa. As many scholars have identified, the ways in which empire was envisaged in the nineteenth century involved more than a one-way projection of metropolitan values, and naval officers played an active part in the interaction of different cultures for the benefit of the anti-slavery cause. Naval officers working on shore often became familiar with local societies and government structures, and as such worked within existing networks of communication concerning anti-slavery, which included colonial governors, missionaries, merchants, explorers and scientists. From the 1830s, imperial administrators, many of whom were military veterans, operated influential personal networks.[24] Naval officers were part of what Richard Huzzey terms 'branches of the anti-slavery state', co-operating for abolitionist purposes.[25] Several officers who had served on the West Africa squadron were later employed as colonial officials, reflecting their experience. Charles Fitzgerald, formerly of the *Buzzard*, was appointed Lieutenant-Governor of British settlements on the Gambia between 1844 and 1847, a role formerly occupied by Captain Henry Vere Huntley (1839), Commander Henry Frowd Seagram (1843) and Commander Edmund Norcott, formerly of the *Curlew* (1843).[26] Edmund Gabriel, who had served for seven years on the African squadron, was appointed Arbitrator and Acting Judge at Luanda, Angola in 1845, and was later promoted to Commissioner.[27] John Hawley Glover, formerly of the

24 Zoe Laidlaw, *Colonial Connections 1815–45: Patronage, The Information Revolution and Colonial Government* (Manchester: Manchester University Press, 2005), pp. 21–27. Colonial networks provided a way of rewarding comrades and exerting authority. For example, Admiral James Stirling became first Governor and Commander-in-Chief of Western Australia in the 1830s.

25 Huzzey, *Freedom Burning*, p. 50, ch. 3. In Luanda in the 1850s, for example, Consul George Brand created a close working relationship with Rear-Admiral Arthur Fanshawe.

26 David Perfect, *Historical Dictionary of the Gambia* (Lanham, MD: Rowman and Littlefield, 2016).

27 Portugal and Britain signed an agreement to set up a Court of Mixed Commission in Luanda in 1842. Gabriel was well regarded for his knowledge of the continuing slave trade from Angola. He was also a keen zoologist, corresponding with Charles Darwin, and presenting items to the Zoological Society of London in 1860. See Tim

gunboat *Handy*, served as Administrator and then Colonial Secretary of Lagos from 1863 until 1872. Glover had great authority over Lagos politics due to his development of a network of relationships with a diverse group of influential Africans and Europeans.[28]

In this context, for the duration of their service on the coast several officers had 'imperial careers', in David Lambert and Alan Lester's words.[29] They fed informed perceptions back to British policy-makers. On the one hand, this was part of officers' official responsibilities; in attempts to create 'an imperial knowledge system', British agents were armed with information about how to interact with and influence local peoples.[30] On the other, as Captain John Proctor Luce's long, descriptive journals of his travels exemplify, cultural encounters were also bound to personal experiences. The value of these knowledge systems in informing official policy was recognized by policy-makers, and naval officers were looked to for insight, remedies and recommendations. For example, Captain H. B. Young of the *Hydra* identified the following fundamental limitations of abolitionist policy in a report to the Admiralty in 1850:

> It seems to me indeed somewhat strange that we should be striving to force upon a reluctant people, even so benevolent a project, without at the same time endeavouring to make them comprehend its advantages and benevolent character. At present the natives perceive the English to be a nation both wise and powerful, but they cannot apprehend the motive, which really gives rise on our part to such violent and incessant attacks on the slave trade.

Young advocated a shift in British thinking. The promotion of 'good will towards this benighted race' was not helped by the practice of 'compelling them ... to reform such of their customs as we have set a mark upon.'[31] Similarly, Commander Henry James Matson believed that the foundations of British influence in West Africa should be 'an empire of opinion' rather

Willasey-Wilsey, 'Edmund Gabriel and the suppression of the Angolan slave trade', *The Victorian Web*, http://www.victorianweb.org/history/antislavery/gabriel.html [accessed 20 March 2018].

28 Kristin Mann, *Slavery and the Birth of an African City: Lagos, 1760–1900* (Bloomington, IN: Indiana University Press, 2007), pp. 106–16. See also Stephanie Williams, *Running the Show: The Extraordinary Stories of the Men who Governed the British Empire* (London: Penguin, 2012), ch. 2.

29 David Lambert and Alan Lester, 'Introduction: imperial spaces, imperial subjects', in Lambert and Lester (eds), *Colonial Lives*, pp. 1–2.

30 Price, *Making Empire*, esp. ch. 7.

31 TNA, ADM 123/173, 'Best means to be adopted for the abolition of the African slave trade, 1850', reply of Captain H. B. Young, 11 July 1850.

than 'an empire of bayonets'. Matson linked these considerations to the perceived 'prestige' he attached to the national character, based on philanthropy and benevolence rather than intimidation and force. He hoped that 'future generations in that country [West Africa] have reason to bless, and not to curse the name of Britain'.[32]

Not all naval officers were so reasoned in their opinions relating to the governance of other peoples, however. Other ideas about national character and the proper use of British power were bound up with perceptions of racial identity and how far freedom was regarded as applicable to non-Europeans. As Alan Lester has argued, the discourses of Britishness overseas encompassed objectives of 'freeing', 'protecting' and 'civilizing' the empire's subjects to a uniquely British standard: 'the essence of Britishness projected on to the wider world'.[33] By their nature, these dialogues raised important questions about race. The moral imperative of the anti-slavery cause to convert African societies and eradicate slave trading was to a large extent based on racially defined understandings of 'others', whereby British, African and other identities were defined and contested in discussions of empire.[34] Complexities surrounding naval officers' racial attitudes abounded. The belief that African peoples were not capable of moral 'improvement' without humanitarian intervention was propounded even by the most sympathetic naval officers. Anti-slavery views did not necessarily affect how officers perceived African peoples, and racial and cultural theories of paternalism and trusteeship gained strength as the century progressed. Many commentators, such as Captain Columbine, deplored the slave trade but believed in racial inequality, and belief in racial tolerance did not necessarily extend from sympathy with the plight of the enslaved. With the publication of his journals, naval surgeon Peter Leonard hoped to encourage 'the abolition of a trade so revolting to every feeling of humanity', yet he also wrote about the Africans he met with vehement racism.[35] The opinions of Captain Luce are another example of the variance and changes in racial attitudes during the century; he expressed a genuine interest in the people he met yet believed that the innate character of African people made missionary attempts futile.

There were two main sites of racial encounters – on board prize vessels and on shore. In contrast to interactions on shore, prize vessels remained British 'territory'. The navy's capture of a slave vessel symbolized the British

32 Matson, *Remarks on the Slave Trade*, p. 67.

33 Lester, 'British settler discourse', pp. 25–26.

34 Derek R. Peterson, 'Introduction', in Peterson (ed.), *Abolitionism and Imperialism*, p. 31.

35 Leonard, *Records of a Voyage*, preface.

dedication to liberty. Officers celebrated this role, with many contributing powerful written accounts of their experiences of the transatlantic slave trade to influence public debates around abolitionism. However, racial attitudes played a part in officers' consideration of those released into their authority. The stark realities of this extraordinary task meant that treatment of recaptives was often influenced by preconceptions and prejudices, and emotions of sympathy and compassion were often matched by indifference and self-interest. In 1848 Lieutenant George Kenyon wrote that he was 'heartly [*sic*] tired of the Bights & the Coast altogether & wish I had done with nigger driving'.[36] Kenyon was a successful officer in relation to the suppression of the slave trade, but his use of the contemporary phrase referring to plantation owners' management of their slaves says much about his belief in the anti-slavery cause, and the treatment received by those who might have come under his command. Officers' narratives often presented African peoples as dependent on certain gifts that were within the British power to bestow – freedom being the predominant example. Undertones of servitude and control continued in the liberation process. British apprenticeship and emigration schemes revealed the ambiguities of freedom for those supposedly liberated by the navy, and notions of debt and obligation continued to frame relations. When Captain Heath received a request for help from the liberated Africans settled at Badagry, in fear that they would 'again fall into the hands of the slave dealers, from the iron-grasp of which our Queen has graciously delivered us', he counselled against naval interference. Heath added that he hoped that 'you will be able to repay the debt of gratitude you owe England by protecting the missionaries & merchants'.[37]

While this book asserts naval officers' engagement with the themes of anti-slavery, empire and identity, many narratives were also written with a sense of detachment and transience. Like any other naval commissions, the anti-slave-trade patrols represented a temporary set of conditions, and officers' experiences of suppression were to an extent formed of a series of transitional moments: at port, searching rivers, conveying a prize vessel or negotiating a treaty in the interior. Naval narratives therefore occupy

36 SRO, DD/X/GRA/11, George Kenyon to an unidentified recipient from the *Cygnet* in the Bight of Benin, 12 December 1848. The letter was probably intended for Commodore Hotham, as Kenyon began: 'My dear Sir, At last I am able to send you another prize ...' Kenyon had been on the coast since 1842. His phrase compares to the similarly abhorrent 'nigger hunting' used by an anonymous officer in a published letter from 1845 to describe service 'on the most miserable station in the wide world' (*Hampshire Advertiser & Salisbury Guardian*, 11 October 1845).

37 CRL, Church Missionary Society Archive, CA2/o5/1-11, correspondence between 'The liberated African subjects at Badagry' and Captain Heath, 23–24 July 1851.

a unique position in the culture of European contact with West Africa in this period. Many British representatives – missionaries, merchants, traders, officials, administrators – were colonizers in the traditional sense, and engaged in colonial relations with a sense of permanence and the need to create settlements and develop lasting relationships.[38] The transience of the anti-slavery patrols, however, gave officers a degree of independence of thought regarding their accounts of West Africa and the slave trade. Outside of their professional obligations, they had no agenda to follow, and those who expressed support for the abolitionist cause in British publications or via membership of anti-slavery societies were not required to do so. Yet the humanitarian project was inseparable from the agency of naval officers because to a large extent its success or failure depended on their work. As seen in this book, several naval officers relished the influence that came with this responsibility.

There are many examples of officers articulating informed and considered reflections on the transatlantic slave trade and on the British presence in West Africa. Their narratives were shaped by notions of racial identity and cultural arrogance, but they were also influenced by their travels, by people they encountered, and by their personal interpretation of humanitarian discourse. These interconnections of the navy, anti-slavery, exploration and empire are personified in the career of Commodore Arthur Eardley-Wilmot. As we have seen throughout this book, Wilmot threw himself wholeheartedly into his anti-slavery mission in West Africa, to the extent that the Admiralty expressed frustration at his independent approach to his role. As he was informed by First Naval Lord, Sir Frederick William Grey:

> I think you sometimes forget that you are employed as a naval officer & not as a diplomatic one, & that in your well-intentioned desire to benefit Africa you are sometimes led to recommend measures which do not belong to your province or fall within the scope of Admiralty business.[39]

Such an assessment, of an independent, often overly zealous attitude towards anti-slave-trade service, could apply to several other naval officers of the West Africa squadron. Wilmot's approach was more positively received in the African societies in which he spent time. A letter from 'Native Merchants and Inhabitants of the West Coast of Africa' in 1865 wished to thank Wilmot 'for the great zeal and interest which you have displayed for the welfare and advancement of Africa and Africans'. The letter concluded

---

38 Hall, 'Introduction', p. 16.
39 DUL, WYL/27/10-11, Frederick William Grey to Commodore Wilmot, 23 March 1864.

by declaring Wilmot's place in an illustrious cast of abolitionists: 'It is with pride we mention the names of Clarkson, Wilberforce, Sharp, Buxton, and many others, and it is with pride and unfeigned pleasure that we now add to that noble list the name of Wilmot.'[40]

Naval officers such as Wilmot considered themselves envoys of the abolitionist cause, responsible for and implicated in many aspects of the wider British anti-slavery campaign. Others regarded their service very differently, and yet the unique and multifaceted conditions of employment in West Africa meant that very few operated in a military bubble. Naval officers' varying and often conflicting perspectives are therefore an important piece in the complex puzzle of motivations and moral imperatives that represents British abolitionism in the early to mid-nineteenth century, offering valuable insight into shifting attitudes and anxieties about the institution of slavery, and the nature of Britain's evolving relationship with West Africa and its peoples.

40 'Address from Native Merchants and Inhabitants of the Western Coast of Africa', 23 December 1865, in *A Brief Statement of the Services of Vice-Admiral Eardley-Wilmot, C.B.* (Totnes, 1878), pp. 37–38.

Bibliography

Primary sources

i. Manuscripts
Bedfordshire Archives
Papers of Samuel Whitbread (W1/4144)

British Library
Letters of Frederick Forbes, 1849 (Add 17817)
Minute books of the British and Foreign Anti-Slavery Society, 1839–68 (MFR 2883)

Cadbury Research Library, University of Birmingham
Church Mission Society Archive: copy correspondence between the Yoruba Mission and naval officers, 1845–63 (C/A2/05) and (C/A2/08)
Journal of William Hall, 1822 (MS 27)

Caird Library and Archive, National Maritime Museum
Letter of Thomas Butter (AGC/B/24)
Papers of Cornelius T. A. Noddall (AGC/N/33)
Volume of watercolour drawings by Henry Need (ART/10)
Papers of William Webb (BGY/W/2)
Letters from Edwin Thomas Hinde to his family, 1829–32 (HIN/1-2)
Letterbook of Dr McIlroy, 1841–43 (LBK/41)
Letterbook of Sir John Barrow, 1815–17 (LBK/65/2)
Logbook of HMS *Sybille* and HMS *Black Joke* by Henry Downes (LOG/N/41)
Sketch books of watercolour drawings by Francis Meynell (MEY/1-2)
Letters from Francis Meynell to his father, 1843–47 (MEY/5)

Uncatalogued letters of Hugh Dunlop, fl 1842–69 (MSS/87/002/1)
George Collier 'Report of the Forts and Settlements on the Coast of Africa',
  c. 1818–20 (WEL/10)

Cambridge University Library
Journals of George Maclaren, 1831–37 (Add. 9528/1-2)

Churchill Archives Centre, Churchill College, Cambridge University
Papers of Henry Hamilton Beamish (BEAM/1/8-9)

Derbyshire Record Office
Letters of Augustus Peter Arkwright (D5991/10)
Letters of Samuel Richardson (D8/B/F/66)

Durham University Library, Special Collections
Correspondence of Charles, 2nd Earl Grey (GRE/B52/9)
Papers of William Henry Wylde (WYL/24, WYL/26, WYL/27, WYL/28,
  WYL/30)

Gloucestershire Archives
Papers of the Sotherton-Estcourt family (D1571)
Papers of the Bowly family (D4582/6)

Hull University Archives, Hull History Centre
Letterbook of copy letters from Charles Hotham, 1846–48 (U DDHO 10/8)
Secret letterbook of copy letters from Charles Hotham, 1847–49 (U DDHO
  10/11)

Ministry of Defence Admiralty Library
Diaries of George Augustus Bedford, 1835–38 (MSS 151)
Journals of Thomas Boteler, 1828 (MSS 73/1)
'Second Annual Report on the coast of Africa by Commodore Sir George
  Collier, 1820' (MSS 45)

Mitchell Library, State Library of New South Wales
Journal of Arthur Alexander Walton Onslow, 1850–52 (MSS 2050)

National Library of Scotland
Papers of General Sir Charles William Pasley (MS 9879)
Correspondence of the 2nd Earl of Minto as First Lord of the Admiralty (MS
  12048-68)
Memoirs of John M'Kie from c. 1850, compiled c. 1905 (MS 24632-6)

National Museum of the Royal Navy
Diaries of Cheesman Henry Binstead, 1823–24 (2005.76/1-2)

National Records of Scotland
Copy letters from Robert Flockhart to his family, 1838 (GD 76/458)
Letters from Alexander Murray to his brother, 1847–49 (GD 219/304)

New York Public Library
Journal of John Thompson, 1852–59
Memoirs of Gordon Gallie MacDonald, c. 1832

Nimitz Library, Special Collections and Archives Department, US Naval Academy
Remark book of Commander Hugh Dunlop, 1847–49 (MS 59)

Private Collections
Journal of Henry Rogers, c. 1849–50
Papers of the Adam family, of Blair Adam (NRAS1454)

Record Office for Leicestershire, Leicester and Rutland
Cross-section of the Spanish schooner *Josefa Maracayera* (DE8170/2)

Royal Anthropological Institute Archive
Journals of Captain J. P. Luce (MS 280)

Somerset Heritage Centre, South West Heritage Trust
Papers of the Shore family (A/AOV)
Papers of the Capel and Keats families (DD/CPL)
Papers of the Kenyon family (DD/X/GRA)

The National Archives
Admiralty Records:
ADM 1/1
ADM 1/2027
ADM 1/5517
ADM 7/606
ADM 30/26
ADM 105/92
ADM 123/173, 176, 181, 182, 183
Colonial Office Records:
CO 267/25, 27, 28
Foreign Office Records:
FO 84/893, 1040
FO 881/824

UK Hydrographic Office Archive
Remark book of James Dacres, 1845–46 (CRB 1846)
Incoming letters (LP 1857/Box M760)
Miscellaneous papers (MP 46/Ac 8)
D. G. Miller, 'Remarks on some parts of the West Coast of Africa', 1832 (MP 90/Ca6)
Remark book of HM sloop *Thalia*, 1836 (MP 90/Ca6)
Remarks of Captain W. Walkhope, 1837 (MP 90/Ca6)
Commander B. Marwood Kelly, 'A Survey of a Bay in the Island of Fernando Po, together with remarks on the NW Coast of that island', 1823 (MP 107)
Commander B. Marwood Kelly, 'Remarks and observations on the probable value of the island of Fernando Po as a British colony', 1823 (MP 107)

University of Illinois at Chicago Library, Special Collections
Papers of Edward H. Columbine (Series III)
Journal of George W. Courtenay, 1823–25 (Series V, Folder 16)

Wellcome Collection
Journals of Fleetwood Buckle, 1866–67 (MS 1395-7)

West Sussex Record Office
Papers of the Buckle family (BUCKLE)

ii. Primary sources published online
Diary of Richard Carr McClement, published at Scottish Catholic Archives, www.scottishcatholicarchives.org.uk/Learning/DiaryofRichardCarr McClement/tabid/142/Default.aspx
Letters of Commodore William Henry Jones, 1845, published at www.pdavis.nl/Jones_3.htm
UK Parliamentary Papers, https://parlipapers.proquest.com

iii. Periodicals and newspapers
The African Repository, and Colonial Journal
The Anti-Slavery Reporter
The Bath Chronicle
The British Review and London Critical Journal
The Bury and Norwich Post, and East Anglian
The Christian Observer
The Colonial Magazine
Devizes and Wiltshire Gazette
Glasgow Herald

Hampshire Advertiser & Salisbury Guardian
Illustrated London News
The Leeds Times
Maidstone Journal and Kentish Advertiser
The Missionary Register
The Morning Chronicle
The Morning Post
The Nautical Magazine
Royal Cornwall Gazette, Falmouth Packet & Plymouth Journal
The Royal Gazette, and Sierra Leone Advertiser
The Times
United Service Magazine (including *The United service journal and naval and military magazine* and *The United service magazine and naval and military journal*)
Western Morning News
Whitby Panorama; And Monthly Chronicle

iv. Printed publications

A Brief Statement of the Services of Vice-Admiral Eardley-Wilmot, C.B. (Totnes, 1878)

A View of the Present State of the African Slave Trade Published by Direction of a Meeting Representing the Religious Society of Friends in Pennsylvania, New Jersey (Philadelphia, 1824)

Allen, William, and Thomson, T. R. H., *A Narrative of the Expedition to the River Niger in 1841 under the Command of Captain H. D. Trotter, R.N,* 2 vols (London: Richard Bentley, 1848)

Ashcroft, William Petty, 'Reminiscences', serialized in *The Naval Review*, part V, 53.1 (1965), pp. 62–70

Baker, Samuel White, *The Albert N'yanza, Great Basin of the Nile, and Exploration of the Nile Sources,* 2 vols (London: Macmillan, 1866)

Beaver, Philip, *African Memoranda: Relative to an attempt to establish a British settlement on the island of Bulama* (London: C. and R. Baldwin, 1805)

Belcher, Captain, 'Extracts from Observations on Various Points of the West Coast of Africa, Surveyed by His Majesty's Ship *Aetna* in 1830–32', *Journal of the Royal Geographical Society of London*, 2 (1832), pp. 278–304

Boteler, Thomas, *Narrative of a voyage of discovery to Africa and Arabia performed by HMS Leven and Barracouta from 1821 to 1826 under the command of Capt. W.F.W. Owen* (London: Richard Bentley, 1835)

Bridge, Horatio, *Journal of an African Cruiser* (London, 1845)

British and Foreign State Papers, 1821–1822, compiled by the Foreign Office (London: J. Harrison and Son, 1829)

British and Foreign State Papers, 1822–1823, compiled by the Foreign Office (London: J. Harrison and Son, 1828)

Bryson, Alexander, *Report on the Climate and Principal Diseases of the African Station; compiled from documents in the office of the Director-General of the Medical Department, and from other sources* (London: William Clowes and Sons, 1847)

Burton, Richard, *The Lake Regions of Central Africa*, 2 vols (London: Longman, 1860)

Burton, Richard, *A Mission to Glele, King of Dahome* (London: Tinsley Brothers, 1864)

Buxton, Charles, *Memoirs of Sir Thomas Fowell Buxton, Baronet, with Selections from his Correspondence* (London: John Murray, 1848)

Buxton, Thomas Fowell, *The African Slave Trade and Its Remedy*, 2nd edn (London: John Murray, 1840)

'Capture of the Spanish Slaver, *Marinerito*, by the *Black Joke*', *United Service Magazine*, part II (1832), pp. 63–65

Case of the Vigilante, a ship employed in the slave trade; with some reflections on that traffic (London: Harvey, Darton & Co., 1823)

Chamier, Frederick, *The Life of a Sailor by a Captain in the Navy*, 3 vols (London: Richard Bentley, 1832)

Clapperton, Hugh, and Lander, Richard, *Journal of a second expedition into the interior of Africa from the Bight of Benin to Soccatoo* (London: John Murray, 1829)

Clarkson, Thomas, *The History of the Abolition of the African Slave-Trade*, 2 vols (1808)

Colomb, P. H., *Memoirs of the Admiral the Right Honorable Sir Astley Cooper Key* (London: Methuen, 1898)

Crowther, Revd Samuel, *Journal of An Expedition Up the Niger and Tshadda Rivers* (London: Church Missionary House, 1855)

Cugoano, Quobna Ottobah, *Thoughts and Sentiments on the Evil of Slavery and Other Writings* (London, 1787)

Denman, Joseph, *Practical Remarks on the Slave Trade* (London: Ridgway, 1839)

Denman, Joseph, *West India Interests, African Emigration and Slave Trade* (1848)

Denman, Joseph, *The African Squadron and Mr Hutt's Committee*, 2nd edn (London: John Mortimer, 1850)

Drake, Richard, *Revelations of a Slave Smuggler* (New York: Robert de Witt, 1850)

Duncan, John, 'Some Account of the Last Expedition to the Niger', *Bentley's Miscellany*, 22 (1847)

Equiano, Olaudah, *The Interesting Narrative of the Life of Olaudah Equiano or Gustavus Vassa the African* (New York: Penguin, 1995), first published 1789

Falconbridge, Alexander, *An Account of the Slave Trade on the Coast of Africa* (London: J. Phillips, 1788)

Foote, Andrew Hull, *Africa and the American Flag* (New York, 1854)

Foote, John, 'A Few Remarks on the Slave-Trade in the Brazils by Commander Foote R.N.', *United Service Magazine*, part II (1845), pp. 378–87

Forbes, Frederick, *Six Months' Service in the African Blockade, from April to October, 1848, in command of H.M.S. Bonetta* (London: Richard Bentley, 1849)

Forbes, Frederick, 'Despatch communicating the discovery of a Native Written Character at Bohmar, on the Western Coast of Africa, near Liberia, accompanied by a Vocabulary of the Vahie or Vei Tongue', *Journal of the Royal Geographical Society*, 20 (1850), pp. 89–113

Forbes, Frederick, *Dahomey and the Dahomans, being the journals of two missions to the King of Dahomey and residence at his capital in the years 1849 and 1850* (Paris: A. and W. Galignani and Co., 1854), first published 1851

Hamilton, Sir Richard Vesey (ed.), *Letters and Papers of Admiral of the Fleet Sir Thomas Byam Martin*, vol. 1 (Navy Records Society, 1903)

Holman, James, *A Voyage Round the World: including travels in Africa, Asia, Australasia, America*, 2 vols (London: Smith, Elder and Co., 1834)

How do we procure sugar? A question proposed for the consideration of the people of Great Britain. By a Naval Officer. Printed for the Whitby Anti-Slavery Society (1828)

Huntley, Sir Henry, *Seven Years' Service on the Slave Coast of Western Africa*, 2 vols (London: Thomas Cautley Newby, 1850)

Industrial Exhibition at Sierra Leone 1865: Its History, French and British Catalogues, Appointment of Jurors, Their Reports, and Lists of Their Awards (London: Hatchard and Co., 1866)

Instructions for the Guidance of Her Majesty's Naval Officers Employed in the Suppression of the Slave Trade (London: T. R. Harrison, 1844)

Jackson, R. M., *Journal of a Voyage to Bonny River on the West Coast of Africa in the Ship Kingston from Liverpool*, ed. Roland Jackson (Letchworth: Garden City Press, 1934)

'Journal of a Naval Officer on the West Coast of Africa', *The Colonial Church Chronicle and Missionary Journal* (July 1858), pp. 250–62

Laird, Macgregor, and Oldfield, R. A. K., *Narrative of an expedition into the interior of Africa by the River Niger*, 2 vols (London: Richard Bentley, 1837)

Lander, Richard, *Records of Captain Clapperton's last expedition to Africa with the subsequent adventures of the author* (London: Richard Bentley, 1830)

Lander, Richard, and Lander, John, *Journal of an expedition to explore the course and termination of the Niger* (London: John Murray, 1832)

Leonard, Peter, *Records of a Voyage to the Western Coast of Africa, in His Majesty's Ship Dryad, and of the Service on that Station for the Suppression of the Slave Trade, in the Years 1830, 1831 and 1832* (Edinburgh: William Tait, 1833)

Macaulay, Thomas Babington, 'Minute of 2 February 1835 on Indian Education', in *Prose and Poetry*, ed. G. M. Young (Cambridge, MA: Harvard University Press, 1957)

Marshall, John, *Royal Naval Biography* (London: Longman, 1825)

Matson, Commander Henry James, *Remarks on the Slave Trade and African Squadron*, 3rd edn (London: James Ridgeway, 1848)

Matthews, John, *A Voyage to the River Sierra Leone on the Coast of Africa; containing an account of the trade and productions of the country, and of the civil and religious customs and manners of the people* (London: B. White and Son, 1791)

McHenry, George, *Visits to Slave Ships* (British and Foreign Anti-Slavery Society, 1862)

Moore, Samuel, *Biography of Mahommah G. Baquaqua, a Native of Zoogoo in the Interior of Africa* (Detroit, 1854)

Nelson, Thomas, *Remarks on the Slavery and Slave Trade of the Brazils* (London: J. Hatchard and Son, 1846)

O'Byrne, William Richard, *A naval biographical dictionary: comprising the life and services of every living Officer in her Majesty's Navy, from the rank of Admiral of the Fleet to that of Lieutenant* (London: John Murray, 1849)

Owen, William Fitzwilliam, *Narrative of voyages to explore the shores of Africa, Arabia and Madagascar performed in HM Ships 'Leven' and 'Barracouta'* (London: Richard Bentley, 1833)

Proceedings of the General Anti-Slavery Convention (1840), vol. 1

Report of the Committee of the African Civilization Society to the Public Meeting of the Society, held at Exeter Hall, 21 June 1842 (London: John Murray, 1842)

Reports of the Directors of the African Institution (1807–22)

'Representation of Captain Huntley's Model of a Slave Ship', *The Mirror – of Literature, Amusement, and Instruction*, 1 June 1839

Schön, J. F., and Crowther, Samuel A., *Journals of the Rev. James Frederick Schön and Mr Samuel Crowther, Who ... Accompanied the Expedition up the Niger in 1841* (London: Hatchard and Son, 1842)

Smith, George, *The case of our West African cruisers and West African settlements fairly considered* (London: J. Hatchard, 1848)

Stoddart, James, 'A Cruise in a Slaver. From the Journal of Admiral James Stoddart', *Blackwood's Magazine*, 245.1480 (1939), pp. 186–99

The Amulet. A Christian and Literary Remembrancer, ed. S. C. Hall (London: Frederick Westley and A. H. Davis, 1832)

The Friend of Africa; by the Society for the Extinction of the Slave Trade, and for the Civilization of Africa, vol. 1 (London, John W. Parker, 1841)

'The Slaver. From the note-book of an Officer employed against the slave trade', *United Service Magazine*, part I (1842), pp. 375–80

The Story of the Sea, Edited by Q (London: Cassell and Co., 1896)

Trial of Pedro de Zulueta, Jun., on a charge of slave trading. On Friday the 27th, Saturday the 28th, and Monday the 30th of October, 1843 at the Central Criminal Court, Old Bailey, London (London: C. Wood & Co., 1844)

Walker, Revd Samuel Abraham, *Missions in Western Africa, among the Soosoos, Bulloms &c, being the First Undertaken by The Church Missionary Society for Africa and the East* (Dublin: William Curry, Jun., and Co., 1845)

Washington, Captain John, 'Some Account of Mohammedu-Siseï, a Mandingo, of Nyáni-Marú on the Gambia', *Journal of the Royal Geographical Society of London*, 8 (1838), pp. 448–54

Wauchope, Robert, *A Short Narrative of God's Merciful Dealings* (privately printed, 1862)

West African Sketches: Compiled from the Reports of Sir G.R. Collier, Sir Charles MacCarthy, and Other Official Sources (London: L. B. Seeley and Son, 1824)

Wilmot, Arthur Parry Eardley-, *A Letter to The Right Honorable Viscount Palmerston on the Present State of the African Slave Trade and on the Necessity of Increasing the African Squadron* (London: James Ridgway, 1853)

Wilmot, Sydney Eardley-, *An Admiral's Memories: Sixty-five Years Afloat and Ashore* (London: Sampson Low, Marston and Co., 1927)

Wilson, Revd J. Leighton, *The British Squadron on the Coast of Africa* (London: James Ridgway, 1851)

Yonge, C. D., *History of the British Navy: from the earliest period to the present time*, 3 vols (London: Richard Bentley, 1863)

Yule, Sir Henry, *The African Squadron Vindicated* (London: James Ridgway, 1850)

Secondary sources

i. Books and articles

Abrahams, Yvette, 'Images of Sara Bartman: sexuality, race, and gender in early-nineteenth-century Britain', in Ruth Roach Pierson and Nupur Chaudhuri (eds), *Nation, Empire, Colony: Historicizing Gender and Race* (Bloomington, IN: Indiana University Press, 1998), pp. 220–36

Ackerson, Wayne, *The African Institution (1807–1827) and the Antislavery Movement in Great Britain* (New York: Edwin Mellen, 2005)

Adderley, Roseanne, *'New Negroes from Africa': Slave Trade Abolition and Free African Settlement in the Nineteenth-Century Caribbean* (Bloomington, IN: Indiana University Press, 2006)

Ajayi, J. F. Ade, and Oloruntimehin, B. O., 'West Africa in the anti-slave trade era', in John E. Flint (ed.), *The Cambridge History of Africa*, vol. 5 (Cambridge: Cambridge University Press, 1976), pp. 200–21

Allain, Jean, 'Nineteenth-century law of the sea and the British abolition of the slave trade', *British Yearbook of International Law*, 78.1 (2007), pp. 342–88

Altick, Richard, *The Shows of London* (Cambridge, MA: Harvard University Press, 1978)

Anderson, Clare, *Subaltern Lives: Biographies of Colonialism in the Indian Ocean World, 1790–1920* (Cambridge: Cambridge University Press, 2012)

Anim-Addo, Joan, 'Queen Victoria's black "daughter"', in Gretchen Holbrook Gerzina (ed.), *Black Victorians/Black Victoriana* (New Brunswick, NJ: Rutgers University Press, 2003), pp. 11–19

Anstey, Roger, 'Capitalism and slavery: a critique', *The Economic History Review*, 21.2 (1968), pp. 307–20

Anstey, Roger, *The Atlantic Slave Trade and British Abolition, 1760–1810* (London: Macmillan, 1975)

Asiegbu, Johnson U. J., *Slavery and the Politics of Liberation, 1787–1861: A Study of Liberated African Emigration and British Anti-slavery Policy* (Harlow: Longman, 1969)

Austen, Ralph, and Smith, Woodruff D., 'Images of Africa and British slave-trade abolition: the transition to an imperialist ideology, 1787–1807', *African Historical Studies*, 2.1 (1969), pp. 69–83

Bank, Andrew, 'Losing faith in the civilizing mission: the premature decline of humanitarian liberalism at the Cape, 1840–60', in Martin Daunton and Rick Halpern (eds), *Empire and Others: British Encounters with Indigenous Peoples 1600–1850* (London: UCL Press, 1999), pp. 364–83

Barker, Anthony J., *The African Link: British Attitudes to the Negro in the Era of the African Slave Trade, 1550–1807* (London: Frank Cass, 1978)

Barringer, Tim, 'Images of otherness and the visual production of difference: race and labour in illustrated texts, 1850–1865', in Shearer West (ed.), *The Victorians and Race* (Aldershot: Scolar Press, 1996), pp. 34–53

Bayly, C. A., *Imperial Meridian: The British Empire and the World 1780–1830* (London: Longman, 1989)

Bayly, C. A., 'The British and indigenous peoples, 1760–1860: power, perception and identity', in Martin Daunton and Rick Halpern (eds), *Empire and Others: British Encounters with Indigenous Peoples, 1600–1850* (London: UCL Press, 1999), pp. 19–41

Beeler, John, 'Maritime policing and the *Pax Britannica*: the Royal Navy's anti-slavery patrol in the Caribbean, 1818–1846', *Northern Mariner*, 16.1 (2006), pp. 1–20

Bethell, Leslie, 'The Mixed Commissions for the suppression of the trans-Atlantic slave trade in the nineteenth century', *The Journal of African History*, 7.1 (1966), pp. 79–93

Bethell, Leslie, *The Abolition of the Brazilian Slave Trade: Britain, Brazil and the Slave Trade Question 1807–1869* (Cambridge: Cambridge University Press, 1970)

Bew, John, '"From an umpire to a competitor": Castlereagh, Canning and the issue of international intervention in the wake of the Napoleonic Wars', in Brendan Simms and D. J. B. Trim (eds), *Humanitarian Intervention: A History* (Cambridge: Cambridge University Press, 2011), pp. 117–38

Bindman, David, *Ape to Apollo: Aesthetics and the Idea of Race in the 18th Century* (Ithaca, NY: Cornell University Press, 2002)

Blake, Richard, *Evangelicals in the Royal Navy 1775–1815: Blue Lights & Psalm-Singers* (Woodbridge: The Boydell Press, 2008)

Blake, Richard, *Religion in the British Navy 1815–1879* (Woodbridge: The Boydell Press, 2014)

Blaubarb, Rafe, and Clarke, Liz, *Inhuman Traffick: The International Struggle Against the Transatlantic Slave Trade: A Graphic History* (Oxford: Oxford University Press, 2015)

Blyth, Robert J., 'Britain, the Royal Navy and the suppression of the slave trades in the nineteenth century', in Douglas Hamilton and Robert J. Blyth (eds), *Representing Slavery: Art, Artefacts and Archives in the Collections of the National Maritime Museum* (Aldershot: Lund Humphries, 2007), pp. 78–91

Bolt, Christine, *Victorian Attitudes to Race* (London: Routledge, 1971)

Bolt, Christine, 'Race and the Victorians', in C. C. Eldridge (ed.), *British Imperialism in the Nineteenth Century* (London: Macmillan, 1984), pp. 126–47

Brantlinger, Patrick, 'Victorians and Africans: the genealogy of the myth of the Dark Continent', *Critical Inquiry*, 12.1 (1985), pp. 166–203

Brantlinger, Patrick, *Rule of Darkness: British Literature and Imperialism, 1830–1914* (Ithaca, NY: Cornell University Press, 1988)

Bratton, J. S., *Acts of Supremacy: The British Empire and the Stage, 1790–1930* (Manchester: Manchester University Press, 1991)

Brown, Christopher L., *Moral Capital: Foundations of British Abolitionism* (Chapel Hill, NC: University of North Carolina Press, 2006)

Brown, Robert T., 'Fernando Po and the anti-Sierra Leonean campaign, 1826–1854', *International Journal of African Historical Studies*, 6.2 (1973), pp. 249–64

Burroughs, Robert, '"[T]he true sailors of Western Africa": Kru seafaring identity in British travellers' accounts of the 1830s and 1840s', *Journal of Maritime Research*, 11.1 (2009), pp. 51–67

Burroughs, Robert, 'Eyes on the prize: journeys in slave ships taken as prizes by the Royal Navy', *Slavery and Abolition*, 31.1 (2010), pp. 99–115

Burroughs, Robert, 'Slave-trade suppression and the culture of anti-slavery in nineteenth-century Britain', in Robert Burroughs and Richard Huzzey (eds), *The Suppression of the Atlantic Slave Trade: British Policies, Practices and Representations of Naval Coercion* (Manchester: Manchester University Press, 2015), pp. 125–45

Burroughs, Robert, 'Suppression of the Atlantic slave trade: abolition from ship to shore', in Robert Burroughs and Richard Huzzey (eds), *The Suppression of the Atlantic Slave Trade: British Policies, Practices and Representations of Naval Coercion* (Manchester: Manchester University Press, 2015), pp. 1–16

Burrows, E. H., *Captain Owen of the African Survey, 1774–1857* (Rotterdam: A. A. Balkema, 1979)

Byrd, Alexander X., *Captives and Voyagers: Black Migrants across the Eighteenth-Century British Atlantic World* (Baton Rouge, LA: Louisiana State University Press, 2008)

Cannadine, David, *Ornamentalism: How the British saw their Empire* (London: Allen Lane, 2001)

Canney, Donald, *Africa Squadron: The US Navy and the Slave Trade, 1842–1861* (Washington, DC: Potomac Books, 2002)

Carey, Brycchan, *British Abolitionism and the Rhetoric of Sensibility: Writing, Sentiment, and Slavery 1760–1807* (Basingstoke: Palgrave Macmillan, 2005)

Carey, Hilary M. (ed.), *Empires of Religion* (Basingstoke: Palgrave Macmillan, 2008)

Christopher, Emma, *Slave Ship Sailors and their Captive Cargoes, 1730–1807* (New York: Cambridge University Press, 2006)

Christopher, Emma, '"Tis enough that we give them liberty"? Liberated Africans at Sierra Leone in the early era of slave-trade suppression', in Robert Burroughs and Richard Huzzey (eds), *The Suppression of the Atlantic Slave Trade: British Policies, Practices and Representations of Naval Coercion* (Manchester: Manchester University Press, 2015), pp. 55–72

Christopher, Emma, Pybus, Cassandra and Rediker, Marcus (eds), *Many Middle Passages: Forced Migration and the Making of the Modern World* (Berkeley, CA: University of California Press, 2007)

Clendinnen, Inga, *Dancing with Strangers: The True History of the Meeting of the British First Fleet and the Aboriginal Australians, 1788* (Edinburgh: Canongate, 2003)

Coates, Tim (ed.), *King Guezo of Dahomey, 1850–1852: The Abolition of the Slave Trade on the West Coast of Africa* (London: The Stationery Office, 2001)

Colley, Linda, *Britons: Forging the Nation, 1707–1837* (New Haven, CT: Yale University Press, 1992)

Colley, Linda, *Captives: Britain, Empire and the World, 1600–1850* (London: Jonathan Cape, 2002)

Conley, Mary, *From Jack Tar to Union Jack: Representing Naval Manhood in the British Empire, 1870–1918* (Manchester: Manchester University Press, 2009)

Costello, Ray, *Black Salt: Seafarers of African Descent on British Ships* (Liverpool: Liverpool University Press, 2012)

Coupland, Sir Reginald, *The British Anti-Slavery Movement* (London: Thornton Butterworth, 1933)

Creighton, Mandell, *Memoir of Sir George Grey, G.C.B.* (privately printed, 1884)

Curtin, Philip D., *The Image of Africa: British Ideas and Action 1780–1850* (Madison, WI: University of Wisconsin Press, 1964)

Curtin, Philip D. (ed.), *Africa Remembered: Narratives by West Africans from the Era of the Slave Trade* (Madison, WI: University of Wisconsin Press, 1967)

Curtin, Philip D., *Death by Migration: Europe's Encounter with the Tropical World in the Nineteenth Century* (Cambridge: Cambridge University Press, 1989)

Davidson, Basil, *Africa in History* (London: Phoenix Press, 2001)

Davis, David Brion, *The Problem of Slavery in Western Culture* (Oxford: Oxford University Press, 1966)

Davis, David Brion, *The Problem of Slavery in the Age of Revolution, 1770–1823* (Ithaca, NY: Cornell University Press, 1975)

De Groot, Joanna, 'Sex and race: the construction of language and image in the nineteenth century', in Susan Mendus and Jane Rendall (eds), *Sexuality and Subordination: Interdisciplinary Studies of Gender in the Nineteenth Century* (London: Routledge, 1989), pp. 89–128

Desmond, Adrian, and Moore, James, *Darwin's Sacred Cause: Race, Slavery and the Quest for Human Origins* (London: Allen Lane, 2009)

Deveneaux, Gustav, 'Buxtonianism and Sierra Leone: the 1841 Timbo expedition', *Journal of African Studies*, 5.1 (1978), pp. 34–54

Diouf, Sylviane A., *Dreams of Africa in Alabama: The Slave Ship Clotilda and the Story of the Last Africans Brought to America* (Oxford: Oxford University Press, 2007)

Domingues da Silva, Daniel, Eltis, David, Misevich, Philip and Ojo, Olatunji, 'The diaspora of Africans liberated from slave ships in the nineteenth century', *The Journal of African History*, 55 (2014), pp. 347–69

Drayton, Richard, 'Knowledge and empire', in P. J. Marshall (ed.), *The Oxford History of the British Empire: Volume II: The Eighteenth Century* (Oxford: Oxford University Press, 2001), pp. 231–52

Drescher, Seymour, *Econocide: British Slavery in the Era of Abolition* (Pittsburgh, PA: University of Pittsburgh Press, 1977)

Drescher, Seymour, 'Public opinion and the destruction of British colonial slavery', in J. Walvin (ed.), *Slavery and British Society 1776–1846* (London: Macmillan, 1982), pp. 22–48

Drescher, Seymour, *Capitalism and Antislavery: British Mobilization in Comparative Perspective* (London: Macmillan, 1986)

Drescher, Seymour, *The Mighty Experiment: Free Labor versus Slavery in British Emancipation* (Oxford: Oxford University Press, 2002)

Drescher, Seymour, *Abolition: A History of Slavery and Antislavery* (Cambridge: Cambridge University Press, 2009)

Drescher, Seymour, 'Emperors of the world: British abolitionism and imperialism', in Derek R. Peterson (ed.), *Abolitionism and Imperialism in Britain, Africa, and the Atlantic* (Athens, OH: Ohio University Press, 2010), pp. 129–49

Dumas, Paula, *Proslavery Britain: Fighting for Slavery in an Era of Abolition* (Basingstoke: Palgrave Macmillan, 2016)

Edwards, Bernard, *Royal Navy Versus the Slave Traders: Enforcing Abolition at Sea* (Barnsley: Pen and Sword Maritime, 2007)

Eltis, David, *Economic Growth and the Ending of the Transatlantic Slave Trade* (Oxford: Oxford University Press, 1987)

Eltis, David, and Richardson, David, 'A new assessment of the transatlantic slave trade', in David Eltis and David Richardson (eds), *Extending the Frontiers: Essays on the New Transatlantic Slave Trade Database* (New Haven, CT: Yale University Press, 2008), pp. 1–60

Eltis, David, and Richardson, David, *Atlas of the Transatlantic Slave Trade* (New Haven, CT: Yale University Press, 2010)

Evans, Eric J., *The Forging of the Modern State: Early Industrial Britain, 1783–1870*, 3rd edn (Harlow: Longman Pearson, 2001)

Everill, Bronwen, *Abolition and Empire in Sierra Leone and Liberia* (Basingstoke: Palgrave Macmillan, 2013)

Fett, Sharla M., *Recaptured Africans: Surviving Slave Ships, Detention, and Dislocation in the Final Years of the Slave Trade* (Chapel Hill, NC: University of North Carolina Press, 2017)

Fyfe, Christopher, 'Four Sierra Leone recaptives', *The Journal of African History*, 2.1 (1961), pp. 77–85

Gagnier, Regina, *Subjectivities: A History of Self-representation in Britain, 1832–1920* (Oxford: Oxford University Press, 1991)

Gallagher, Catherine, 'Floating signifiers of Britishness in the novels of the anti-slave-trade squadron', in Wendy S. Jacobson (ed.), *Dickens and the Children of Empire* (Basingstoke: Palgrave, 2000), pp. 78–93

Gallagher, J., 'Fowell Buxton and the New African Policy, 1838–1842', *The Cambridge Historical Journal*, 10.1 (1950), pp. 36–58

Gibson Wilson, Ellen, *John Clarkson and the African Adventure* (London: Macmillan, 1980)

Gilliland, Herbert C., *Voyage to a Thousand Cares: Master's Mate Lawrence with the Africa Squadron 1844–1846* (Annapolis, MD: Naval Institute Press, 2003)

Goodman, Jordan, *The Rattlesnake: A Voyage of Discovery to the Coral Sea* (London: Faber and Faber, 2005)

Gray, Todd, *Devon and the Slave Trade: Documents on African Enslavement, Abolition and Emancipation from 1562 to 1867* (Exeter: The Mint Press, 2007)

Grindal, Peter, *Opposing the Slavers: The Royal Navy's Campaign against the Atlantic Slave Trade* (London: I. B. Tauris, 2016)

Halévy, Elie, *The Birth of Methodism in England*, trans. and ed. Bernard Semmel (Chicago: University of Chicago Press, 1971)

Hall, Catherine, 'Going a-trolloping: imperial man travels the Empire', in Clare Midgley (ed.), *Gender and Imperialism* (Manchester: Manchester University Press, 1998), pp. 180–99

Hall, Catherine, 'Introduction: thinking the postcolonial, thinking the empire', in Catherine Hall (ed.), *Cultures of Empire: Colonizers in Britain and the Empire in the Nineteenth and Twentieth Centuries* (Manchester: Manchester University Press, 2000), pp. 1–33

Hall, Catherine, *Civilising Subjects: Metropole and Colony in the English Imagination, 1830–1867* (Oxford: Polity Press, 2002)

Hall, Catherine, 'An empire of God or of man? The Macaulays, father and son', in Hilary M. Carey (ed.), *Empires of Religion* (Basingstoke: Macmillan, 2008), pp. 64–83

Hall, Catherine, 'Troubling memories: nineteenth-century histories of the slave trade and slavery', *Transactions of the Royal Historical Society*, 21 (2011), pp. 147–69

Hall, Catherine, Draper, Nicholas, and McClelland, Keith (eds), *Emancipation and the Remaking of the British Imperial World* (Manchester: Manchester University Press, 2014)

Hall, Catherine, and Rose, Sonya O. (eds), *At Home with the Empire: Metropolitan Culture and the Imperial World* (Cambridge: Cambridge University Press, 2006)

Hamilton, C. I., 'Naval hagiography and the Victorian hero', *The Historical Journal*, 23.2 (1980), pp. 381–98

Hamilton, Douglas, 'Slave life in the Caribbean', in Douglas Hamilton and Robert J. Blyth (eds), *Representing Slavery: Art, Artefacts and Archives in the Collections of the National Maritime Museum* (Aldershot: Lund Humphries, 2007), pp. 52–61

Hamilton, Douglas, and Blyth, Robert J. (eds), *Representing Slavery: Art, Artefacts and Archives in the Collections of the National Maritime Museum* (Aldershot: Lund Humphries, 2007)

Hamilton, Keith, 'Zealots and helots: the slave trade department of the nineteenth-century Foreign Office', in Keith Hamilton and Patrick Salmon (eds), *Slavery, Diplomacy and Empire: Britain and the Suppression of the Slave Trade, 1807–1975* (Eastbourne: Sussex Academic Press, 2009), pp. 20–41

Hamilton, Keith, and Salmon, Patrick (eds), *Slavery, Diplomacy and Empire: Britain and the Suppression of the Slave Trade, 1807–1975* (Eastbourne: Sussex Academic Press, 2009)

Hargreaves, J. D., *Prelude to the Partition of West Africa* (London: Macmillan, 1963)

Harries, Patrick, 'The hobgoblins of the Middle Passage: the Cape of Good Hope and the trans-Atlantic slave trade', in Ulrike Schmeider, Katja Fullbery-Stolberg and Michael Zeuske (eds), *The End of Slavery in Africa and the Americas: A Comparative Approach* (Berlin: Global, 2011), pp. 33–42

Harrison, Mark, 'An "important and truly national subject": the West Africa Service and the health of the Royal Navy in the mid nineteenth century', in David Boyd Haycock and Sally Archer (eds), *Health and Medicine at Sea, 1700–1900* (Woodbridge: Boydell Press, 2009), pp. 108–27

Heartfield, James, *The British And Foreign Anti-Slavery Society, 1838–1956: A History* (Oxford: Oxford University Press, 2016)

Helfman, Tara, 'The Court of Vice Admiralty at Sierra Leone and the abolition of the West African slave trade', *The Yale Law Journal*, 115 (2006), pp. 1122–56

Holt, Thomas C., *The Problem of Freedom: Race, Labor and Politics in Jamaica and Britain, 1832–1938* (Baltimore, MD: Johns Hopkins University Press, 1992)

Hopkins, A. G., *An Economic History of West Africa* (London: Longman, 1973)

Hopkins, A. G., 'Property rights and empire building: Britain's annexation of Lagos, 1861', *Journal of Economic History*, 40.4 (1980), pp. 777–98

Hopkins, A. G., 'The "new international economic order" in the nineteenth century: Britain's first development plan for Africa', in Robin Law (ed.), *From Slave Trade to 'Legitimate' Commerce: The Commercial Transition in Nineteenth-Century West Africa* (Cambridge: Cambridge University Press, 1995), pp. 240–64

Howard, Allen M., 'Nineteenth-century coastal slave trading and the British abolition campaign in Sierra Leone', *Slavery and Abolition*, 27.1 (2006), pp. 23–49

Howell, Raymond, *The Royal Navy and the Slave Trade* (London: Croom Helm, 1987)

Hurston, Zora Neale, 'Cudjo's own story of the last African slaver', *The Journal of Negro History*, 12.4 (1927), pp. 648–63

Huzzey, Richard, *Freedom Burning: Anti-Slavery and Empire in Victorian Britain* (Ithaca, NY: Cornell University Press, 2012)

Huzzey, Richard, 'Concepts of liberty: freedom, laissez-faire and the state after Britain's abolition of slavery', in Catherine Hall, Nicholas Draper and Keith McClelland (eds), *Emancipation and the Remaking of the British Imperial World* (Manchester: Manchester University Press, 2014), pp. 149–71

Huzzey, Richard, 'The politics of slave-trade suppression', in Robert Burroughs and Richard Huzzey (eds), *The Suppression of the Atlantic Slave Trade: British Policies, Practices and Representations of Naval Coercion* (Manchester: Manchester University Press, 2015), pp. 17–52

Huzzey, Richard, and McAleer, John, 'History, memory and commemoration', in Robert Burroughs and Richard Huzzey (eds), *The Suppression of the Atlantic Slave Trade: British Policies, Practices and Representations of Naval Coercion* (Manchester: Manchester University Press, 2015), pp. 166–88

Jordan, Gerald, and Rogers, Nicholas, 'Admirals as heroes: patriotism and liberty in Hanoverian England', *The Journal of British Studies*, 28.3 (1989), pp. 201–24

Kaufmann, Chaim D., and Pape, Robert A., 'Explaining costly international moral action: Britain's sixty-year campaign against the Atlantic slave trade', *International Organization*, 53 (1999), pp. 631–68

Kennedy, Dane, *The Last Blank Spaces: Exploring Africa and Australia* (Cambridge, MA: Harvard University Press, 2013)

Kennedy, Paul, *The Rise and Fall of British Naval Mastery* (London: Allen Lane, 1976)

Kielstra, Paul Michael, *The Politics of Slave Trade Suppression in Britain and France, 1814–48: Diplomacy, Morality and Economics* (Basingstoke: Macmillan, 2000)

Koivunen, Leila, *Visualizing Africa in Nineteenth-Century British Travel Accounts* (London: Routledge, 2009)

Laidlaw, Zoe, *Colonial Connections 1815–1845: Patronage, The Information Revolution and Colonial Government* (Manchester: Manchester University Press, 2005)

Lambert, Andrew, 'Slavery, free trade and naval strategy, 1840–1860', in Keith Hamilton and Patrick Salmon (eds), *Slavery, Diplomacy and Empire: Britain and the Suppression of the Slave Trade, 1807–1975* (Eastbourne: Sussex Academic Press, 2009), pp. 65–80

Lambert, David, 'Sierra Leone and other sites in the war of representation over slavery', *History Workshop Journal*, 64 (2007), pp. 103–22

Lambert, David, '"Taken captive by the mystery of the Great River": towards an historical geography of British geography and Atlantic slavery', *Journal of Historical Geography*, 35 (2009), pp. 44–65

Lambert, David, and Lester, Alan (eds), *Colonial Lives across the British Empire: Imperial Careering in the Long Nineteenth Century* (Cambridge: Cambridge University Press, 2006)

Land, Isaac, *War, Nationalism and the British Sailor, 1750–1850* (Basingstoke: Palgrave Macmillan, 2009)

Lavery, Brian, *Nelson's Navy: The Ships, Men and Organisation, 1793–1815* (London: Conway Maritime, 1989)

Law, Robin, 'An African response to abolition: Anglo-Dahomian negotiations on ending the slave trade, 1838–77', *Slavery and Abolition*, 16.3 (1995), pp. 281–310

Law, Robin (ed.), *From Slave Trade to 'Legitimate' Commerce: The Commercial Transition in Nineteenth-Century West Africa* (Cambridge: Cambridge University Press, 1995)

Law, Robin, 'Abolition and imperialism: international law and the British suppression of the Atlantic slave trade', in Derek R. Peterson (ed.), *Abolitionism and Imperialism in Britain, Africa, and the Atlantic* (Athens, OH: Ohio University Press, 2010), pp. 150–74

Lawrance, Benjamin N., '*La Amistad*'s "interpreter" reinterpreted: James "Kaweli" Covey's distressed Atlantic childhood and the production of knowledge about nineteenth-century Sierra Leone', in Paul E. Lovejoy and Suzanne Schwarz (eds), *Slavery, Abolition and the Transition to Colonialism in Sierra Leone* (Trenton, NJ: Africa World Press, 2015), pp. 217–55

Lester, Alan, *Imperial Networks: Creating Identities in Nineteenth-century South Africa and Britain* (London: Routledge, 2001)

Lester, Alan, 'British settler discourse and the circuits of empire', *History Workshop Journal*, 54 (2002), pp. 22–48

Lewis, Michael, *A Social History of the Royal Navy 1793–1815* (London: George Allen and Unwin, 1960)

Lewis, Michael, *The Navy in Transition 1814–1864: A Social History* (London: Hodder and Stoughton, 1965)

Lincoln, Margarette, *Representing the Royal Navy: British Sea Power, 1750–1815* (Aldershot: Ashgate, 2002)

Linebaugh, Peter, and Rediker, Marcus, *The Many-headed Hydra: Sailors, Slaves, Commoners and the Hidden History of the Revolutionary Atlantic* (Boston: Beacon Press, 2000)

Lipschutz, Mark R., and Rasmussen, R. Kent (eds), *Dictionary of African Historical Biography* (Berkeley, CA: University of California Press, 1992)

Lloyd, Christopher, *The Navy and the Slave Trade: The Suppression of the African Slave Trade in the Nineteenth Century* (London: Longman, 1949)

Lockhart, Jamie Bruce, *A Sailor in the Sahara: The Life and Travels in Africa of Hugh Clapperton, Commander RN* (London: I. B. Tauris, 2008)

Lorimer, Douglas A., *Colour, Class and the Victorians: English Attitudes to the Negro in the Mid-nineteenth Century* (Leicester: Leicester University Press, 1978)

Lovejoy, Paul E., *Transformations in Slavery: A History of Slavery in Africa* (Cambridge: Cambridge University Press, 1983)

Lovejoy, Paul E., and Richardson, David, 'The initial "crisis of adaptation": the impact of British abolition on the Atlantic slave trade in West Africa, 1808–1820', in Robin Law (ed.), *From Slave Trade to 'Legitimate' Commerce: The Commercial Transition in Nineteenth-Century West Africa* (Cambridge: Cambridge University Press, 1995), pp. 32–56

Lovejoy, Paul E., and Schwarz, Suzanne (eds), *Slavery, Abolition and the Transition to Colonialism in Sierra Leone* (Trenton, NJ: Africa World Press, 2015)

Lynn, Martin, 'The "imperialism of free trade" and the case of West Africa, c. 1830–c.1870', *Journal of Imperial and Commonwealth History*, 15 (1986), pp. 22–40

Lynn, Martin, *Commerce and Economic Change in West Africa: The Palm Oil Trade in the Nineteenth Century* (Cambridge: Cambridge University Press, 1997)

MacGaffey, Wyatt, 'Commodore Wilmot encounters Kongo Art, 1865', *African Arts* (summer 2010), pp. 52–53

Macmillan, John, 'Myths and lessons of liberal intervention: the British campaign for the abolition of the Atlantic slave trade to Brazil', *Global Responsibility to Protect*, 4 (2012), pp. 98–124

Mamigonian, Beatriz G., 'In the name of freedom: slave trade abolition, the law and the Brazilian branch of the African Emigration Scheme (Brazil–British West Indies, 1830s–1850s)', *Slavery and Abolition*, 30.1 (2009), pp. 41–66

Mangan, J. A., and Walvin, James, *Manliness and Morality: Middle Class Masculinity in Britain and America 1800–1940* (Manchester: Manchester University Press, 1991)

Mann, Kristin, 'The original sin: British reform and imperial expansion at Lagos', in Robin Law and Silke Strickrodt (eds), *Ports of the Slave Trade: Bights of Benin and Biafra* (Stirling: Centre of Commonwealth Studies, 1999), pp. 169–89

Mann, Kristin, *Slavery and the Birth of an African City: Lagos, 1760–1900* (Bloomington, IN: Indiana University Press, 2007)

Marshall, P. J., 'Empire and British identity: the maritime dimension', in David Cannadine (ed.), *Empire, the Sea and Global History: Britain's Maritime World, c.1763–c.1840* (New York: Palgrave Macmillan, 2007), pp. 41–59

Marshall, P. J., and Williams, Glyndwr, *The Great Map of Mankind: British Perceptions of the World in the Age of Enlightenment* (London: Dent, 1982)

Martinez, Jenny, *The Slave Trade and the Origins of International Human Rights Law* (Oxford: Oxford University Press, 2011)

Martins, Luciana, and Driver, Felix, 'John Septimus Roe and the art of navigation, c. 1815–30', in Tim Barringer, Douglas Fordham and Geoff Quilley (eds), *Art and the British Empire* (Manchester: Manchester University Press, 2007), pp. 53–66

McAleer, John, and Petley, Christer (eds), *The Royal Navy and the British Atlantic World, c. 1750–1820* (London: Palgrave Macmillan, 2016)

McCaskie, T. C., 'Cultural encounters: Britain and Africa in the nineteenth century', in Andrew Porter (ed.), *The Oxford History of the British Empire: Volume III: The Nineteenth Century* (Oxford: Oxford University Press, 1999), pp. 665–89

McClintock, Anne, *Imperial Leather: Race, Gender and Sexuality in the Colonial Conquest* (London: Routledge, 1995)

McLeod, Hugh, 'Protestantism and British national identity, 1845–1945', in Peter Van Der Veer and Hartmut Lehmann (eds), *Nation and Religion: Perspectives on Europe and Asia* (Princeton, NJ: Princeton University Press, 1999), pp. 44–70

McLynn, F. J., *Hearts of Darkness: The European Exploration of Africa* (London: Hutchinson, 1992)

Meer, Sarah, *Uncle Tom Mania: Slavery, Minstrelsy and Transatlantic Culture in the 1850s* (Athens, GA: University of Georgia Press, 2005)

Midgley, Clare, *Women Against Slavery: The British Campaigns 1780–1870* (London: Routledge, 1992)

Miers, Suzanne, *Britain and the Ending of the Slave Trade* (London: Longman, 1975)

Miers, Suzanne, *Slavery in the Twentieth Century: The Evolution of a Global Problem* (Walnut Creek, CA: Altamira Press, 2003)

Mitchell, Charles, and Turano, Leslie, 'Burón v Denman (1848)', in Charles Mitchell and Paul Mitchell (eds), *Landmark Cases in the Law of Tort* (Oxford: Hart Publishing, 2010), pp. 33–68

Moore, Grace, *Dickens and Empire: Discourses of Race, Class and Colonialism in the Works of Charles Dickens* (Aldershot: Ashgate, 2004)

Mouser, Bruce L., 'Coasters and conflict in the Rio Pongo from 1790 to 1808', *The Journal of African History*, 14.1 (1973), pp. 45–64

Mulligan, William, and Bric, Maurice (eds), *A Global History of Anti-Slavery Politics in the Nineteenth Century* (London: Palgrave Macmillan, 2013)

Murray, David, *Odious Commerce: Britain, Spain and the Abolition of the Cuban Slave Trade* (Cambridge: Cambridge University Press, 1980)

Myers, Norma, *Reconstructing the Black Past: Blacks in Britain, 1780–1830* (London: Frank Cass, 1996)

Myers, Walter Dean, *At Her Majesty's Request: An African Princess in Victorian England* (New York: Scholastic, 1999)

Nicholson, Andrea, 'Transformations in the law concerning slavery: legacies of the nineteenth century anti-slavery movement', in William Mulligan and Maurice Bric (eds), *A Global History of Anti-Slavery Politics in the Nineteenth Century* (London: Palgrave Macmillan, 2013), pp. 214–36

Northrup, David, 'African mortality in the suppression of the slave trade: the case of the Bight of Biafra', *Journal of Interdisciplinary History*, 9.1 (1978), pp. 47–64

Northrup, David, *Indentured Labour in the Age of Imperialism, 1834–1922* (Cambridge: Cambridge University Press, 1995)

Northrup, David, 'Becoming African: identity formation among liberated slaves in nineteenth-century Sierra Leone', *Slavery and Abolition*, 27.1 (2006), pp. 1–21

Northrup, David, *Africa's Discovery of Europe: 1450–1850*, 2nd edn (Oxford: Oxford University Press, 2009)

Oldfield, J. R., *Popular Politics and British Anti-Slavery: The Mobilisation of Public Opinion against the Slave Trade 1787–1807* (Manchester: Manchester University Press, 1995)

Oldfield, J. R., 'Palmerston and anti-slavery', in David Brown and Miles Taylor (eds), *Palmerston Studies II* (Southampton: Hartley Institute, University of Southampton, 2007), pp. 24–38

Oldfield, J. R., *Transatlantic Abolitionism in the Age of Revolution: An International History of Anti-Slavery, c. 1787–1820* (Cambridge: Cambridge University Press, 2013)

Olusoga, David, *Black and British: A Forgotten History* (Basingstoke: Pan Macmillan, 2016)

Perfect, David, *Historical Dictionary of the Gambia* (Lanham, MD: Rowman and Littlefield, 2016)

Pole, Len, *Iwa L'Ewa: Yoruba and Benin Collections in the Royal Albert Memorial Museum* (Exeter Museums, 1999)

Powell, Roger, *Why Here? Why Then? The Roles of John and Thomas Clarkson in the Abolition of the Slave Trade 1807* (Wisbech and Fenland Museum, 2007)

Pearson, Andrew, *Distant Freedom: St Helena and the Abolition of the Slave Trade, 1840–1872* (Liverpool: Liverpool University Press, 2016)

Pearson, Andrew, 'Waterwitch: a warship, its voyage and its crew in the era of anti-slavery', *Atlantic Studies*, 13.1 (2016), pp. 99–124

Pearson, Andrew, Jeffs, Ben, Witkin, Annsofie, and MacQuarrie, Helen, *Infernal Traffic: Excavation of a Liberated African Graveyard in Rupert's Valley, St Helena* (York: Council for British Archaeology, 2011)

Peterson, Derek R. (ed.), *Abolitionism and Imperialism in Britain, Africa, and the Atlantic* (Athens, OH: Ohio University Press, 2010)

Peterson, John, *Province of Freedom: A History of Sierra Leone 1787–1870* (London: Faber, 1969)

Porter, Andrew, '"Commerce and Christianity": the rise and fall of a nineteenth-century missionary slogan', *The Historical Journal*, 28.3 (1985), pp. 597–621

Porter, Andrew, 'Introduction: Britain and empire in the nineteenth century', in Andrew Porter (ed.), *The Oxford History of the British Empire: Volume III: The Nineteenth Century* (Oxford: Oxford University Press, 1999), pp. 1–28

Porter, Andrew, 'Trusteeship, anti-slavery, and humanitarianism', in Andrew Porter (ed.), *The Oxford History of the British Empire: Volume III: The Nineteenth Century* (Oxford: Oxford University Press, 1999), pp. 198–221

Porter, Andrew, *Religion versus Empire? British Protestant Missionaries and Overseas Expansion, 1700–1914* (Manchester: Manchester University Press, 2004)

Pratt, Mary Louise, *Imperial Eyes: Travel Writing and Transculturation* (London: Routledge, 2002)

Price, Richard, *Making Empire: Colonial Encounters and the Creation of Imperial Rule in Nineteenth-Century Africa* (Cambridge: Cambridge University Press, 2008)

Pybus, Cassandra, *Epic Journeys of Freedom: Runaway Slaves of the American Revolution and Their Global Quest for Liberty* (Boston: Beacon Press, 2006)

Pybus, Cassandra, '"A less favourable specimen": the abolitionist response to self-emancipated Slaves in Sierra Leone, 1763–1808', in Stephen Farrell, Melanie Unwin and James Walvin (eds), *The British Slave Trade: Abolition, Parliament and People* (Edinburgh: Edinburgh University Press, 2007), pp. 97–112

Quilley, Geoff, *Empire to Nation: Art, History and the Visualization of Maritime Britain 1768–1829* (New Haven, CT: Yale University Press, 2011)

Quirk, Joel, 'Uncomfortable silences: contemporary slavery and the "lessons" of history', in Alison Brysk and Austin Choi-Fitzpatrick (eds), *From Human Trafficking to Human Rights: Reframing Contemporary Slavery* (Philadelphia, PA: University of Pennsylvania Press, 2011), pp. 25–43

Quirk, Joel, and Richardson, David, 'Anti-slavery, European identity and international society: a macro-historical perspective', *The Journal of Modern European History*, 7.1 (2009), pp. 68–92

Qureshi, Sadiah, *Peoples on Parade: Exhibitions, Empire, and Anthropology in Nineteenth-Century Britain* (Chicago: University of Chicago Press, 2011)

Rankin, John, 'Nineteenth-century Royal Navy sailors from Africa and the African diaspora: research methodology', *African Diaspora*, 6 (2013), pp. 179–95

Rankin, John, *Healing the African Body: British Medicine in West Africa 1800–1860* (Columbia, MO: University of Missouri Press, 2015)

Rattansi, Ali, *Racism: A Very Short Introduction* (Oxford: Oxford University Press, 2007)

Rediker, Marcus, *Between the Devil and the Deep Blue Sea: Merchant Seamen, Pirates and the Anglo-American Maritime World, 1700–1750* (Cambridge: Cambridge University Press, 1987)

Rediker, Marcus, *The Slave Ship: A Human History* (London: John Murray, 2007)

Rees, Sian, *Sweet Water and Bitter: The Ships that Stopped the Slave Trade* (London: Chatto & Windus, 2009)

Richards, Jake Christopher, 'Anti-slave-trade law, "liberated Africans" and the state in the South Atlantic World, c. 1839–1852', *Past and Present*, 241 (2018), pp. 179–219

Richardson, David, 'Shipboard revolts, African authority and the Atlantic slave trade', *William and Mary Quarterly*, 58.1 (2001), pp. 69–92

Richardson, David, 'Through African eyes: the Middle Passage and the British slave trade', in Douglas Hamilton and Robert J. Blyth (eds), *Representing Slavery: Art, Artefacts and Archives in the Collections of the National Maritime Museum* (Aldershot: Lund Humphries, 2007), pp. 42–49

Richardson, David, 'Cultures of exchange: Atlantic Africa in the era of the slave trade', *Transactions of the Royal Historical Society*, 19 (2009), pp. 151–79

Roberts, Shirley, *Charles Hotham: A Biography* (Melbourne: Melbourne University Press, 1985)

Rodger, N. A. M., *The Wooden World: An Anatomy of the Georgian Navy* (Glasgow: William Collins, 1986)

Ryan, Maeve, 'The price of legitimacy in humanitarian intervention: Britain, the right of search, and the abolition of the West African slave trade, 1807–1867', in Brendan Simms and D. J. B. Trim (eds), *Humanitarian Intervention: A History* (Cambridge: Cambridge University Press, 2011), pp. 231–56

Ryan, Maeve, '"A most promising field for future usefulness": the Church Missionary Society and the liberated Africans of Sierra Leone', in William Mulligan and Maurice Bric (eds), *A Global History of Anti-Slavery Politics in the Nineteenth Century* (London: Palgrave Macmillan, 2013), pp. 37–59

Said, Edward, *Orientalism* (London: Chatto & Windus, 1993)

Salmond, Anne, *Bligh: William Bligh in the South Seas* (Berkeley, CA: University of California Press, 2011)

Samson, Jane, *Imperial Benevolence: Making British Authority in the Pacific Islands* (Honolulu, HI: University of Hawaii Press, 1998)

Bibliography

Samson, Jane, 'Too zealous guardians? The Royal Navy and the South Pacific labour trade', in David Killingray and David Omissi (eds), *Guardians of Empire: The Armed Forces of the Colonial Powers c. 1700–1964* (Manchester: Manchester University Press, 1999), pp. 70–90

Samson, Jane, 'Hero, fool or martyr? The many deaths of Commodore Goodenough', *Journal for Maritime Research*, 10.1 (2008), pp. 1–22

Saunders, Christopher, 'Liberated Africans in Cape Colony in the first half of the nineteenth century', *International Journal of African Historical Studies*, 18.2 (1985), pp. 223–39

Scanlan, Padraic X., 'The rewards of their exertions: prize money and British abolitionism in Sierra Leone, 1808–1823', *Past and Present*, 225 (2014), pp. 113–42

Schama, Simon, *Rough Crossings: Britain, the Slaves and the American Revolution* (London: BBC Books, 2005)

Schwarz, Suzanne, 'Commerce, civilization and Christianity: the development of the Sierra Leone Company', in David Richardson, Suzanne Schwarz and Anthony Tibbles (eds), *Liverpool and Transatlantic Slavery* (Liverpool: Liverpool University Press, 2008), pp. 252–76

Schwarz, Suzanne, 'Reconstructing the life histories of liberated Africans: Sierra Leone in the early nineteenth century', *History in Africa*, 39 (2012), pp. 175–207

Shaikh, Farida, 'Judicial diplomacy: British officials and the Mixed Commission courts', in Keith Hamilton and Patrick Salmon (eds), *Slavery, Diplomacy and Empire: Britain and the Suppression of the Slave Trade, 1807–1975* (Eastbourne: Sussex Academic Press, 2009), pp. 42–64

Sherwood, Marika, 'Britain, the slave trade and slavery, 1808–1843', *Race and Class*, 46 (2004), pp. 54–77

Slavery in Diplomacy: The Foreign Office and the Suppression of the Transatlantic Slave Trade, Foreign and Commonwealth Office Historians History Note, 17 (2007)

Smalls, James, 'Art and illustration', in Seymour Drescher and Stanley Engerman (eds), *A Historical Guide to World Slavery* (Oxford: Oxford University Press, 1998), pp. 65–76

Smith, Billy G., *Ship of Death: A Voyage that Changed the Atlantic World* (New Haven, CT: Yale University Press, 2013)

Smith, Robert, 'The Lagos consulate, 1851–1861: an outline', *The Journal of African History*, 15.3 (1974), pp. 393–416

Soumanni, E. A., 'The compatibility of the slave and palm oil trades in Dahomey, 1818–1858', in Robin Law (ed.), *From Slave Trade to 'Legitimate' Commerce: The Commercial Transition in Nineteenth-Century West Africa* (Cambridge: Cambridge University Press, 1995), pp. 78–92

Southam, Brian, *Jane Austen and the Navy* (London: National Maritime Museum, 2000)

Spence, Daniel, *Colonial Naval Culture and British Imperialism, 1922–67* (Manchester: Manchester University Press, 2015)

Stepan, Nancy, *The Idea of Race in Science: Great Britain 1800–1960* (Basingstoke: Macmillan, 1982)

Stoler, Ann Laura, *Race and the Education of Desire: Foucault's 'History of Sexuality' and the Colonial Order of Things* (Durham, NC: Duke University Press, 1995)

Talbott, John E., *The Pen and Ink Sailor. Charles Middleton and the King's Navy, 1778–1813* (London: Frank Cass, 1998)

Temperley, Howard, *British Antislavery 1833–1870* (London: Longman, 1972)

Temperley, Howard, 'Anti-slavery as a form of cultural imperialism', in Christine Bolt and Seymour Drescher (eds), *Anti-Slavery, Religion and Reform* (Folkestone: Dawson, 1980), pp. 335–50

Temperley, Howard, *White Dreams, Black Africa: The Antislavery Expedition to the River Niger, 1841–42* (New Haven, CT: Yale University Press, 1991)

Thomas, Hugh, *The Slave Trade: The History of the Atlantic Slave Trade 1440–1870* (London: Picador, 1997)

Thorne, Susan, *Congregational Missions and the Making of an Imperial Culture in Nineteenth Century England* (Stanford, CA: Stanford University Press, 1999)

Tinnie, Dinizulu Gene, 'The slaving brig *Henriqueta* and her evil sisters: a case study in the 19th-century illegal slave trade to Brazil', *The Journal of African American History*, 93.4 (2008), pp. 509–31

Towards Liberty: Slavery, the Slave Trade, Abolition and Emancipation: Study Sources Available at Sheffield Local Studies Library and Sheffield Archives (Sheffield City Council, 2007)

Turley, David, *The Culture of English Antislavery, 1780–1860* (London: Routledge, 1991)

Twells, Alison, *The Civilising Mission and the English Middle Class, 1792–1850: The 'Heathen' at Home and Overseas* (Basingstoke: Palgrave Macmillan, 2009)

Ukpabi, S. C., 'West Indian troops and the defence of British West Africa in the nineteenth century', *African Studies Review*, 17.1 (1974), pp. 133–50

Van Der Linden, Marcel (ed.), *Humanitarian Intervention and Changing Labor Relations: The Long-Term Consequences of the Abolition of the Slave Trade* (Leiden: Brill, 2011)

Vance, Norman, *The Sinews of Spirit: The Ideal of Christian Manliness in Victorian Literature and Religious Thought* (Cambridge: Cambridge University Press, 1985)

War, Art, Racism & Slavery (London: Michael Graham-Stewart, 2009)

Ward, William, *The Royal Navy and the Slavers: The Suppression of the Atlantic Slave Trade* (London: George Allen & Unwin, 1969)

Waters, Hazel, *Racism on the Victorian Stage* (Cambridge: Cambridge University Press, 2007)

Watt, Sir James, 'The health of seamen in anti-slavery squadrons', in Andrew Lambert (ed.), *Naval History 1850–Present* (Aldershot: Ashgate, 2007), pp. 69–78

Wheeler, Roxann, 'Limited visions of Africa: geographies of savagery and civility in early eighteenth-century narratives', in James Duncan and Derek Gregory (eds), *Writes of Passage: Reading Travel Writing* (London: Routledge, 1999), pp. 14–44

Williams, Stephanie, *Running the Show: The Extraordinary Stories of the Men who Governed the British Empire* (London: Penguin, 2012)

Winton, John, 'Life and education in a technically evolving navy 1815–1925', in J. R. Hill (ed.), *The Oxford Illustrated History of the Royal Navy* (Oxford: Oxford University Press, 1995), pp. 250–79

Wood, Marcus, *Blind Memory: Visual Representations of Slavery in England and America, 1780–1865* (London: Routledge, 2000)

Wood, Marcus, *Slavery, Empathy and Pornography* (Oxford: Oxford University Press, 2002)

Wood, Marcus, 'Popular graphic images of slavery and emancipation in nineteenth-century England', in Douglas Hamilton and Robert J. Blyth (eds), *Representing Slavery: Art, Artefacts and Archives in the Collections of the National Maritime Museum* (Aldershot: Lund Humphries, 2007), pp. 138–51

ii. Unpublished theses and articles

Doulton, Lindsay, 'The Royal Navy's anti-slavery campaign in the western Indian Ocean, c. 1860–1890: race, empire and identity', PhD thesis, University of Hull, 2010

iii. Online publications

Blake, Richard, 'Gambier, James, Baron Gambier (1756–1833)', *Oxford Dictionary of National Biography*, Oxford University Press, September 2004, www.oxforddnb.com/view/article/10321 [accessed 4 October 2016]

Blouet, Olwyn Mary, 'Buxton, Sir Thomas Fowell, first baronet (1786–1845)', *Oxford Dictionary of National Biography*, Oxford University Press, September 2004, www.oxforddnb.com/view/article/4247 [accessed 23 September 2015]

Chapman, Peter, 'Wilmot, Sir John Eardley Eardley-, first baronet (1783–1847)', *Oxford Dictionary of National Biography*, Oxford University Press, September 2004, www.oxforddnb.com/view/article/52438 [accessed 15 March 2016]

Hodgson, Kate, 'Slave trades, slavery and emancipation in nineteenth-century European travel narratives', EURESCL: European political cultures of anti-slavery, www.eurescl.eu/images/stories/essays_wp1/Slave%20trades%20slavery%20and%20emancipation%20in%20travel%20narratives.pdf [accessed 27 January 2018]

Jones, Gareth H., and Jones, Vivienne, 'Denman, Thomas, first Baron Denman (1779–1854)', *Oxford Dictionary of National Biography*, Oxford University Press, September 2004, www.oxforddnb.com/view/article/7495 [accessed 4 October 2015]

Lambert, Andrew, 'Collier, Sir George Ralph, baronet (1774–1824)', *Oxford Dictionary of National Biography*, Oxford University Press, September 2004, www.oxforddnb.com/view/article/58443 [accessed 3 March 2018]

Laughton, J. K., 'Hayes, John (1775–1838)', rev. Roger Morriss, *Oxford Dictionary of National Biography*, Oxford University Press, September 2004, www.oxforddnb.com/view/article/12758 [accessed 3 March 2016]

Terrell, Christopher, 'Columbine, Edward Henry (1763–1811)', *Oxford Dictionary of National Biography*, Oxford University Press, 2004, www.oxforddnb.com/view/article/64853 [accessed 9 March 2017]

Watt, J., 'Ramsay, James (1733–1789)', *Oxford Dictionary of National Biography*, Oxford University Press, September 2004, www.oxforddnb.com/view/article/23086 [accessed 4 October 2016]

Willasey-Wilsey, Tim, 'Edmund Gabriel and the suppression of the Angolan slave trade', *The Victorian Web*, http://www.victorianweb.org/history/antislavery/gabriel.html [accessed 20 March 2018]

iv. Online sources

British Library collections, https://www.bl.uk/collection-items/polyglotta-africana

Cromford Village in Derbyshire, www.cromfordvillage.co.uk/arkwrights.html

Legacies of British Slave-ownership, https://www.ucl.ac.uk/lbs/

Liberated Africans, liberatedafricans.org

National Maritime Museum collections, http://collections.rmg.co.uk/collections/

Saltford Environment Group, http://www.saltfordenvironmentgroup.org.uk/history/history010.html

Sierra Leone Heritage, www.sierraleoneheritage.org/sites/monuments/kingsyard/

St George's News, Waterlooville's Parish Magazine, www.stgeorgesnews.org/2004/06f11.htm

The African Origins Project, http://www.african-origins.org/

The History of Parliament, http://www.historyofparliamentonline.org/

The Trans-Atlantic Slave Trade Voyages Database, www.slavevoyages.org

Visualizing Abolition: A Digital History of the Suppression of the African Slave Trade, visualizingabolition.org.

William Loney RN – Victorian Naval Surgeon, www.pdavis.nl/Jones_3.htm

Index

Printed and bound by CPI Group (UK) Ltd, Croydon, CR0 4YY

06/09/2023

08109358-0001